MW01252943

Making Religion Safe for Democracy

Transformation from Hobbes to Tocqueville

Does the toleration of liberal democratic society mean that religious faiths are left substantively intact, so long as they respect the rights of others? Or do liberal principles presuppose a deeper transformation of religion? Does life in democratic society itself transform religion? In *Making Religion Safe for Democracy*, J. Judd Owen explores these questions by tracing a neglected strand of Enlightenment political thought that presents a surprisingly unified reinterpretation of Christianity by Thomas Hobbes, John Locke, and Thomas Jefferson. Owen then turns to Alexis de Tocqueville's analysis of the effects of democracy on religion in the early United States. Tocqueville finds a religion transformed by democracy in a way that bears a striking resemblance to what the Enlightenment thinkers sought, while offering a fundamentally different interpretation of what is at stake in that transformation. *Making Religion Safe for Democracy* offers a novel framework for understanding the ambiguous status of religion in modern democratic society.

J. Judd Owen is Associate Professor of Political Science, an associated faculty member in the Department of Religion, and Senior Fellow at the Center for the Study of Law and Religion at Emory University. He has held fellowships with the National Endowment for the Humanities and with the Institute for Advanced Studies in Culture at the University of Virginia. He is the author of *Religion and the Demise of Liberal Rationalism* (2001) and the coeditor of *Religion, Enlightenment, and the New World Order* (2010). His articles have appeared in the *American Political Science Review*, the *Journal of Politics*, and *Perspectives on Politics*.

Making Religion Safe for Democracy

Transformation from Hobbes to Tocqueville

J. JUDD OWEN

Emory University

CAMBRIDGE
UNIVERSITY PRESS

CAMBRIDGE
UNIVERSITY PRESS

32 Avenue of the Americas, New York, NY 10013-2473, USA

Cambridge University Press is part of the University of Cambridge.

It furthers the University's mission by disseminating knowledge in the pursuit of
education, learning, and research at the highest international levels of excellence.

www.cambridge.org
Information on this title: www.cambridge.org/9781107036796

© Cambridge University Press 2015

First published 2015

A catalog record for this publication is available from the British Library.

Library of Congress Cataloging in Publication Data
Owen, J. Judd, author.
Making religion safe for democracy : transformation
from Hobbes to Tocqueville / J. Judd Owen.
pages cm
Includes bibliographical references and index.
ISBN 978-1-107-03679-6 (Hardback)
1. Democracy–Religious aspects–Christianity. 2. Democracy–Philosophy. 3. Church
and state. 4. Christianity and politics. I. Title.
BR115.P7O96 2014 322'.1–dc23
2014027890

ISBN 978-1-107-03679-6 Hardback

For Marion

Contents

Preface

Religion is back as a topic of discussion among Western scholars and intellectuals. The renewed interest in religion is largely driven by daily headlines, but years before Islamism commanded so much public attention scholars had begun to observe a resurgence of religion as a public and politically vital force across many faiths, both within the West and without. This resurgence may well seem stunning from the vantage point of several generations of Western intellectuals, to whom it was obvious that religion was progressively weakening in the modern era. Whether it was observed with delight, dismay, or indifference, the trend of modernity had seemed unmistakable until not long ago.

This resurgence has caused the sociology of religion to be turned on its ear with the crisis, if not the demise, of "secularization theory." According to Peter Berger, "the key idea of the theory can be traced to the Enlightenment … Modernity necessarily brings with it a decline of religion, both in society and in the minds of individuals" (1999, 1). Jose Casanova observes that nearly all of the founding fathers of sociology accepted some version of secularization theory, which "may have been the only theory that has been able to attain a truly paradigmatic status in the modern social sciences" (1994, 17). But today, he asks, "who still believes in the myth of secularization?" (11). In fact the field has become divided, but a clear sign of the shift is that Berger, once one of secularization theory's leading proponents, has changed his mind and now declares the theory to have been empirically "falsified."

What is the importance of this changing landscape for political theorists? Is political theory, and in particular liberal political theory, as we find it today capable of responding, or even of grasping what is at stake? The leading school of liberal theory today is known as "political liberalism," which stems from the teaching of John Rawls. Defenders of political liberalism see it as especially well equipped to address the problem of radically conflicting worldviews, including non-liberal religion. For political liberalism gets its name by distinguishing itself from "metaphysical" liberalism, that is to say, liberalism that is grounded in some foundational doctrine or worldview that justifies liberal principles. Political liberalism is not, like Enlightenment liberalism, grounded in a modern scientific worldview – Rawls is explicit: "Political liberalism is not a form of Enlightenment liberalism" (1996, xl). Similarly, political liberalism is not grounded in any religious doctrine. Political liberalism is as a matter of principle or necessity not grounded at all, but "free-standing." Or rather, political liberalism would leave the question of the grounding of liberal principles to individuals, as and whether they feel the need for such grounding.

According to Rawls, "the philosophical question [political liberalism] primarily addresses" "should be … sharply put this way: how is it possible for those affirming a religious doctrine that is based on religious authority, for example, the Church or the Bible, also to hold a reasonable political conception that supports a just democratic regime?" (1996, xxxix) Yet Rawls constructs the doctrine of political liberalism in such a way that this "philosophical question" is not addressed. For it does not matter to political liberalism *how* believers might hold those views required by a just democratic regime; it matters only that they do so, provided that they distinguish between properly political conceptions and properly "metaphysical" and hence politically irrelevant conceptions. The result would be an "overlapping consensus" around liberal political principles among those who differ deeply on theological and philosophical questions.

But here is the crucial difficulty for political liberalism: the line between the political and the metaphysical (which includes the theological), and indeed whether there is such a line at all, is deeply controversial. Moreover the question is not simply or primarily one of the foundation of liberal democratic principles, but the rightness and goodness of those principles. The foundational disagreement among liberals remains a crucial difficulty (cf. Chapter 1), but liberal democracy itself is at issue, and not merely the foundations of liberal democracy among those who already accept it. Political liberalism is attractive in appearing broadly inclusive of those who disagree about the most fundamental issues, but in fact it presupposes acceptance of (a certain interpretation of) liberal democratic principles. It can address only what Rawls calls a "reasonable pluralism," not pluralism as such, where reasonableness is defined by acceptance of political liberalism. Both religious and non-religious challenges to political liberalism (perhaps even challenges of "metaphysical liberalisms" such as Enlightenment liberalism) are not met but excluded beforehand as unreasonable (cf. Owen 2001, ch. 5).

The leading school of liberal theory, then, is not well equipped to confront a world of resurgent religion, particularly religion that is uneasy with or rejects liberal democratic principles. In this respect, political liberalism is manifestly inferior to Enlightenment liberalism. For insofar as political liberalism looks to religion, it looks to "reasonable" religion, that is, religion that supports or at least does not conflict with liberal democratic principles. Enlightenment liberalism, in contrast, engaged a world in which religion permeated politics and which saw questions of orthodoxy and church authority as central to the highest purposes of law. It engaged a world in which what Rawls too loosely calls the "metaphysical" was entwined with and guided the political.

Here we approach the theme of the present study. Nothing is more characteristic of the difference between the early liberal philosophy of the Enlightenment and contemporary liberal theory than the fact that the early liberals engaged religion substantively and extensively. They engaged in disputes over theology and biblical interpretation with a view to transforming religion, as evidenced by writings that are largely neglected today, such as Locke's *First Treatise* and *Reasonableness of Christianity*, parts II and III of Hobbes's *Leviathan*, and Spinoza's *Theologico-political Treatise*. Contemporary liberal theory would not dream of offering its own theology or of attempting the correct or rational interpretation of scripture. Political liberalism, for example, refrains from speaking to substantive religious questions in a manner akin to the United States Supreme Court's refusal to engage in theological disputes, with the aim of "neutrality between religion and religion, and between religion and nonreligion."[1] The Supreme Court, however, presupposes a foundation of legitimacy among American citizens that political theory cannot presuppose in the contest of ideas. It must make its case. Enlightenment liberalism recognized implicitly that liberalism is not

[1] *Epperson v. Arkansas*, 393, U.S. 97, 104 (1968).

and cannot be neutral with respect to religion, making it more suited to the challenge of politically resurgent religion.

Yet it would be absurd to assert that politically resurgent religion returns us to the situation faced by Enlightenment philosophy. We highlight two crucial differences that seem to be in tension with one another.

First and most obviously, the Enlightenment philosophers wrote at the dawn of the modern era. They looked forward to, or hoped to accelerate, a radical and still nascent break from the past scientifically, politically, theologically, and technologically, whereas we find ourselves far into the unforeseeably complicated advance of what they helped to initiate. More specifically, liberal democracy, which found its original theoretical justification in Enlightenment doctrines, has proved tremendously successful and resilient over the span of centuries. Its moral and practical superiority over its two great modern rivals, communism and fascism, famously led Francis Fukuyama to ask whether history had come to an end, in the sense that political and economic liberalism had proved to be the last man standing, the regime that had no serious rival on the horizon and was therefore bound to complete its sweep of the globe. If the resurgence of political religion, and the rise of Islamism in particular, has made Fukuyama's question appear premature (he has continued to defend his "end of history" thesis), the very recent plausibility of his argument nevertheless suffices to show how very different our situation is from that of the seventeenth century in regard to religiously based politics – the degree to which the balance has shifted.

The second difference is the emergence of what has been called the postmodern condition. Paradoxically, at the same time that liberal democracy appears so ascendant, faith in the universal validity of liberal democratic principles has perhaps never been lower. Liberals themselves, especially but not only liberal intellectuals, have lost confidence that there is any universally valid moral standard, including their own. This loss of confidence is not always in view, but it becomes most visible in comparison to the hopeful confidence once found among Enlightenment liberals, who spoke of natural and universal rights of man and who triumphed in the prospect of the victory of reason over benighted particularistic traditions. Today, liberals themselves are frequently inclined to speak of liberal principles as peculiarly Western or, as Richard Rorty put it, "ethnocentric." The attachment to liberal democracy remains, but without the belief that this attachment or any other can be defended rationally.

Moreover, this postmodern sense cannot be separated from at least the occasional dissatisfaction with the modern way of life that prevails in liberal societies. Liberals, like other modern human beings, commonly regret the weakening of at least certain aspects of tradition owing to the rise of modern, individualistic, commercial "monoculture." We feel both the attraction of human rights, freedom, and limited government, on the one hand, and an aversion to the materialistic and spiritually thin way of life fostered in modern democratic society, on the other.[2] As Jurgen Habermas has observed, even or precisely the most secular liberal may feel "an awareness of what is missing," that is, spiritually missing from secular reason (2010). It is unlikely to be a coincidence that a resurgence of political religion would occur amid postmodern doubts about the capacity of secular reason to establish universally valid moral and political principles.

From an American perspective, however, the story of religion and modern democracy looks rather different from that of decline and resurgence. The United States is as modern as any country in the world, and its political founding occurred in the heyday and under the profound influence of Enlightenment political philosophy. And yet America has long stood out among modern nations for its religiosity. Alexis de Tocqueville used the American example to refute an early version of "secularization theory," which he associated with "the philosophers of the eighteenth century," that is, those French *philosophes* whose bold critique of religion subsequently became closely associated with the Enlightenment (282). Tocqueville explains America's exceptional religiosity largely by pointing to Puritan influence, but he also shows the profound transformation of American religion under the influence of democratic society as Puritanism faded. The religion of the Americans Tocqueville observed was in place and owed much of its character to the Puritans, but that religion had changed markedly from Puritanism.

We now approach still closer to the theme of the present study. For while Tocqueville attributes the transformation of American religion to the nature of democracy, not to the influence of the Enlightenment – which he chiefly associates with French thinkers of the eighteenth century – the transformation he observed closely resembles the religious transformation sought by certain *English* Enlightenment thinkers of the *seventeenth century*. For, despite their clear disagreement on religious toleration, Hobbes and Locke were in considerable agreement on how

---

[2] "Even if the typical character types of liberal democracy are bland, calculating, petty, and unheroic, the prevalence of such people may be a reasonable price to pay for political freedom." (Rorty 1991, 190)

religion needed to be changed in order to make it compatible with the new political science. They sought, in remarkably similar ways, to prepare religion for an era of enlightenment.

This transformative agenda is the clearest sign that liberal philosophy in its original form understood that liberalism could not be neutral to religion in the way that political liberalism seeks to be neutral to religion. Liberalism cannot be neutral in its foundations; it cannot be "freestanding." As we shall see in the opening chapter, this does not mean that in its historical origins and development, liberalism was or has ever been foundationally unified on the question of religion. But agreement on certain liberal policies amid foundational tension or struggle should not be confused with foundational neutrality.

The transformative agenda that we will explore in the following also indicates the extent to which a modern liberal democratic society can sustain religion of a certain sort, or within certain bounds. This takes us to another, perhaps surprising, reason to reconsider early Enlightenment liberal philosophy today – with a view to addressing Habermas's sense of "what is missing" from a thoroughgoing secularism that is more clearly associated with the later Enlightenment. Did both Hobbes and Locke simply seek to make religion more rational, as they saw it, and tame it? Or did either of them promote religious transformation as they did in part also out of a concern with the spiritual thinness of the materialistic individualism that otherwise permeated their political doctrines? To what extent does religion make a positive contribution to their teachings, and to what extent does it remain as a concession to the limits of enlightenment? Or, as a further alternative that we will explore, did they suppose that, because "the people are enlightened little by little" (Hobbes, *Opera Philosophica* 2:128), an enlightened transformation of religion would start a process of a more thoroughgoing secularization over time? If so, with a view to what end?

It is far more clearly the case for Tocqueville than for either Hobbes or Locke that religion speaks to a vital need of both individual and society in enlightened democratic times. This is one of the chief reasons for his keen interest in America. He not only saw in America the most democratic nation in a world moving toward an ever more democratic future, but also observed the strength of American religion, which stood in contrast to the weakening of religion amid the advance of European democracy. Could American religion serve as a much-needed model for the future of democracy? The answer to that question required a careful assessment of how religion in America had been transformed by democracy, for better and worse.

The study that follows begins and ends with religion in American democracy, but we seek ultimately a better understanding of the place of religion in modern democracy by tracing certain tensions and ambiguities found in the American case to their theoretical core. We will see that the simple opposition of the religious and secular, as it is often spoken of today, is inadequate. The trend of modern democracy remains one of secularization, but at least in its early Enlightenment and American forms, that secularization remains bound up with and profoundly influences religion. Religion remains, but transformed. This transformed religion is ambiguous, and what we could call the different views of Hobbes, Locke, and Tocqueville of the same phenomena lead us to the heart of the disagreement among their political teachings.

Our first view of this ambiguity comes from a comparison between two strong defenders of religious freedom in the American revolutionary era: Thomas Jefferson and Isaac Backus. Jefferson, the Enlightenment rationalist, and Backus, the Calvinist-Baptist, may initially seem tailor-made for the foundational neutrality of political liberalism, but closer examination reveals that religious freedom for them was not only an extension of their radically opposed views on religion but also an instrument for the promotion of those views throughout society. We see, not foundational neutrality, but an unsettled contest for hearts and minds.

Acknowledgments

This book was a long time in the making and I have incurred many debts along the way. For financial support, I thank the National Endowment for the Humanities, the Institute for Advanced Studies in Culture at the University of Virginia, and the Earhart Foundation. The Department of Political Science at Emory has been extremely supportive, as has Emory's Center for the Study of Law and Religion. My thinking on the questions and texts covered here has been aided by more individuals than I could possibly list, but I do want particularly to acknowledge my undergraduate students at Emory and my former colleagues Robert Bartlett and the late Randy Strahan. Publication of the book was delayed in part because I was forced to rethink several questions in light of a seminar on *Democracy in America* that I co-taught with Randy last year. I dedicate the chapter on Tocqueville to his memory. Last, for their patience and support, I thank my children, Dorothy and Isaac, and my dear wife, Marion.

A third way of religious freedom?

Thomas Jefferson, Isaac Backus, and
the struggle for the American soul

Painting with a broad brush, there were two distinctive sources of support for the strict separation of church and state and religious freedom at the time of the American Founding – sources that were theoretical or theological antagonists of one another, but nevertheless political allies: on the one hand, the theologically skeptical political science of the Enlightenment, and, on the other hand, an array of devout religious beliefs – for the most part, Protestant Christian ones.[1] The religiously devout supporters of religious freedom and disestablishment differed among themselves theologically, as they also differed in the reasons for their support. In some cases, there was a theological basis for opposing a political establishment of religion – such as the protection of the purity of God's church from the corrupting influence of man's politics; in other cases, minority religions simply sought to protect themselves through religious liberty.

In William Lee Miller's account of these two sources of religious freedom in *The First Freedom* (2003), he proceeds largely by way of historical narratives featuring, principally, Thomas Jefferson and James Madison (representing the Enlightenment) and Roger Williams (representing devout Protestant Christianity, though long before the American Founding). Miller is mainly interested in the ideas, rather than the history. But his historical approach to the ideas is called for, since, as he points out, religious freedom has come to mean something different for

---

[1] This is not to say that there were only two camps or two sources of American political thought as a whole. Cf. Witte 2000, 24; Adams and Emmerich 1990, 21–31; McConnell 1990, 1409–1517; Powell 1993, 52–86.

Americans today than it did for either Jefferson and Madison or Williams; hence both the Enlightenment rationalists and the devout believers of old are somewhat alien to us, their heirs.

It may appear, then, that we have a "third way" of religious freedom today that is distinct from either Enlightenment rationalism or old-style piety. Certainly Miller views religious freedom today as a salutary blend of its two main original sources (233–54). Yet certain aspects of his presentation support the conclusion that the Enlightenment's influence has in fact predominated. In Miller's book, he repeatedly is forced to remind his reader of how central and vitally important religion used to be, even in the widely "enlightened" early United States. Speaking, for example, of Jefferson's "Bill for Establishing Religious Freedom," Miller writes, "The politics of this affair, to a degree that may be difficult for a modern American to comprehend, revolved around the debates from within, and rivalries among, the denominations" (2003, 32). It is difficult to comprehend owing to what Miller calls "a modern view," according to which "one should not believe in any religious affirmation 'too strongly'" (153), lest one be tempted to violate the principle of toleration. Jefferson and Madison would perhaps be heartened to find that a history lesson would be required for later generations to learn of the intense religious concerns they struggled against. Yet as a sign that they have not received all they might have wished for, the idea of natural right also requires a history lesson.

It will be helpful to set our situation in sharper relief by looking more closely at these two sources of religious freedom in America. As my representative of the devout Protestant justification of religious freedom, let us consider a figure who is not as famous as Roger Williams, but who was active at the time of the Founding: the Massachusetts Baptist Isaac Backus. One can find no better representative of the Enlightenment among the American Founders than Thomas Jefferson.

Among the myriad positions on church and state that one finds at the time of the American Founding, those of Jefferson and Backus stand out for two reasons. First, both were unusually strict separationists at a time when prevailing opinion, at least at the state level, supported some form of religious establishment, which, although extremely mild by earlier standards, would not pass constitutional muster today. The policy of strict separation that they supported eventually won the day. And yet, Jefferson and Backus also stand out because the reasons that each supported strict separation differed radically. However *politically* compatible their views may have been, the basis of their views – for

Backus, a distinctly Calvinist theology, and for Jefferson, a distinctly rationalist political science – were fundamentally antagonistic to one another. This antagonism, as we shall see, forces us to qualify substantially their political agreement on religious freedom.

Jefferson, as author of the Declaration of Independence and president, is, of course, far more famous than Backus, whose political efforts were generally (though by no means exclusively) limited to Massachusetts and whose foremost concern was, in any case, the Christian Church. Backus remains a historically important figure for American Baptist Christianity, but this fact underscores one reason that his name is not remembered as widely as Jefferson's: Backus as a Baptist was (to use Jeffersonian terminology) sectarian. Jefferson, on the other hand, spoke of mankind more readily than the church, eschewed all forms of sectarianism, and is therefore seen as a more universal figure – or, at any rate, as belonging to America as a whole rather than to one part, such as the Baptists. This is one reason that the courts readily make reference to Jefferson, but not to Backus or other sectarian supporters of religious freedom.[2]

But increasingly it has come to be doubted that any such broad universalism is possible. Increasingly, the Enlightenment is seen as just another sectarian camp and its universalism as a boast. Moreover, appeals by the courts to what Rawls would call Jefferson's "comprehensive doctrine" – in particular, his deeply heterodox views on religion – would no doubt prove highly controversial. Jefferson himself only hinted at his views on religion in his public and political writings and expressed his hesitancy to reveal them even in his private correspondence, our main access to those views.

It is tempting in the case of Jefferson and even Backus simply to draw a line between the public-political principle of religious freedom and private views on religion, along the lines of John Rawls's distinction between the political and the "metaphysical," which would include the theological. Perhaps this is our "third way" of religious freedom. The prevailing view of both the U.S. Supreme Court and liberal theory in America today is that liberal principles are neither essentially secular nor essentially religious, but somehow foundationally neutral. As Justice

---

[2] William McLoughlin argues, however, that Backus is the better representative of American thinking on religious freedom at the time of the American Revolution. Although "in the secular mood of the twentieth century the United States Supreme Court has drawn heavily upon Jefferson and Madison," they "were too indifferent, if not hostile, toward revealed religion to be entirely representative of the American approach to church-state relationships" (1968, 1392).

Fortas put it in *Epperson v. Akansas*, "The First Amendment mandates
government neutrality between religion and nonreligion."[3] The attractive
possibility presented in Jefferson and Backus is of two men who are
profoundly at odds in their views on religion and yet remain compatriots
in agreement on basic political freedoms. (Backus has been called
"a Jeffersonian in politics" [Backus 1968, 61].) Surely Jefferson's practice
of keeping his views on religion private indicates that Jefferson
maintained some such distinction.

But that distinction proves to be deeply problematic upon closer examination. Such a distinction fails to capture a crucial aspect of Backus's
support for religious freedom, and the same can be said of Jefferson
on the basis of his "private" views as they are found precisely in his
correspondence. Both Backus and Jefferson viewed the policy of religious
freedom, not only as extensions of their views on religion, but as *instruments* for the spread of those views in a struggle for the soul of the new
republic. Backus supported religious freedom in large part in order to
remove human interference from the work of the Holy Spirit. Religious
freedom would, he earnestly hoped, lead to revival and the spread of the
true church (Calvinist-Baptist) throughout New England and the New
World. Jefferson, on the other hand, hoped that religious freedom would
have nearly the opposite result. Jefferson despised Calvinism, and he
hoped that religious freedom would entail the spread of a "religion of
reason" or a rational Christianity. Or, as he stated in one letter, "I trust
there is not a young man now living in the United States who will not die a
Unitarian" (1904, 15:385). Jefferson and Backus were thus not merely
antagonists in their private opinions but, despite their agreement
on religious freedom, in politics as well. Each sought a profound
transformation of religion, though the transformations they sought were
profoundly at odds.

Isaac Backus

The Reverend Isaac Backus was the leader of the Baptist Separatist movement in Massachusetts and the most prominent spokesman of the pietist
case for religious freedom at the time of the American Revolution.
"Separatist" was not, in the first place, a political designation, but rather
a denominational one. The Separatists broke from the mainstream Baptists

---

[3] 393 U.S. 97, 104 (1968). This passage was cited as a statement of the Court's "touch-
stone" in its recent decision in *McCreary County v. ACLU of Ky.*

in the wake of the Great Awakening of the 1740s. Yet one cannot ultimately divorce this denominational separatism from the cause of political separation, or religious disestablishment, which cause the Baptist Separatists, under the leadership of Backus, staunchly championed.

Backus's theology was rooted in Calvinism, and central to all of his thinking was the notion of the election of individuals by God's mysterious grace. The elect are those who have experienced God's call and whose understanding has thus been illuminated by God for the first time. Owing to this emphasis on a radically new divine illumination, Backus and other like-minded Christians became known as the "New Lights" (a radically different sort of enlightenment). The true church, according to Backus, is the body of true believers. Not all who call themselves Christians, nor all those who have been raised as Christians from birth, are true believers. Only those who have experienced God's new light as mature adults and accepted it of their own volition are true believers and members of Christ's church. Backus thus stressed the purity of the church, and he maintained that the church could not be purified through reform, but only through separation by the elect. Only the church of true believers was under the leadership of Christ, rather than some merely human authority. The bogus church from which they separated was, in contrast, hopelessly mired in the intrusive institutions of man.

Backus's theology led to a doctrine of religious freedom because it mistrusted all attempts by man to direct Christ's church or otherwise lead human beings to God. In contrast, the theology that dominated Massachusetts Christianity – known as covenant theology and inherited from the early Massachusetts Puritans – viewed religious establishment as essential to the mission of both church and state. We can draw out the political implication of Backus's theology more clearly by setting it in contrast, as Backus himself does, to covenant theology.

Covenant theology formed the basis of Puritan Christianity and experienced its fullest bloom in America in the early Massachusetts Bay Colony under the leadership of John Winthrop and John Cotton. Although Puritanism maintained a distinction between secular and religious authority, both were emphatically understood to be ministers of God's will and to form two parts of a single orthodox Christian community. The model for Puritan covenant theology was the theocracy of the ancient Hebrews under the Mosaic Law. And although Winthrop's Puritans dedicated themselves to liberty, they did not mean by this "natural liberty" or natural right since, as Winthrop declared, "our nature is now corrupt." Natural liberty is "the liberty to do evil as well as good," whereas "civil or federal" liberty, which "may also be termed moral, in reference to the covenant between God and man ... is a liberty to that only which is good, just, and honest" and is of a piece with "the liberty of the church under the authority of Christ, her king and husband."[4] Temporal authority was ultimately subordinate to spiritual authority, and the instruments of political and communal life were to be directed emphatically toward salvation as the ultimate end of human life, both individually and collectively. Covenant theology was thus emphatically communal – the community as a whole, though under the spiritual leadership of the clergy, was responsible for teaching, nurturing, and chastising children, youth, and those adults who strayed. Accordingly, the distinction between church and state for the Puritan entailed very limited religious freedom in the modern (not Winthrop's) sense and was not extended to, for example, Quakers, Baptists, or even dissident Puritans such as Roger Williams and Anne Hutchinson.

Although by Backus's time, covenant theology had been greatly moderated or diluted,[5] it remained at the core of the political theology of his chief Christian opponents. Vestiges of the old Puritan system remained in political institutions and in the opinions that supported them. Massachusetts maintained, for example, a parish system, with approved clergy (including the mainstream Baptists, but not the Separatists) receiving financial support from taxation. Backus opposed this system long before the Revolution, and he welcomed the Revolution in large part in hope of a providential overturning of the religious establishment. In the years leading to the Revolution, he reports in his history of New England, the Baptist faith had spread in "revivals" throughout the colonies: "Within seven years past several thousand had been hopefully converted from the errors of their ways," and these conversions "bespoke a design of final deliverance" of the true church from oppression (1871, II:198).

Backus more fully developed the political implications of his theology after the war in the debates surrounding the new Massachusetts constitution, which sought to maintain the basic outline of colonial ecclesiastical law. The new constitution had provisions for the protection of religious free exercise, but as William McLoughlin notes with some exaggeration, "no one in New England, except the Baptists, thought that

---

[4] John Winthrop, "On Liberty."
[5] Critical changes occurred in Puritan thought in the late seventeenth and early eighteenth centuries owing to the influx of the new thinking of the Enlightenment, especially that of John Locke; see Newlin 1962.

'the free exercise' of religion implied separation of Church and State" (1967, 138), that is, full disestablishment. Backus rejected the Puritan notion of a covenant between God and a community that assumes responsibility for the salvation of individuals by enforcing God's laws. This, according to Backus, was indeed God's way to salvation before Christ. But the New Testament rejects all human attempts to enforce God's law. Puritanism, like any attempt at a Christian political establishment, was the product of "men's jumbling the Old Testament Church and the New together" (1968, 159): that is, of "confounding law and grace together" (413). The Christian revelation in the New Testament replaced law as a path to salvation with the direct dispensation of grace to individuals.

We return, then, to Backus's theological starting point: individual salvation, understood to be accepted *directly* from God's mysteriously bestowed grace. Human attempts to enforce God's law, and thereby mediate between God's will and human responsibility, he saw as human usurpations of Christ's leadership of believers on earth. Backus's approach to the political doctrine of religious freedom and separation of church and state is therefore emphatically salvation and the "purity and life of religion" (1968, 333).

This does not mean, however, that Backus was unconcerned with the welfare of political society as well. His theological and political opponents insisted on state support and at least some degree of regulation of religion, not only as a means of guidance to salvation, but also on the grounds that public morality and hence sound government depend on religion. Religion is vitally necessary for political society, and therefore political society ought to promote and even help guide it. Backus agreed on the political necessity of religion, and indeed of true Christianity: "True Christianity ... is as necessary for the well-being of human society as salt is to preserve from putrefaction or as light is to direct our way and to guard against our enemies, confusion, and misery" (1968, 371). But true Christianity, he argued, and hence the sound morality that government requires, is found only in the true church, with Christ and Christ alone at its head. So although he supported public worship, he opposed the state's either dictating or in any way favoring one Christian denomination over another. Allowing human government, which God set over temporal affairs, any hand in maintaining or regulating the church "evidently tends to destroy the purity and life of religion" (Backus 1968, 333). Backus did not view disestablishment as leaving religion to "the humors of the multitude," as one political opponent characterized it, but rather to the leadership of Christ through the Holy Spirit. "How came," asks Backus, "the kingdoms of *this world* to have a right to govern in Christ's kingdom which is *not of this world*!" (333).[6]

Although Backus's theological disagreement with the Puritans made him a political ally of Enlightenment proponents of religious freedom, his radical difference from these allies is seen in the first place in his notion of what freedom means. His most systematic presentation appeared in a pamphlet written in 1778 entitled "Government and Liberty Described; and Ecclesiastical Tyranny Exposed." Backus begins with an account of liberty that is closer to Winthrop's than to the Enlightenment's – Backus makes clear that the rights he speaks of are not natural rights (Backus 1968, 328). Liberty is not the freedom to do as one pleases: "Judgment and righteousness are essential to freedom ... Freedom is not acting at random but by reason and rule," which results from "the flow of mercy and grace from God to men," as well as "its effects in them in producing obedience unto him" (350). Freedom properly understood requires government – there is no natural freedom or natural right prior to government. But freedom is also, as a product of "the flow of mercy and grace from God to men," stronger than the merely human forces of tyranny and licentiousness. Government must provide order in temporal matters. But it must also remove all obstacles to true liberty (judgment and righteousness):

Streams and rivers are of great use and cause a constant flow of refreshment and blessing wherever they come; so does the exercise and administration of judgment and righteousness among all people that enjoy them. Hence, ... the command of Heaven is, Let them run down; put no obstruction in their way. No, rather be in earnest to remove everything that hinders their free course. (350–51).

---

[6] Backus did not object to Article Two of the proposed Massachusetts constitution, which began by asserting "the right as well as the duty of all men in society, publicly and at stated seasons to worship the Supreme Being, the great Creator and Preserver of the universe." Nor did he object to the beginning of Article Three, which stated that "the happiness of a people, and the good order and preservation of civil government, essentially depend upon piety, religion, and morality, and ... these cannot be generally diffused through a community but by the institution of public worship of God, and of the public instruction in piety, religion, and morality" (quoted at McLoughlin 1967, 148). Backus never objected to the notion that Massachusetts was and should remain a Christian commonwealth, provided church and state were not conflated. Backus does not blame the Puritans for being "earnestly concerned to frame their constitution both in church and state by divine rule" (Backus 1871, I:37). He objects to "how unscripturally they had confounded church and state together" (36).

It is the duty – emphatically the Christian duty – of the civil rulers to prevent merely human institutions from usurping Christ's leadership. For Backus, church and state were distinct, but both – like all of God's creation – were ultimately subject to God.

Thus liberty, for Backus unlike for the Enlightenment, did not mean "self-determination," which he called a "horrid impiety" (404). Self-determination means that "men have assumed the judgment seat and have arraigned the sayings of God to their bar" (403). They (and "they," as we will see, includes Jefferson) have "set up their reason above divine revelation" (402). But "all mankind in their natural condition is in a state of revolt against [the] heavenly ruler"; and "of themselves," through their "unassisted reason," are "never able to come to the knowledge of the truth" (402, 403).

Backus trusted that if man would step aside, subordinate his reason and his pride to God's revelation, which meant among other things permitting an unqualified freedom of conscience, God would work in hearts and minds. Backus insisted on religious freedom, because he trusted that the Great Awakening, "when God was pleased remarkably to pour out his Spirit and gloriously revive religion [in New England]" (424), would continue to spread in the New World. The American Revolution would issue in "the advancement and completion of the Redeemer's kingdom,"[7] for "the truth is great" (1968, 402).

Thomas Jefferson

Although the "Bill for Establishing Religious Freedom" was written not as an expression of Jefferson's own views, but rather as a legal document for Virginia, it nevertheless provides a helpful point of access to Jefferson's doctrine.[8] The bill mostly comprises a long list of justifications for religious freedom. And while Backus may have approved of the policy of religious freedom that follows, he would reject many of the claims on which Jefferson depends in his list of justifications. Perusing that list in search of common ground with Backus, we come upon two main points: the denial at the beginning of free will regarding religious belief and

[7] Quoted at McLoughlin 1967, 186.
[8] In his autobiography, Jefferson wrote that his two proudest accomplishments were the Declaration of Independence and the "Bill Establishing Religious Freedom." It should be noted that Virginia did not adopt Jefferson's draft in its entirety – including some of the elements to be discussed here. Our discussion will concern Jefferson's full draft.

the affirmation near the end that "the truth is great and will prevail if left to herself" (947). But even here – indeed precisely here – in these two points, we see the theological gulf that separates these two political allies. For when Jefferson denies human free will in religious belief, he does not point to our bondage to sin, on the one hand, and our need for God's grace, on the other, as Backus would.[9] Instead, Jefferson says that "the opinions and belief of men depend not on their own will, but follow involuntarily the evidence proposed to their minds" (946). One's beliefs are not freely chosen; they are, rather, dependent on evidence, as evaluated by the mind. Thus religion cannot be determined by legislation or compulsion, no matter how great, but by "reason alone." Although Backus at times employs language akin to Jefferson's, speaking, for example, of each person's "unalienable right to act in all religious affairs according to the full persuasion of his own mind" (1968, 487), he, unlike Jefferson, places that mind in relation to God's "revealed will." Jefferson speaks of Nature's God, not the revealed God, since, according to Jefferson, "reason is our only oracle" (Letter to Carr). As McLoughlin explains, whereas Jefferson "trusted entirely to man's reason and free will," Backus "insisted that only through the supernatural grace of God would men find the Truth that is in Jesus Christ" (1968, 144).[10]

Thus, too, when Jefferson affirms alongside Backus that "truth is great" and therefore in no need of state sponsorship, he does not mean, as did Backus, that the truth of God's revelation will triumph over the folly of man's attempt to establish himself as judge. Rather "the truth [itself] is the proper and sufficient antagonist to error, and has nothing to fear from the conflict unless by human interposition disarmed of her natural weapons, free argument and debate" (947). Human folly does indeed provide the obstacle; but the solution lies precisely in the free judgment of unassisted human reason.

Jefferson provides a fuller account of this confidence in unassisted truth to defeat error in his *Notes on the State of Virginia*, the second most public elaboration of his doctrine of religious freedom. In Query 17, we see Jefferson repeating his claim: "It is error alone which needs the support of government. Truth can stand by itself" (675). And again the gulf separating the grounds of Jefferson's confidence from those of Backus is clear: "Reason and free inquiry are the *only* effectual agents against error. Give a loose to them, they will support the true religion by

---

[9] See McLoughlin's account of Backus's conversion experience at 1967, 14–15.
[10] Cf. Yarbrough 1998, 183–84 and McLoughlin 1967, 170.

bringing every false one to their tribunal, to the test of their investigation" (my emphasis). Jefferson suggests not merely that the truth in religion is discernable by human reason, but that the success of human reason in determining the true religion will become evident to all. Just as the discoveries in the natural sciences are stifled or hindered by government interference, so too in the case of religion. Even the true religion is not served by government interference, since the truth is more firmly established where reason, and not faith, is free and sovereign: "The Newtonian principle of gravitation is now more firmly established, on the basis of reason, than it would be were the government to step in, and to make it an article of necessary faith." For Jefferson, a student of the philosophy of the Enlightenment, there is a gulf between reason and faith.

In these published accounts of his position, the size of the gulf separating Jefferson from Backus is somewhat obscured by the fact that Jefferson leaves it as an open question just what religion will pass the bar of reason – indicating in the bill only that it is "our religion." Perhaps their disagreement, however profound in itself, is limited to whether or not the true religion, on which they generally agree, can and must be vindicated by reason. This ambiguity may serve Jefferson's rhetorical purpose (particularly in the bill), but we must turn to Jefferson's private correspondence in order to explore more fully just what in religion he thought could and could not be rationally vindicated, or, in other words, what this true religion was that Jefferson supposed would triumph publicly as a result of religious freedom.

As he indicates on more than one occasion in his correspondence, Jefferson rarely permitted himself to discuss religion, "and never but in a reasonable society" (14:233). Yet some of his letters provided the occasion, it seems, for reasonable society, and thus offer many revealing discussions of his views on religion, including his views on the religion that he hoped would come to prevail in American society. Jefferson identified that religion alternatively as rational Christianity, primitive Christianity, and Unitarianism. It was, he at times would claim, the religion of Jesus himself, as opposed to the various strands of Christianity that followed. Jesus' religious teaching, according to Jefferson, was simple and incomparably better for society than the multifarious Christian creeds that arose after Jesus' time, and even among his followers. Indeed, those followers who provide us our only access to Jesus' teaching had already miserably corrupted it. We are forced to sift through "the groundwork of vulgar ignorance, of things impossible, of superstitions, fanaticisms, and fabrications" laid down by Jesus' "biographers"

(15:259). Mixed with these "follies and falsehood" (258) is a simple religion, which Jefferson reduces to three main doctrines: 1) that there is only one God, and that he is perfect; 2) that there is a future state of rewards and punishments; 3) that to love God with all your heart and your neighbor as yourself is the sum of religion (15:384). These doctrines "are far beyond the powers of [the] feeble minds ... of the groveling authors who relate them" (15:259). Jefferson's praise of Jesus is dependant on a harsh critique of the Gospels. Jefferson went so far as to extract those portions of the Gospels that he thought worth preserving – by literally cutting up Bibles – and compiling the results, a task he apparently completed in the White House while president. The task, he wrote to William Short, involved "abstracting what is really His from the rubbish in which it is buried, easily distinguished by its luster from the dross of His biographers, and as separable from that as the diamond from the dunghill" (15:220).

Jefferson set this "primitive Christianity" most vividly against the Christianity of Calvin (among whose followers Backus counted himself), whom Jefferson called an "impious dogmatist" (15:384). Jefferson opposed, in particular, Calvin's "demoralizing" denial that good works count toward salvation, his repudiation of reason in religion, his notion of mysterious election by grace, and what Jefferson called "tritheism," that is, the belief in the Trinity – Father, Son, and Holy Spirit. These are doctrines in which Backus also believed; and Jefferson shows no signs that he knew of Backus or those strands of Calvinism, such as Baptist Separatism, that supported religious freedom. Jefferson associated Calvinism instead with the Presbyterians, who Jefferson thought accepted religious freedom only reluctantly and who would eagerly establish their own religious tyranny if they could. Indeed, Presbyterian Calvinism seems to have epitomized for Jefferson the fanaticism that endangers religious freedom and republican government.

The deeper problem, however, lay not with Calvin, but with the "deliria of crazy imaginations" that have plagued Christianity from the start. The recovery of Jesus' own religion would mean that "we shall have unlearned everything which has been taught since His day" (15:323). Among the "artificial systems, invented by ultra-Christians" (15:221) that must be "unlearned," as Jefferson casually lists in a footnote, are "e.g. the immaculate conception of Jesus, His deification, the creation of the world by Him, His miraculous powers, His resurrection and visible ascension, His corporeal presence in the Eucharist, the Trinity, original sin, atonement, regeneration, election, orders of Hierarchy, etc."

(15:221). In opposing such traditional, and it seems in many cases elemental, Christian doctrines, Jefferson denied that he was anti-Christian as many accused him of being. "I am a Christian," Jefferson wrote to Benjamin Rush, "in the only sense in which [Jesus] wished anyone to be; sincerely attached to his doctrines, in preference to all others; ascribing to him every *human* excellence" (10: 380; Jefferson's emphasis).

Thus the most salient answer to our question of what the true religion is that Jefferson supposed would win out is what he calls primitive Christianity, that is, the religion of Jesus himself, which would reject nearly all traditional Christian doctrines. This in fact radically novel Christianity would replace the authority of Scripture with the authority of reason. It would, as Jefferson's amended gospel makes clear, reject the miracles reported in the Bible, as well as Jesus' divinity and resurrection.[11] It would, however, affirm the existence of one God; it would be theologically unitarian. Jefferson, in fact, comes close to identifying this primitive Christianity with contemporary Unitarianism. Be that as it may, he clearly viewed Unitarianism as the vanguard of reasonable religion in America.

Jefferson saw America as embroiled in a religious struggle, which he followed with great interest,[12] between the forces of superstition and intolerance, on the one hand, and reason and toleration, on the other. "The atmosphere of our country," he wrote to Thomas Cooper in 1822, "is unquestionably charged with a threatening cloud of fanaticism, lighter in some parts, denser in others, but too heavy in all" (15:403). Yet, despite this threatening cloud, Jefferson repeatedly iterates his hope, and indeed confidence, in the ultimate defeat of fanaticism, a defeat that could be brought about in part through the advance of Unitarianism. Later in his letter to Cooper, Jefferson writes: "The diffusion of instruction, to which there is now so growing an attention, will be the remote remedy for this fever of fanaticism; while the more proximate one will be the progress of Unitarianism" (405). A month later, in a letter to James Smith that he urges be kept private, Jefferson gives a brighter assessment: "The pure and simple unity of the Creator of the Universe, is now all but ascendant in the Eastern states; it is dawning in the West, and advancing towards the South; and I confidently expect that the present generation will see Unitarianism become the general religion of

---

[11] Jefferson's *Life of Jesus* ends this way: "Now in the place where he was crucified, there was a garden; and in the garden a new sepulcher, wherein was never man yet laid. There laid they Jesus, and rolled a great stone to the door of the sepulcher and departed" (147).

[12] See, for example, his letters at 15:265, 323, 383, 391, 403, 430.

the United States" (409).[13] In June, he had gone further: "I trust that there is not a young man now living in the United States who will not die a Unitarian" (385).

Thus "the genuine doctrine of the one only God [i.e., the rejection of Jesus' divinity] is reviving," Jefferson wrote, owing to "free inquiry and belief" (15:385). Whereas Backus trusted that religious freedom would lead to a widespread revival of Calvinism, Jefferson trusted it would lead to death of the entire "artificial scaffolding" of the Christian religion, including Calvinism above all: "We may hope that the dawn of reason and freedom of thought in these United States, will do away all this artificial scaffolding, and restore to us the primitive and genuine doctrines of [Jesus] the most venerated Reformer of human errors" (430). What is more, not only does freedom of thought in religion lead to the eradication of fanaticism and superstition; genuine religious freedom – that is, the freedom to reason for oneself – exists only as they wane. That is, Jefferson distinguishes between a merely legal religious freedom and genuine religious freedom: "If the freedom of religion, guaranteed to us by law in theory, can ever rise in practice under the overbearing inquisition of public opinion, truth will prevail over fanaticism, and the genuine doctrines of Jesus, so long perverted by His pseudo-priests, will again be restored to their original purity" (288). True freedom of religion does not entail simply a legal right, but moreover a free mind, subject to neither priests nor dogma nor public opinion, but to reason alone.[14]

There is a loose thread remaining, however, that is worth noticing. Despite Jefferson's promotion of primitive or rational Christianity and despite his profession "I am a Christian," Jefferson admits that he does not subscribe to Jesus' religion without qualification. Commenting on his "syllabus" of Jesus' doctrines, Jefferson wrote to William Short: "But while this syllabus is meant to place the character of Jesus in its true light and high light, as no impostor Himself, but a great Reformer of the Hebrew code of religion, it is not to be understood that I am with him in all his doctrines ... The syllabus is therefore of *His* doctrines, not *all* of *mine*" (15:244, 245; Jefferson's emphasis). Jefferson, for example, identifies himself as a materialist, while Jesus "takes the side of spiritualism" (244). It is "very possible" that Jesus might have to be included among the deluded and superstitious interpreters of his own genuine excellence. All blame may not lie with his biographers, for Jesus

---

[13] Cf. Luebke 1963, 346.   [14] Cf. Cooke 1973, 568.

may have "believed himself inspired from above," having mistaken "the coruscations of His own fine genius for the inspirations of an higher order" (15:261).[15] Being a materialist, Jefferson is willing to identify himself as an Epicurean (15:219). The Epicurean believes in "matter and void alone" – nothing spiritual – and believes that "the universe is eternal" – no creation (223).

Jefferson attempted at one point to defend materialism as a Christian doctrine, going so far as to speak of the "heresy of spiritualism," introduced into Christianity at some unknown time (15:266). But given his admission that Jesus himself was a "spiritualist," the question arises whether, not just this attempt to defend Christian materialism, but Jefferson's primitive Christianity as a whole must be taken with a grain of salt. Is even primitive Christianity, in Jefferson's view, true? Is it the "true religion" that reason and free inquiry will firmly establish? Or is "rational Christianity" only a feasible, though revolutionary, approximation of and pointer toward a fully rational human life, given the deep and millennia-old roots of the Christian religion? Is it, like Unitarianism, only a proximate remedy? Moreover, if this is merely an approximation, is it then a stepping stone to the ultimate predominance of a fuller rationality that is not necessarily Christian, or that does not have to claim as a chief authority any single human being, especially one who, however great his genius, was nevertheless of "an enthusiastic mind," and who, though he "set out with no pretensions to divinity, ended in believing them" (6:260)?[16] Or, given that "for one man of science, there are thousands who are not," is an approximation the best Jefferson thought he could expect as "the general religion of the United States"?

Possible evidence that Jefferson was completely sincere in his professions of Christianity is the fact that they occur in private letters, in which he repeatedly pleads that his comments on religion in particular be kept from the public. He never published his expurgated gospel. Although we do not know how open Jefferson felt he could be with these

---

[15] In a pedagogic letter to his nephew Peter Carr, Jefferson offers two alternative claims about Jesus to be considered: "1, of those who say he was begotten by God, born of a virgin, suspended and reversed the laws of nature at will, and ascended bodily into heaven; and 2, of those who say he was a man of illegitimate birth, of a benevolent heart, enthusiastic mind, who set out without pretension of divinity, ended in believing them and was punished capitally for sedition." In weighing these claims, "keep your reason firmly on the watch ... your own reason is the only oracle given you by heaven" (1904, 6:260–61).

[16] Cf. 1904 10:376–77.

correspondents, or in any letter, which might well someday be made public, there is little sign that he did much to promote publicly this "rational Christianity." At the age of seventy-nine, he wrote: "Happy in the prospect of a restoration of primitive Christianity, I must leave to younger athletes to encounter and lop off the false branches which have been engrafted into it by the mythologists of the middle and modern ages" (15:391).

And yet, though Jefferson clearly followed with great interest "the progress of reason in its advances towards rational Christianity," he acknowledged that the United States was early in that progress – at the "dawn of reason and freedom of thought" (15:430). In a letter to Thomas Cooper on the University of Virginia, Jefferson agreed with Cooper that "a professorship of Theology should have no place in our institution" – that is, not even a professor of primitive Christianity. Yet Jefferson continues: "Those with whom we act, entertaining different views have the power and the right of carrying them into practice. Truth advances, and error recedes step by step only; and to do to our fellow men the most good in our power, we must lead them where we can, follow where we cannot, and still go with them, watching always the favorable moment for helping them to another step" (14:200). "The establishment," Jefferson wrote to William Short, "of the inno-cent and genuine character of this benevolent Moralist [Jesus], and rescuing it from the imputation of imposture ... *would in time, it is to be hoped, effect a quiet euthanasia* of bigotry and fanaticism which have so long triumphed *over human reason*, and so generally and deeply afflicted mankind; but *this work is to be begun* by winnowing the grain from the chaff of the historians of His life" (15:221; my emphasis). Perhaps Jefferson supposed that euthanasia would be made quiet by leading Americans toward what claimed to be the original Christianity, Jesus' own religion, disinterred under the sole guidance of reason. Attracted by the authority of Jesus, Christians who followed Jefferson's lead would find that authority quietly replaced by the sole authority of reason alone.

Has Jefferson triumphed?

It seems that the hopes of neither Backus nor Jefferson for religious freedom have been realized. Considering Backus first: although there have been subsequent "great awakenings" and other revivals of devout Protestant Christianity, they have remained, even if defined in broader theological terms than Backus might allow, outside the mainstream, and in part as reactions against it. Perhaps Backus would be content that at least some version of the "New Lights" still exists in significant numbers and is free to evangelize in the United States. But from a Backian point of view, the need for revival remains despite that freedom, and the religion to be revived appears, to the American mainstream, as a remnant of an ever more distant past. As for Jefferson, even the proximate remedy of Unitarianism, to say nothing of the "religion of reason," has made little headway. Indeed, so far is Unitarianism from being the general religion of the United States, Jefferson may have lived to see the heyday of American Unitarianism. Moreover, many of the "spiritualist" beliefs that Jefferson considered vulgar superstitions remain widely held by Americans.

Yet matters are not equal on both sides. The United States has taken a far more Jeffersonian turn than a Backian one. One clear victory for Jefferson concerns the specific legal implications of religious freedom, where Jefferson's view has largely won the day. As we noted previously, for Backus religious freedom was directed toward moving human beings to lives in conformity with God's will, rather than a Jeffersonian indifference so long as one's own leg is not broken or pocket picked. Accordingly Backus never opposed the fact that the Westminster Confession of Faith was mandatory for all Massachusetts schoolchildren; nor did he object to laws against "profanity, blasphemy, gambling, theater-going, and desecration of the Sabbath, which [he] accepted as within the domain of the government in its preservation of a Christian society" (McLoughlin 1968, 149). Jefferson opposed all such laws, and the courts have sided squarely with him.

Moreover, it is likely that "the general religion of the United States" – mainstream American religion – is far closer to what Jefferson hoped for than what Backus or other devout believers of his day hoped for. Central to Jefferson's critique of traditional Christianity was the critique of theology as a whole, and in particular the exploration and articulation of religious doctrine – dogma or creeds. Jefferson's attempt to return to primitive Christianity is less an attempt to restore the true Christian doctrines than it is an attempt to set aside questions of "true Christian doctrine." In his letters, Jefferson repeatedly inveighs against the "metaphysical insanities" (15:288), the "mysticisms, fancies, and falsehoods" (323), the "deliria of crazy imaginations" (384), and the "hocus-pocus phantasms" (409) discussed by "the metaphysical heads" (13:378) and "commentators" (15:384). Concern with creeds – with truths regarding spiritual matters – was at best a waste of time, since human beings are incapable of knowing any truths in spiritual matters.[17] Jefferson wrote to the Reverend Isaac Story:

The laws of nature have withheld from us the means of physical knowledge of the country of spirits, and revelation has, for reasons unknown to us, chosen to leave us in the dark as we were. When I was young I was fond of the speculations which seemed to promise me some insight into that hidden country, but observing at length that they left me in the same ignorance in which they had found me, I have for very many years ceased to read or to think concerning them. (10:299)

Jefferson told Story (who had sent him some of his own theological reflections) that such speculations may be fine if "only the amusement of leisure hours."

Elsewhere, however, Jefferson appears to suggest that such speculations are best avoided altogether. Jefferson wrote to the Reverend Thomas Whittemore:

I have never permitted myself to mediate a specified creed. These formulas have been the bane and ruin of the Christian church, its own fatal invention, which through so many ages, made Christendom a slaughter-house, and to this day divides it into castes of inextinguishable hatred of one another. (15: 373–74)

Thus, although the primitive Christianity Jefferson hoped to promote can be said to be characterized by certain doctrines – such as the rejection of trinitarianism, and the primacy of reason over faith – he is also concerned to identify primitive Christianity with an indifference to doctrinal questions, owing to the "mischiefs of creeds and confessions of faith" (374).

The promotion of this indifference entailed severing the link between correct belief (orthodoxy) and salvation. Although our utter ignorance of "the country of spirits" would seem to entail ignorance of the way to salvation or even the possibility of salvation (i.e., the existence of an afterlife), Jefferson seems not to have been opposed to the notion that belief in an afterlife may provide an inducement to morality.[18] And so when he did refer to an afterlife, he insisted that what one *believes* is of no

---

[17] We will explore the basis of such theological skepticism in the following chapters.

[18] Whether Jefferson believed in an afterlife is far less clear. Adrienne Koch writes: "It is difficult to determine whether Jefferson approved the argument of immortality only as an extra incentive to moral behavior, a kind of Benthamite 'religious sanction,' but without literal or ascertainable truth value, or whether he actually believed in its promise. Unfortunately, Jefferson was reluctant to air his views on this subject" (1943, 33). Regardless of whether Jefferson's reluctance in itself suggests an answer, Koch does offer more concrete grounds for speculation: Jefferson felt "that the belief in an immaterial, immortal soul would open all avenues to mysteries, miracles, and incomprehensible 'logomachies'" (35). Cf. Yarbrough 1998, 180.

importance for securing it. Only the observance of basic, commonly accepted moral principles matters: "I believe ... that he who steadily observes those moral precepts in which all religions concur, will never be questioned at the gates of heaven, as to the dogmas in which they differ" (13:377). Even the most elementary religious dogmas, such as the belief in God, do not matter. When Jefferson encouraged his nephew Peter Carr to "question with boldness even the existence of a God," he reassured him that whatever he determined in this or any religious inquiry, there is no reason for "any fear of its consequences. If it ends in a belief that there is no God, you will find incitements to virtue in the comfort and pleasantness you feel in its exercise" (6:258, 260).

Carr, of course, may have feared for his soul at least as much as for the inducements to virtue. But it is the latter – morality, judged by its utility – that most concerns Jefferson. To be more precise, when Jefferson makes morality alone the standard for judging religion, he most often judges with a view to what is good for society, not what is good for the salvation of one's soul. "The interests of society," he wrote to James Fishback, "require the observation of those moral precepts only in which all religions agree (for all forbid us to murder, steal, plunder, or bear false witness) and that we should not intermeddle with the particular dogmas in which all religions differ, and which are totally unconnected with morality" (12:315). The loss of interest in "particular dogmas" is in the interest of society.

In this light, Jefferson's predictions about the rise of Unitarianism appear not so far off as they might at first glance. Unitarianism remains a small sect today, to be sure. But if by "Unitarianism" we mean in part the placement of toleration and simple morality above doctrinal and institutional orthodoxy, could we not say that, for example, today's Episcopalians and Presbyterians are far closer to the Unitarians of Jefferson's day than the Episcopalians and Presbyterians of Jefferson's day? If Jefferson was wrong that Unitarianism would become the general religion of the United States, perhaps American religion has generally "unitarianized."

We arrive, then, at the following question. Are not the toleration, peace, and morality Jefferson hoped for in American religion possible without conformity to primitive Christianity or Unitarianism? In a letter to Thomas Cooper, in which he hopes for "the progress of Unitarianism," he nevertheless observes that in Virginia (where Unitarianism had made little progress), "Episcopalian and Presbyterian, Methodist and Baptist, meet together, join in hymning their Maker, listen with attention and devotion to each others' preachers, and all mix in society with perfect harmony" (15:405). In the *Notes on the State of Virginia*, moreover, immediately after suggesting that the true religion will prevail if government allows free reign to rational inquiry, Jefferson suggests that it is best if no religion prevails: "Is uniformity of opinion desirable? No more than of face and stature ... Difference of opinion is advantageous in religion." Note that Jefferson does not say that difference of opinion is advantageous *for religion*, but rather *in religion*. As the paragraph proceeds, it becomes clear that he means that difference of opinion in religion is advantageous for society. New York and Pennsylvania, he notes, "flourish infinitely" without any religious establishment: "Religion is well supported; of various kinds, indeed, but all good enough; all sufficient to preserve peace and order" (1943, 676). In that chapter, Jefferson points not to a conformity to primitive Christianity or Unitarianism, but to religious pluralism. Yet the pluralism favored by Jefferson subordinates the importance of doctrinal disagreement for the sake of peace and order in society. There was, he reports, a variety of religious groups in New York and Pennsylvania, "but all good enough." Whatever you believe, if you are peaceful and tolerant, your religion is good enough. In a letter to John Adams, Jefferson wrote that if one's life "has been honest and dutiful to society, the religion which has regulated it cannot be a bad one" (1817). Here Jefferson does not point to the rational investigation of religious truth, but to an indifference to religious truth that would remove the incentive for such an investigation.

In fact, religious apathy stands in an ambiguous relation to the intentions of Jefferson and the Enlightenment more generally. On the one hand, Jefferson sought to promote reason and a rational or natural religion. On the other hand, he sought to promote a disinclination to reflect on religion at all, rational or other. These two intentions, or two aspects of his intention, appear to be in tension with one another and suggest a theoretical muddle. As sophisticated as Jefferson was as a thinker, for a comprehensive philosophical approach and help sorting out that muddle it is necessary to go in search of the theoretical roots of his approach to religion. The philosopher who exercised the most direct and unambiguous influence on Jefferson was John Locke, to whom we will turn in Chapter 3. En route to Locke, we turn to a philosopher whose influence Jefferson squarely denounced, but who nevertheless provides the clearest and most forceful articulation of that strand of Enlightenment thought that, though markedly transformed, leads to Jefferson's ambiguous approach to religion and religious indifference. That philosopher is Thomas Hobbes.

2

Hobbes and the new minimalist Christianity

Though the effect of folly in them that are possessed of an opinion of being inspired be not visible always in one man by any very extravagant action that proceedeth from such passion, yet when many of them conspire together, the rage of the multitude is visible enough. For what argument of madness can there be greater than to clamour, strike, and throw stones at our best friends? Yet this is somewhat less than such a multitude will do. For they will clamour, fight against, and destroy those by whom all their lifetime before they have been protected and secured from injury. And if this be madness in the multitude, it is the same in every particular man. For as in the midst of the sea, though a man perceive no sound of that part of the water next to him, yet he is well assured that part contributes as much to the roaring of the sea as any other part of the same quantity, so also, though we perceive no great unquietness in one or two men, yet we may be well assured that their singular passions are parts of the seditious roaring of a troubled nation. And if there were nothing else that bewrayed their madness, yet that very arrogating such inspiration to themselves is enough. (Leviathan 8.21)

If this superstitious fear of spirits were taken away, and with it prognostics from dreams, false prophecies, and many other things depending thereon, by which crafty and ambitious persons abuse the simple people, men would be much more fitted than they are for civil obedience. (Leviathan 2.8)

Thomas Hobbes lays the philosophical groundwork for liberalism's political project of religious transformation, although he does so in the context of a political solution markedly different from that of later liberals. Hobbes's approach to religion differs from that of later liberals most obviously in that he denied a right in political society to the free exercise of religion. The sovereign may establish any religion he sees fit, including non-Christian ones, or he may establish no religion at all. The sovereign has authority over religious worship and professions of belief (as opposed to what one believes in one's heart or mind), should he choose to exercise it, and the sovereign must be obeyed even if he commands idolatry. This part of Hobbes's approach to religion – what we might call his illiberalism – is familiar to students of his thought: self-preservation through absolute submission in word and deed to the will of the sovereign.[1]

But this most basic statement of Hobbes's formal solution to the problem of religion and politics is inadequate. For it neglects the fact that Hobbes does not simply grant the sovereign absolute authority over religious practice, but lays out an elaborate and extensive reinterpretation of Christianity. The character and intention of this reinterpretation provide a better guide to Hobbes's aim than does the sole fact of sovereign authority over religion alone. The sovereign has the authority to establish whatever religion he sees fit, but not just any religion is well suited to the aim of the leviathan state. Hobbes stressed the fact that the deeds of human beings are guided by their beliefs. Some beliefs are dangerous to the commonwealth, while others support it. Far too much of Christianity as it was understood and practiced was, according to Hobbes, politically disastrous. The practical success of Hobbes's political project depended, he believed, on "this writing of mine [falling] into the hands of a sovereign who will consider it himself ... and by the exercise of entire sovereignty ... protect[] the public teaching of it" (31.41; cf. Latin version).

The obvious core of Hobbes's reinterpretation of Christianity is the notion that religion requires obedience to the sovereign – even, most astoundingly, if he commands the profession and practice of false, non-Christian religion: "When the sovereign is an infidel, every one of his own subjects that resisteth him sinneth against the laws of God (for such are the laws of nature)" (43.23). "Sin," Hobbes asserts, "[is] nothing but the transgression of the law" (29.15), and "besides the laws of nature, and the laws of the Church, which are part of the civil law ... there be no other laws divine" (43.22). But Hobbes's Christianity extends well beyond

---

[1] For my argument that Hobbes's philosophy is liberal, see Owen 2005.

the requirement to obey the sovereign. And he is forced to go beyond that requirement *as a support for that requirement*. Hobbes presents a Christianity whose principles are guided wholly by reason and that is radically skeptical of all theological metaphysics. The doctrines of Hobbes's Christianity are very few and, he claims, easily grasped by all. As far as possible, controversial or obscure parts of religion he dismisses as unnecessary. All that purports to be miraculous or supernatural is subjected to a ruthless skepticism. He rarely misses an opportunity to impress upon the reader how very little anyone, not least the clergy, knows about spiritual matters, while attributing ulterior motives to those who claim to know. And all this for the sake of political order and peace. From here, Jefferson's "rational Christianity" and, indeed, religious indifference, are already coming into view. Hence, however much Jefferson and Hobbes differ as representatives of the Enlightenment (Jefferson despised Hobbes's defense of absolute monarchy), nevertheless Hobbes, like Jefferson, promotes a skepticism or indifference based on the belief that fervent and otherworldly religiosity is detrimental to civic life. This is the guiding belief of the Enlightenment's project of religious transformation, whose philosophical grounds and development we will trace through the next two chapters.

What takes the place of a preoccupation with the spiritual and otherworldly is a preoccupation with the mundane goods of this life – the things necessary for "commodious living," especially peace and safety. The quest for material goods in this life supplants the quest for spiritual goods, especially in the next life. Hobbes's reinterpretation of Christianity is founded on his anthropology. Human beings are by nature preoccupied with mundane goods and the power necessary to secure them. But, by nature, our capacity to secure these goods is very uncertain. Man's natural condition is characterized by fear and insecurity. Almost all human beings have been ignorant of natural causation and have therefore attributed their good and bad fortune to invisible powers – spirits or demons whose mysterious will they seek to appease. All religion (including natural religion) is rooted in natural mundane concerns, and especially fears over one's bodily security and material well being. The high is rooted in and is reducible to the low. But once the human imagination is filled with spirits, demons, and otherworldly powers, a new fear emerges: fear of the afterlife. This fear can overwhelm the natural fears of the ignorant, and thus pose a grave problem for the sovereign. For fear of eternal torment can give one who seizes hold of it and manipulates it greater power over the obedience of subjects than even the sovereign's monopoly of earthly power can do.

Hobbes, then, seeks to weaken supernatural religion and restore or awaken human beings to the natural primacy of their worldly material concerns. When our attention is focused on the hopes and fears of this life and the fear of imaginary powers fades, then the power of the sovereign can be sufficient to do its job. Then it can become like a god – though a "Mortal God" – and the invisible power of imaginary leviathans is replaced by the visible power of Hobbes's "great Leviathan" (17.13). To the extent that the residue of supernatural religion may persist, Hobbes will attempt to employ it to reinforce the great Leviathan. But because even this residue could incubate and be cultivated by an enemy of the sovereign, it must be kept down through public education or control of what beliefs are taught – if you will, through "enlightened propaganda."

The problem of supernatural religion

In approaching the problem of supernatural religion for Hobbes, it is helpful to remind ourselves of the most familiar features of Hobbes's political doctrine. Human beings are, according to Hobbes, by nature equal and are therefore subject to no natural authority. Humans are self-interested creatures, guided by their appetites and aversions, being directed toward pleasure and away from pain. The objects of human desire are essentially mundane, scarce, and ever changing. There is no greatest good or ultimate end of human life, and therefore humans especially seek power for the sake of whatever they may desire from time to time. But though there is no greatest good, there is a greatest evil: violent death. Or, to state it positively, the most powerful human desire is the desire for self-preservation. No one else can be trusted to seek our welfare more certainly than each of us ourselves, and therefore each of us has a right to determine what we may need in pursuit of preservation. But natural scarcity of the means to preservation leads inevitably to war. All human beings by nature have a right to everything, including the right to kill one another: "If any two men desire the same thing, which nevertheless they cannot both enjoy, they become enemies; and in the way to their end, which is principally their own conservation, and sometimes their delectation only, endeavor to destroy or subdue one another ... And from this diffidence of one another, there is no way for any man to secure himself so reasonable as anticipation, that is, by force or wiles to master the persons of all men he can, so long till he see no other power great enough to endanger him" (13.3, 4). "The natural condition of mankind," or state of nature, is therefore a state of war of every person against every other person. "In such a condition," Hobbes says in a famous passage, "there is no place for industry, because the fruit thereof is uncertain, and consequently, no culture of the earth, no navigation, nor use of the commodities that may be imported by sea, no commodious building, no instruments of moving and removing such things as require much force, no knowledge of the face of the earth, no account of time, no arts, no letters, no society, and which is worst of all, continual fear and danger of violent death, and the life of man, solitary, poor, nasty, brutish, and short" (13.9). In such a condition, "nothing can be unjust," because "where there is no common power, there is no law; where there is no law, no injustice" (13.13); nor, for the same reason, is there sin (13.10). Indeed, "force and fraud are the two cardinal virtues" (13.13).

Human beings, however, desire "such things as are necessary to commodious living" and "hope by their industry to obtain them," and above all they fear violent death. And these are "the passions that incline men to peace" (13.14). Reason, Hobbes says, suggests the articles of peace – what he loosely calls the laws of nature. Chief among these articles is the need to surrender or transfer one's natural rights to a single person or body of persons, the sovereign, who will make laws that are known to all and who will have the manifest power to enforce those laws. We are then (and only then) obligated to obey those laws, having taken on ourselves that obligation voluntarily and through a clear-sighted calculation of our own interests, chief among which is our own preservation. Justice, quite simply, is obedience to the sovereign, and injustice is disobedience. We have no right to dispute the judgment of the sovereign, the value of which lies not in its correctness but in its decisiveness. We may dispute the judgment of the sovereign neither on the grounds of human wisdom or right reason, nor on the grounds of divine wisdom or revelation (cf. 5.3). For the only way to settle such disputes is through war, which Hobbes hopes already to have shown to be the worst possible human condition. All that is left, it may seem, is to elaborate the consequences of these fundamental insights.

There has been much discussion over the last several decades of the extent to which religion plays a role in Hobbes's basic account of the origins and grounds of political society. There are two dominant trends of interpretation. One of these tends to view Hobbes's discussions of religion as incidental to his political theory, and thus to neglect Hobbes's lengthy passages on religion, including the second half of *Leviathan*. The other views religion as essential to Hobbes's political theory and insists that Hobbes must ultimately be interpreted as a religious thinker.[2] Both lines of interpretation are partly correct. Religion can be said to be incidental to Hobbes's thought insofar as he sought to base his political doctrine on the principles of nature alone. Hobbes's God may support the principles of nature, but not contradict or even add to them. Anything in religion that is supernatural, including God's own characteristics, is radically unknowable to human beings. Hobbes

---

[2] The former line of interpretation remains the prevailing view, but it has lost ground in recent years to the latter. The latter line of interpretation, initiated by A. E. Taylor and elaborated by Howard Warrender, maintains that God, and indeed divine command, is essential to Hobbes's account of the laws of nature – those principles or maxims that lead human beings to peace. Warrender bases his interpretation on the following comments of Hobbes about the law of nature: "These dictates of reason, men used to call by the name of laws, but improperly: for they are but conclusions, or theorems concerning what conduceth to the conservation and defense of themselves; whereas law, properly, is the word of him that by right hath command over others. But yet if we consider the same theorems, as delivered by the word of God, that by right commandeth all things, then they are properly called laws" (*Leviathan* 15.41). Warrender goes so far as to assert that God's commands obligate "from the fact that they were God's will alone, and not because breach of these laws would entail divine punishment though it would of course do so" (1957, 300). Yet according to Hobbes, fear is a much firmer basis for obedience (whether or not one would consider this true moral obligation) than respect for the will of another. And, as we will see, religion, according to Hobbes is the fear of "invisible powers." Yet the problem with the state of nature is that "there is no *visible* power to keep [men] in awe" (17.1, emphasis added). If the commonwealth depended on God's commands and fear of His invisible power (to say nothing of respect for His will), men would still find themselves in the state of nature. Later in *Leviathan*, Hobbes says, apparently in his own name and without qualification, that "the laws of nature ... in the condition of mere nature ... are not properly laws, but rather qualities that dispose men to peace and to obedience" (36.8). He makes no mention of considering them as God's commands. Instead, these qualities become law, not by God's command, but by the sovereign's: "For though it be naturally reasonable, yet it is by the sovereign power that it is law; otherwise it were a great error to call the laws of nature unwritten laws" (36.22).

   More recently, A. P. Martinich has pointed out that Hobbes says that "before the time of civil society, or in the interruption thereof by war, there is nothing can strengthen covenant of peace agreed upon, against the temptations of avarice, ambition, lust, or other strong desire, but the fear of that invisible power, which they every one worship as God; and fear as a revenger of their perfidy" (*Leviathan*; cited at Martinich 1992, 80). Martinich interprets this to mean something a bit different from what Hobbes actually says, namely, that "nothing other than God has the unfailing strength to enforce a covenant made in the state of nature" (80–81). Yet if Hobbes thought that God does have such an unfailing strength to enforce covenants, it is hard to see why he says so emphatically that "before the names of just and unjust can have place, there must be some coercive power to compel men equally to the performance of their covenants, by the terror of some punishment greater than the benefit they expect by the breach of their covenant ... *and such a power there is none before the erection of the commonwealth*" (15.3, emphasis added). Moreover, as we will discuss at greater length later, Hobbes makes no mention of God or religion in his account of the state of nature in chapter 13 of *Leviathan*.

seeks to provide political and moral principles that are compelling independently of their having been ordained by God. And yet it is highly misleading to treat religion as simply incidental to Hobbes's thought. Sharon Lloyd points us in the right direction when she observes: "There are countless examples of the human capacity for pursuing religious or moral convictions even at the expense of one's own life... We all know this. Hobbes knew it too, and it worried him deeply. It worried him because he believed that transcendent interests very often cause civil wars... The sort of transcendent interests that particularly worried Hobbes were religious interests" (1992, 1, 2). We also are aware of examples of the sort to which Lloyd alludes, despite their being less common in our day than they were in Hobbes's in no small part owing to the religious transformation we are considering. Such obvious examples make what is supposed to be the firm basis of Hobbes's political doctrine, namely, the fear of violent death as the strongest or most fundamental human passion, manifestly inadequate. It is not as clear as Hobbes claims that human beings' passions do in fact incline them toward peace.

This difficulty helps to reveal something paradoxical in Hobbes's doctrine. Hobbes's basic argument, as sketched earlier, depends on an account of human beings as basely selfish – creatures unrestrained by moral principle, incapable of sacrificing their own interests, least of all their lives. He appeals, it seems, to the worst in us. And yet he does so precisely in an attempt to establish a solid basis for membership in political society, and indeed for justice itself. Most of us are inclined to admire the willingness to subordinate self-interest, including or especially "the ultimate sacrifice." But Hobbes found that inclination dangerous and hoped to weaken if not eradicate it.

To help us to understand Hobbes's concern, consider the difference between battling a band of mercenaries and battling a band of religious zealots. Precisely because the mercenaries are self-consciously pursuing their own worldly interests, they are far easier to negotiate with or dissuade than the zealots. The mercenaries may take a simple payoff or, if the fighting gets too hot, decide that fighting is not worth the risk. Precisely because the religious zealots understand themselves to be subordinating their self-interest to a higher will or cause, and may even be eager to demonstrate that subordination, they are far harder to deal with. That part in us that admires the capacity for self-sacrifice is, to Hobbes's mind, the potential fanatic in us. And, as we shall see, he understands that part of us to be essentially linked to religious hopes, whether we are conscious of the link or not. Consequently, the high-minded lover of justice, and in particular one who fears God more than the sovereign, is a greater obstacle to the establishment of Hobbesian justice than the criminal. Hobbes puts Jesus' words to his own use: "No man can serve two masters; nor is he less, but rather more a master, whom we believe we are to obey for fear of damnation, than he whom we obey for fear of temporal death" (*De Cive* 6.11). The selfish and petty calculator pursuing his worldly interests is easier for Hobbes to persuade.

Consider Hobbes's famous refutation of the fool in chapter 15 of *Leviathan*, under the heading "justice not contrary to reason" (15.4–8). The passage begins with a refutation of "the fool" who "hath said in his heart: 'there is no such thing as justice'" (15.4). Not only in his heart, but also sometimes with his tongue this fool alleges that "every man's conservation and contentment being committed to his own care, there could be no reason why every man might not do what he thought conduced thereunto, and therefore also to make or not make, keep or not keep, covenants was not against reason, when it conduced to one's benefit." The fool may even aspire to seizing the throne himself: "The kingdom of God is gotten by violence; but what if it could be gotten by unjust violence?" (15.4)

The fool is one we would commonly think of as unjust. He is out for himself, for his own "conservation and contentment," even if that means breaking his word or the law. The fool fancies himself no fool at all, but rather shrewd and even wise – a "wise guy." He makes the seemingly commonsense observation that there are times when breaking a contract, or injustice, is to one's own advantage. The fool views justice the way most of us do: as a constraint on the pursuit of our own interests. What could be more obvious? Unlike most of us, however, the fool concludes that justice is for suckers. Justice will not constrain the fool's pursuit of his interests. He is therefore a problem for the leviathan state, as for any other.

Hobbes sets out to refute the fool. Because in the state of nature there is no justice or injustice and the cardinal virtues are force and fraud (13.13), Hobbes's chief concern is breaking the laws of the commonwealth. Once the commonwealth, and therefore justice, have been established, Hobbes insists that it is never reasonable to break a contract. For a commonwealth requires a sovereign with tremendous police powers and, although some fools are lucky enough to get away with their crimes on occasion, the risk of being caught and punished is so great as to make the attempt unreasonable. The example of a lottery winner does not make it reasonable to spend the rent money on a ticket. Moreover, once one becomes known for breaking contracts, one becomes an untrustworthy partner, even or especially for political society itself, on which one's survival depends.

Whether or not we find Hobbes's refutation of the fool compelling, this much is clear: Hobbes's understanding of human nature and what it means to be a reasonable human being is very close to the fool's. Hobbes and the fool agree that reason dictates that everyone do what conduces to his own "conservation and contentment." Moreover, the fool's argument requires "taking away the fear of God," that is, the supernatural punishment of God either in this world or the next. "For the same fool," Hobbes says, "hath said in his heart there is no God" (15.4). Hobbes lets the fool's atheistic premise stand. The case for the reasonableness of justice can be made, Hobbes supposes, *without appeal to the fear of God*. The case can be made, moreover, without contradicting, and indeed by *clarifying*, the calculation of self-interest. The fool's foolishness lies not in his calculating selfishness, but in his poor calculations.

Before ending this section, however, Hobbes takes up a case that is often neglected by commentators, one that is quite different from that of the fool: "As for the instance of gaining the secure and perpetual felicity of heaven by any way, it is frivolous, there being but one way imaginable, and that is not breaking, but keeping of covenant" (15.6). Hobbes addresses not the atheist calculating for worldly advantage, but the believer in heavenly happiness, who may break his covenant (that is, disobey the sovereign) because he supposes himself to be obeying a higher authority and greater power.

Hobbes's initial response is to assert that the only imaginable way to heaven is to obey the sovereign. This response is remarkably weak, and indeed obviously false. Of course, someone could imagine another way to heaven besides simple obedience to the sovereign, as Hobbes reveals a few lines later: "There be some that will not have the law of nature to be those rules which conduce to the preservation of man's life on earth, but to the attaining of an eternal felicity after death, to which they think the breach of covenant may conduce, and consequently be just and reasonable (such are they that think it a work of merit to kill, or depose, or rebel against the sovereign power constituted over them by their own consent)" (15.8). These differ from the fool, not only in their theism, but also in the fact that they do not maintain that injustice is reasonable. That is, they see themselves, even or precisely in their rebellion against an impious sovereign, in their obedience to God rather than man, as both just and reasonable. Paradoxically, these most intense lovers of justice are harder for Hobbes to persuade to adhere to justice as *he* understands it than the self-consciously unjust fool. For as believers in supernatural revelation and life after death, they are not as strictly rationalist as either Hobbes or the fool: reason is not their sole or even principal guide.

The weakness of his initial response to this second category of lawbreakers now being plain, Hobbes reveals his more radical response: "But because there is no natural knowledge of man's estate after death, much less of the reward that is then to be given to breach of faith, but only a belief grounded upon other men's saying that they know it supernaturally, or that they know those that knew them that knew others that knew it supernaturally, breach of faith cannot be called a precept of reason or nature" (15.8). Hobbes's more radical response is to promote doubt about all claims regarding the way to heaven. We leave as a question for now how this relates to Hobbesian Christianity, except to say that, like Jefferson, Hobbes credits only the "precept[s] of reason or nature" and will seek to reform Christianity as much as possible by their lights.

The Hobbesian solution cannot ignore supernatural religion, and Hobbes was keenly aware that supernatural religion presented a potentially explosive danger for that solution. He begins his chapter "The Signification of Eternal Life, Hell, Salvation, the World to Come, and Redemption" thus:

The maintenance of civil society depending on justice, and justice on the power of life and death (and other less rewards and punishments) residing in them that have the sovereignty of the commonwealth, it is impossible a commonwealth should stand where any other than the sovereign hath a power of giving greater rewards than life, and of inflicting greater punishments than death. Now seeing eternal life is a greater reward than the life present, and eternal torment a greater punishment than the death of nature, it is a thing worthy to be well considered, of all men that desire (by obeying authority) to avoid the calamities of confusion and civil war, what is meant in Holy Scripture by life eternal and torment eternal; and for what offences, and against whom committed, men are to be eternally tormented, and for what actions they are to obtain eternal life. (38.1)

We note that Hobbes's audience is not those who seek to secure eternal life for themselves, but those "men that desire ... to avoid the calamities of confusion and war," that is, those concerned with "the maintenance of civil society." The danger Hobbes confronts is not merely a divided sovereignty, which would in itself dissolve the commonwealth (29.12). As Pierre Bayle put it, in commenting on the *Leviathan*, "Fear of arms cannot bring peace to those who are motivated to fight one another through an evil more terrible than death, that is to say: through dissention over matters that are necessary for salvation" (2000, 87). The danger to the commonwealth is the belief in a power superior to that of the sovereign, which would weaken, if not break, the hold the sovereign has over his subjects' obedience.

This admission leaves us with one of the great puzzles in Hobbes's writings. For, as Hobbes says more prominently and typically, "death is the greatest of all evils" (*De Homine* 1.6), and it is the "fear of death and wounds" that "disposeth men to obey a common power" (*Leviathan* 11.4; cf. 13.14), that is, the sovereign. But is it not all too clear that for many, death is *not* the greatest of all evils, and that these in particular may not be disposed to obey the sovereign? Hobbes confronted a gulf between human religiosity as he witnessed it and the rational solution to the political problem he supposed he had discovered.

Thus the identification of the state of nature and the natural laws that lead human beings from that state into political society can only be one level of Hobbes's solution. The full solution is still more radical, as Hobbes conceived of advancing a popular enlightenment. He conceived, that is, the radical notion of removing the gulf separating religion as he found it and the reasonable disposition required by Natural Law by transforming or rationalizing religion. Hobbes sought to initiate the movement to which Jefferson, among others, was heir – the assault on supernatural religion for the sake of civil peace and order. In order to discover the philosophical grounds for this ambition of Hobbes's, as well as its scope and character, let us look more closely at Hobbes's treatment of religion in the *Leviathan*.

The natural seeds of religion

The most obvious beginning point for considering Hobbes's treatment of religion is chapter 12, "Of Religion." Chapter 12, however, is in fact a continuation of Hobbes's discussion of religion that began in chapter 11, "Of the Difference of Manners." By "manners," Hobbes means "those qualities of mankind that concern their living together in peace and unity" (11.1). Like Hobbes's discussion of salvation in chapter 43, his discussion of religion in chapters 11 and 12 arises out of concern for the essentially this-worldly desire for peace and not out of a distinctly religious concern. Hobbes's discussion of manners, moreover, is mostly a discussion of those qualities of mankind that are *obstacles* to living together in peace and unity: the restless desire of power, love of competition, hate, vainglory, ambition, and – now approaching the discussion of religion – want of science, want of understanding, adherence to custom, adherence to private men, and credulity from ignorance of nature.

The sequence of topics leading to the discussion of religion that concludes the chapter indicates Hobbes's strategy and begins from what might seem an odd obstacle to peace and unity, namely, "want of science, that is, ignorance of natural causes" (11.17). We have, in the modern era, become accustomed to politicians calling for improved scientific education, with a justification in keeping with the spirit of Hobbes: the promotion of technological advancement and economic growth. Hobbes, however, identifies the want of science as an obstacle to peace and unity, because it "disposeth, or rather constraineth, a man to rely on the advice and authority of others. For all men whom the truth concerns, if they rely not on their own, must rely on the opinion of some other whom they think wiser than themselves (and see not why he should deceive them)." Hobbes is concerned about individuals' gaining authority over others, who think them unusually wise and benevolent. We can see easily enough how a naïve trust in the benevolence of others, a trust that Hobbes seeks to undermine at every turn, could aid the ambitious in their search for authority. But how precisely are the plans of the ambitious helped by a want of science, or ignorance of natural causes? Hobbes still does not make plain the problem he has in mind when he reiterates the difficulty in section 23:

Ignorance of natural causes disposeth a man to credulity, so as to believe many times impossibilities; for such know nothing to the contrary, but that they may be true, being unable to detect the impossibility. And credulity, because men love to be hearkened unto in company, disposeth them to lying; so that ignorance itself without malice is able to make a man both to believe lies and tell them, and sometimes also to invent them.

What is Hobbes talking about? What impossibilities does ignorance of natural causes lead one to believe? What lies does it dispose one to repeat and even to invent? And how are such lies about impossibilities an obstacle to peace and unity?

At the end of the chapter, Hobbes at last reveals what he has in fact been discussing for some pages without naming it. Those who make "profound inquiry into natural causes are inclined thereby to believe there is one eternal God," that is, "some cause, whereof there is no former cause, which is it men call God," even though "they cannot have any idea of him in their mind answerable to his nature" (11.23). But few indeed have made such profound inquiries into natural causes as to arrive at what Hobbes calls "natural religion," that is, the belief in some first cause, whose nature is otherwise radically unknowable. As for the rest:

They that make little or no inquiry into the natural causes of things, yet from the fear that proceeds from the ignorance itself of what it is that hath the power to do them much good or harm[3] are inclined to suppose and feign unto themselves several kinds of powers invisible, and to stand in awe of their own imaginations, and in time of distress to invoke them, as also in the time of unexpected good success to give them thanks, making the creatures of their own fancy their gods. By which means it hath come to pass that, from the innumerable variety of fancy, men have created in the world innumerable sorts of gods. And this fear of things invisible is the natural seed of that which everyone in himself calleth religion, and in them that worship or fear that power otherwise than they do, superstition.[4]

Here are the lies and impossibilities those ignorant of natural causes are inclined to believe: not the first cause of natural religion, but invisible powers, figments of the imagination of the ignorant, who suppose these powers responsible for their good and bad fortune. Ignorance of natural causes leads, in short, to supernatural religion, which is as endlessly varied as the human imagination.

This supernatural religion Hobbes now (and typically throughout) calls simply "religion," being merely what one calls one's own superstitious belief in invisible powers. These invisible powers may be imaginary, but the belief in invisible powers is a potentially extraordinary source of earthly power for those who are able to channel and manipulate it: "And this seed of religion having been observed by many, some of those that have observed it have been inclined thereby to nourish, dress, and form it into laws, and to add to it, of their own invention, any opinion of the causes of future events by which they thought they should be best able to govern others, and make unto themselves the greatest use of their powers" (11.27).

It is to religion thus understood that Hobbes turns, initially at least, in chapter 12, "Of Religion." As Hobbes's succinct and revealing conclusion to chapter 11 confirms, religion is rooted in fear – in particular, the "fear of things invisible," which is the "natural seed" of religion. The seed of religion is natural – not supernatural – and "only in man" (12.1), that is, in no other animal. For the other animals, felicity consists only in "the enjoying of their quotidian food, ease, and lusts" (12.4). Only human beings have, or at least have to an unusually high degree, the capacity to think in terms of cause and effect, to puzzle over the causes of their own good and evil fortune, and therefore to worry about those causes, which

---

[3] The Latin version reads: "whether or not there is some power by which they can be helped or harmed."

[4] Hobbes thus clarifies or corrects an earlier definition at 6.36.

"for the most part are invisible." No human being is free of anxiety over his future, which, as Hobbes describes it, can be an all-consuming evil in itself:

> For being assured that there be causes of all things that have arrived hitherto or shall arrive hereafter, it is impossible for a man who continually endeavoreth to secure to himself against the evil he fears, and procure the good he desireth, not to be in a perpetual solicitude of the time to come; ... so that man which looks too far before him, in the care of future time, hath his heart all the day gnawed on by fear of death, poverty, or other calamity, and has no repose, or pause of his anxiety, but in sleep. (12.5)

Although no human being is free of anxiety over future evils, there are degrees of such anxiety. And whereas in section 5, Hobbes suggests that the most extreme anxiety is the result of looking forward "too far" or being "over-provident," he immediately suggests an additional or alternative cause in section 6: "This perpetual fear [i.e., this anxiety in its extreme form], always accompanying mankind in the ignorance of causes (as it were in the dark), must needs have for an object something. And therefore, when there is nothing to be seen, there is nothing to accuse, either of their good or evil fortune, but some power or agent invisible" (12.6).

This *perpetual* fear, the endless torture of wondering what terrible event may befall one next – and when and from what quarter and why – is always with human beings *when* they are ignorant of natural causes, that is, when their minds are in the grip of superstition/religion. Here the imagination runs wild; and Hobbes presents a long list of the "absurd opinions of Gentilism" respecting invisible powers – attributing powers to ghosts and spirits; inanimate objects, such as the ocean and fire, animals of every sort; as well as such things as time, peace, love, rust, fever, and on and on. Fear of invisible powers leads to the attempt to gain their favor through thanks, honor, sacrifices, and worship, the forms of which also vary endlessly. The fear and ignorance that are the seed of religion can, as Hobbes had already suggested at the end of chapter 11, be cultivated. That is, many have been able to take the seed of religion and form the religion springing from it into laws, manipulating the fear of the many and the desire to appease the object of their fear, that "they should best be able to govern others, and make unto themselves the greatest use of their powers," or simply to "induce others to serve them" (11.27, English and Latin versions).

Here, then, is the extraordinary – indeed, uniquely powerful – political significance of religion. And we can easily see how an ambitious individual who could manipulate these tremendous fears of invisible powers and could induce others to believe that the favor of those powers was tied to obedience to him would enjoy far greater power than one who simply depended on earthly punishments and rewards. We can easily see, furthermore, why Hobbes would be concerned that ambitious individuals might play on fear and ignorance in a bid to undermine the sovereign authority.

But our reading of Hobbes thus far faces an obvious objection. Hobbes's depiction of religion in chapters 11 and 12 is not principally of the threat to sovereign power, but rather of a, if not the, chief *basis* of sovereign power. As Hobbes presents matters here, supernatural religion is not a problem for the sovereign, but is on the contrary for him a gift from heaven, as it were. One obvious reading of Hobbes is that he too seeks to channel religion in support of political obedience through a single-minded reinterpretation of Christianity as requiring obedience to the sovereign and little else. Thus Rousseau wrote: "Of all the Christian writers, the philosopher Hobbes is the only one who correctly saw the evil and the remedy, who dared to propose the reunification of the two heads of the eagle and the complete return to unity, without which no state will ever be well constituted" (*Social Contract* IV.8). Part III of *Leviathan* as a whole provides the most massive evidence for this reading.

Hobbes surely does wish to transform Christianity in a way that will reinforce, rather than divide, sovereignty. That is not in dispute. Moreover, the core of his doctrine of salvation (the way to eternal life) is obedience to the sovereign. He grants to the sovereign the right to declare what is a miracle and what is prophecy. Hobbes seems to allow, in other words, for the continued belief in invisible powers.

This forces us to sharpen our guiding question in this chapter. For even if we grant the obvious fact that Hobbes wishes to reinterpret Christianity with a view to bolstering civil obedience, the character of that reinterpretation is still in question. Hobbes does not in fact follow the pagan founders in seeking to heighten the fear of invisible powers in order to intensify the spur to obedience. He seeks instead to weaken those fears, even to do away with them entirely. He casts doubt on those invisible and supernatural powers time and again. Whatever allowances he makes for the continued belief in invisible powers must be placed alongside and interpreted in light of his claim that if the "superstitious fear of spirits were taken away, and with it prognostics from dreams, false prophecies, and many other things depending thereon, by which crafty and ambitious persons abuse the simple people, men would be much more fitted than they are for civil obedience" (2.8).

We will see better how Hobbes's pursuit of this improved citizenship unfolds later. For now suffice it to say that Hobbes does not reveal to us how individuals have manipulated religion to empower themselves in order to present us with a model to emulate. He has instead exposed for us the ugly truth about the origins of "all formed religion" (12.24). Recall that people are vulnerable to religious manipulation where they are ignorant of natural causes and "rely on the opinion of some other whom they think wiser than themselves (and see not why he should deceive them)" (11.17). Part I of *Leviathan* has thus far been focused on the natural causes of such things as dreams and visions (chapter 2, "Of Imagination"), conscience (7.4), and inspiration (8.24), as well as the passions, revealing the self-interest that lies behind them, even love (6.3), honor, and the admiration of beauty (6.8). Hobbes, in other words, is seeking to enlighten us about natural causation (especially where religious inspiration or prophecy might be claimed) and the selfishness of human nature, causing us to doubt the good faith of those who claim special religious knowledge. Hobbes's chapter on religion is not yet part of his positive reinterpretation of religion. It is instead the climax of an exposé that clears the way for that reinterpretation, which in turn must be somehow compatible with that exposé. It is only at the end of chapter 12 that Hobbes raises the question of "the causes of change in religion" (12.23–32).

Hobbes's focus in that concluding section, however, is less on the causes of *change* in religion (i.e., from one religion to another) than on what causes a "formed religion" to be "contradicted and rejected" (12.24), or as he later puts it, what causes "the weakening of men's faith" (12.29). It would, it seems, be only a first step in a change in religion (though a weakening of faith in itself is surely a change in religion). These causes include the loss of reputation of wisdom and sincerity "in him that formeth a religion (or addeth to it when it is already formed)" (12.25–26), and doubt in miracles that are necessary signs of divine calling – that doubt being in part a consequence of the loss of reputation. The poor reputation, Hobbes tells us, of the pagan priests was "a great part" of the successful "planting of the Christian religion," as well as of the decline of Roman Catholicism in England and elsewhere. Now, Hobbes has relentlessly attempted to persuade us of the ulterior motives of *all* those who wish to seem wise, righteous, and charitable. The problem of "unpleasing priests" is indeed "not only among Catholics, but even in that church that hath presumed most of reformation" (12.32), although Hobbes leaves unclear which church he has in mind. What is clear is that

Christianity, both Catholic and Protestant, is not invulnerable to a weakening or loss of faith. Such is Hobbes's pregnant conclusion to his chapter on religion.

Religion and the state of nature

Before turning more directly to Hobbesian Christianity, it will be helpful to consider briefly Hobbes's puzzling sequel to the religion chapter. For it is here that we might expect some indication of the change in religion that Hobbes hoped for. But Hobbes instead turns abruptly to his account of the state of nature, in the most famous chapter of *Leviathan*, "Of the Natural Condition of Mankind, as Concerning Their Felicity, and Misery." In light of the fact that Hobbes has been treating the question of religion at some length, the way he opens the chapter is striking: "Nature hath made men …" (13.1). This is not a story of God's handiwork or benevolence. There is no Eden. There is no Fall. And although the deeds human beings may commit in the state of nature are horrifying, there is no sin (13.10). Indeed, apart from Hobbes's denial of the presence of sin, there is not so much as an allusion to religion in chapter 13, even in the list of goods that the state of nature precludes and that await us in a commonwealth (13.9).[5] That is, not only does Hobbes's account of the state of nature give no evidence of being rooted in religion, but religion is not present in the account itself. The latter is more puzzling than the former.

Could Hobbes mean to suggest that there was no religion in the state of nature, that religion entered human life only with the invention of political society? Hobbes had suggested in chapter 12 that "formed religion" was the invention of political founders, but he had also asserted that the "first seeds" of religion are part of human nature. And not only the seeds: where "the life of man [is] solitary, poor, nasty, brutish, and short," and where there is no leisure for the study of natural causation,

---

[5] The Latin version does mention Cain's killing of Abel: "But someone may say: there has never been a war of all against all. What! Did not Cain out of envy kill his brother Abel, a crime so great he would not have dared it if there had at that time been a common power which could have punished him?" (12.11). As Edwin Curley notes, however, "The Biblically alert reader might object that Cain was living under a common power able to punish misdeeds. (Genesis 4:6–16 relates that God punished him immediately)" (Hobbes 1994, 77 n. 7). In other words, Hobbes tells the Cain and Abel story without God – the state of nature without religion.

and therefore where man was certainly ignorant, must there not also have been fear of invisible powers, that is, religion? After all, not all religion is necessarily "formed" religion.

Perhaps Hobbes leaves us, on the basis of chapter 12, to assume that of course the state of nature was filled with primitive religion. But it would have been easy for him to have made mention of what would surely have been a vital element of the state of nature. And so we must ask, How would the account of the state of nature have differed with the fear of invisible powers as a vivid presence? More importantly, how would the account of the way out of the state of nature have differed?

The state of nature, as Hobbes presents it, is a terrible problem, the solution to which is the invention of the commonwealth:

The final cause, end, or design of men (who naturally love liberty and dominion over others) in the introduction of that restraint upon themselves in which we see them live in commonwealths is the foresight of their own preservation, and of a more contented life thereby; that is to say, of getting themselves out from that miserable condition of war, which is necessarily consequent (as hath been shown) to the natural passions of men, when there is no visible power to keep them in awe, and tie them by fear of punishment to the performance of their covenants and observations of those laws of nature set down in the fourteenth and fifteenth chapters. (17.1)

The problem in the state of nature is the lack of a *visible power* to keep them in awe. The sovereign is to have "the use of so much power and strength conferred on him that by terror thereof he is enabled to conform the wills of them all to peace at home and mutual aid against their enemies abroad" (17.13). How much more problematic would Hobbes's account of the origins of the commonwealth be if he were to consider the fear of invisible powers alongside the lack of a visible power, and the even greater fears those invisible powers are capable of inspiring? Indeed, would not Hobbes's presentation of the commonwealth as the clearly rational solution to the problem lose its plausibility?

We are confronted with the possibility that the state of nature is fictional, in the sense that it is not meant to be a historical account. Prior to the emergence of the commonwealth, human beings would have had no leisure for the scientific inquiry into nature necessary to dispel the superstitious beliefs in invisible powers, and their intense fears and insecurity would have driven them to such beliefs. But such a condition would not be, strictly speaking, the natural condition of mankind. That is, by nature, human beings are guided decisively by a concern for their own preservation and a more contented life – by real and concrete, or at any rate, *natural* goods and evils. And Hobbes's state of nature views human beings only in light of these natural concerns and the natural means at their disposal and therefore abstracts from the supernatural, that is, merely imaginary. Human beings are led to establish the commonwealth, according to Hobbes, by the "laws of nature," which are not strictly speaking laws (unless we consider them as ordained by God), but "dictates of reason" (15.41). That is, the story (one is tempted to say "myth") of the emergence of the commonwealth out of the state of nature is the story of rational individuals. It is the story, in other words, of enlightened individuals, that is, individuals who have, it seems, already benefited from the sort of education in both political and natural science that only emerged with the leisure that the commonwealth makes possible.

Looking back, then, at the puzzling transition from Hobbes's chapter on religion to his chapter on the state of nature, we can make the following tentative suggestion: that Hobbes has in fact not set aside the question of the change in religion at which he aims, but means in a way to indicate it. He does not, of course, mean to lead human beings to their natural condition, if by that we mean the state of war described in chapter 13. But does he not, in another sense, mean to lead human beings *for the first time* to their natural condition – to a condition free of superstition and unnatural fears and hopes?[6] Does he not mean, as he implied in chapter 2, to take away the superstitious fear of spirits, that is, supernatural forces, with a view to making human beings more fit for civil obedience and less susceptible to the manipulation of "crafty ambitious persons" (2.8)? If, however, Hobbes entertained such a hope, this would mean taking away religion, as he had defined it in 11.26–27, altogether.

What, then, was Hobbes's ultimate hope regarding religion? Bearing in mind that Hobbes did not wish for his *Leviathan* to be classed with the utopian political philosophies of Plato and Thomas More, what did he hope to see come about with the fullest success of his project? The most obvious possibility is the one we have been considering throughout, namely, that he wished to see religion – in particular, of course, Christianity – transformed so as to have become more reasonable. For Hobbes, this transformed religion would be relatively enlightened, suspicious of claims to supernatural wisdom and of those making such claims. It would be unambiguously supportive of the sovereign authority, and its central tenet would be to seek peace through civil obedience. Yet we have now

---

[6] Cf. Ahrensdorf 2000.

arrived at another, admittedly less obvious, possibility, namely, that he sought a more thoroughgoing popular enlightenment and hoped to see religion ultimately vanish altogether. But if Hobbes did entertain such a radical hope, what are we to make of his massive effort to reinterpret Christianity in parts III and IV of *Leviathan*? With these two main possibilities in mind, let us turn to a more direct consideration of Hobbesian Christianity.

Hobbesian Christianity

The Enlightenment tradition followed Hobbes's lead in several fundamental respects, despite significant and indeed momentous departures. Hobbes's arguments in favor of absolute monarchy were almost universally rejected by those who on the whole accepted the principles of his political philosophy.[7] So beyond the pale do Hobbes's institutional recommendations now seem that Hobbes's status as a member of the liberal tradition remains deeply controversial.

Nowhere is Hobbes's illiberality more apparent, well beyond the first glance, than in his policy concerning religion. For, as we noted at the beginning of this chapter, Hobbes asserts that the sovereign has the right to dictate religious worship and even professions of faith, though admitting that the sincerity of those professions is beyond the sovereign's reach and is not, in fact, his concern. This right of the sovereign is intrinsic to sovereignty, and Hobbes allows that the sovereign may exercise that right to establish whatever religion he sees fit – including Roman Catholicism (42.80) or any non-Christian religion (43.23) – or he may tolerate many religions (47.20; cf. 12.21) and establish no religion at all (31.37). But the fact that such latitude is intrinsic to sovereignty does not imply that all arrangements are equally suited to a rational commonwealth. Who could read part IV of *Leviathan* and conclude that Hobbes would have no

---

[7] Cf. Israel 2006, 226–27: "Radical authors, then, while mostly viewing Hobbes as an apologist for tyranny, calumniator of republican assemblies, champion of censorship, and a thinker who had drawn an excessively pessimistic picture of natural humanity, and especially its proneness to aggression and conflict, consistently did so in a curiously equivocal, even paradoxical, way ... In particular, Hobbes was a key stimulus to the kind of 'anti-Scripturalism,' materialism, and atheism which writers such as Bayle, Collins, and Diderot saw as integral to the radical attitudes they strove to propagate." It is worth noting in this context that, in the preface to *De Cive*, Hobbes admits that his argument for the superiority of monarchy to aristocracy and democracy is "the one thing in this book which I admit is not demonstrated but put forth with probability" (§22).

reservations about making Roman Catholicism the established religion? And, as we will consider more carefully later, Hobbes comments that "perhaps the best" condition with respect to religion is akin to the "independency of the primitive Christians, to follow Paul, or Cephas, or Apollos, every man as he liketh best, if it be without contention" (47.20).

The fact that Hobbes does not think it sufficient simply to leave religion to the sovereign, the fact that he means to guide the sovereign in his handling of religion, is evident from the elaborate reinterpretation of Christianity presented in part III of *Leviathan*. Hobbes presents his own doctrine of salvation, prophecy, miracles, the authority of Scripture and of the clergy. Hobbes may grant the sovereign great latitude with respect to religious policy, but Hobbesian Christianity has its own distinct catechism. Moreover, Hobbes insists that the success of his project depends on an enlightened sovereign's "protecting the public teaching" of *Leviathan* and thus of its teaching on religion (31.41; cf. Review and Conclusion §16). And crucial features of Hobbesian Christianity, which aims "to offer new wine to be put into a new cask," anticipate the radical transformation of religion that Jefferson and other liberals hoped to see take place in and through liberal society.

Consistent with his understanding of the political problem posed by religion, as we have laid it out, Hobbes's reinterpretation of Christianity aims to weaken religious zeal and cast radical doubt on claims of miracles, prophecy, and divinely inspired Scriptural interpretation that might exploit that zeal for the sake of temporal power. It is true that Hobbes seeks to place ultimate religious authority in the sovereign, so that the sovereign alone may declare what is a true miracle, true prophecy, even true Scripture. But, as we will see, this grant of religious authority to the sovereign is based not only on the requirements of peace, but also on the radical uncertainty surrounding all religious claims. It is this radical uncertainty that makes adhering to the sovereign's essentially arbitrary declaration necessary. Here, however, is one of the basic puzzles of Hobbes's teaching on civil religion: the religion that would support the sovereign has been softened or weakened, perhaps even undermined, by Hobbes's skeptically rationalist approach to religion as such.

Part III begins by claiming a shift in the grounds of argumentation from the previous two parts – from a dependence only on nature and natural reason to a dependence on "supernatural revelations of the will of God" as well (32.1). Hobbes immediately stresses that revelation, or prophecy, does not provide alternative grounds, but additional grounds. For there is nothing in prophecy, in true prophecy, that contradicts natural reason, "though there may be many things in God's word above reason (that is to say, which cannot by natural reason be either demonstrated or confuted)" (32.2). Thus many commentators have concluded from this introduction that Hobbes means to reconcile reason and revelation – an eminently respectable aim, to be sure, even if it is not clear why reason (parts I and II) alone would not suffice.[8]

How are we to approach that part of revelation that is above reason and presumably sets part III apart from parts I and II? Hobbes states, "When anything is too hard for our examination, we are bidden to captivate our understanding to the words, and not to labour in sifting out a philosophical truth by logic, of such mysteries as are not comprehensible, nor fall under any rule of natural science" (32.3). But Hobbes makes clear that, by "captivate our understanding," he does not mean that we sacrifice the intellect, nor even that we believe what is beyond our understanding.

By the captivity of our understanding is not meant a submission of the intellectual faculty to the opinion of any other man, but of the will to obedience, where obedience is due. For sense, memory, understanding, reason, and opinion are not in our power to change, but always and necessarily such as the things we see, hear, and consider suggest unto us; and therefore are not effects of our will, but our will of them. We then captivate our understanding and reason when we forbear contradiction, we so speak as (by lawful authority) we are commanded, and when we live accordingly; which, in sum, is trust and faith reposed in him that speaketh, though the mind be incapable of any notion at all from the words spoken. (32.4)

One cannot be forced, or force oneself, to believe what one does not understand. So belief is not at issue. Instead, we "captivate our understanding" when we *speak* (not believe) as we are commanded "by lawful authority." One can speak without believing, and in this case one would be obligated to do so. Hobbes will paradoxically call such obedient speech faith in revelation – or rather, in the prophet – even though this "faith" may well accompany disbelief. Hobbesian "faith" is fully compatible with hypocrisy.

Hobbes does not here speak of faith in God, and in this he is consistent throughout. For unless one is the recipient oneself of God's supernatural revelation, one is trusting not God, but another human being, who claims to be the recipient of revelation (cf. 7.5–6 and 43.1). Hobbes in effect severs faith in prophecy from faith in God. This is a crucial move, for faith in prophecy becomes a merely human question. More importantly, doubt

---

[8] See, e.g., Martinich 1997, 64–68.

of prophecy is simply doubt of a man, one whom Hobbes has trained us to suspect of being either a charlatan or superstitious. It is not necessarily impious to doubt a man. Hobbes tells us that God speaks to human beings "either immediately or by mediation of another man to whom he had formerly spoken by himself immediately" (32.5). For those who are not prophets, prophecy is always encountered as a human claim of immediate revelation. Because the hearer of such a claim has received no supernatural insight himself, there is no way for him to know that what is being reported is in fact genuine revelation. Indeed, without the benefit of experiencing revelation oneself, it is hard, if not impossible to know how revelation is possible at all. It is therefore hard, if not impossible to know that revelation exists at all. Hobbes (speaking in the first person) goes so far as to say that the sovereign "may oblige me to obedience (so as not by act or word to declare I believe him not), but not to think any otherwise than my reason persuades me." And where one claiming revelation has no sovereign authority, "there is nothing that exacteth either belief or obedience."

Revelation is "beyond reason," and Hobbes insists that there are no grounds to believe anything that is "beyond reason." How can one tell the difference between what is beyond reason and what is simply lacking reason? Someone may claim that "he speaks by supernatural inspiration," but to Hobbes this looks as if he merely "finds an ardent desire to speak, or some strong opinion of himself, for which he can allege no natural or sufficient reason" (32.6). Similarly, for a man "to say that [God] hath spoken to him in a dream is no more than to say he dreamed that God spake to him," and "to say he hath seen a vision, or heard a voice, is to say that he dreamed between sleeping and waking; for in such a manner a man doth many times naturally take his dream for a vision, as not having well observed his own slumbering." Hobbes will not deny that God *can* speak to man in dreams and visions, "yet [God] obliges no man to believe he hath so done to him that pretends it, who (being a man) may err, and (which is more) may lie." There is a gap between acknowledging what God can do and believing in any given instance that He has done it, a gap we will see Locke exploit in the next chapter.

All of this is to say, however, only that one is not obligated to take any alleged prophet at his word. Does that go for the Bible as well? To recall again Hobbes's definition of faith in chapter 7, "when we believe the Scriptures are the word of God, having no immediate revelation from God himself, our belief, faith, and trust is in the church, whose word we take, and acquiesce therein ... So that it is evident that whatsoever we believe upon no other reason than what is drawn from authority of men and their writings, whether they be sent from God or not, is *faith in men only*" (7.7, emphasis added). Hobbes assures us that if a historian claims that God speaks and we do not believe it, we doubt the historian, not God. Be that as it may, Hobbes opens part III by leading us to wonder how *any* claimed revelation can be believed, even though in the case of Scripture, he makes sure by neither "act or word to *declare* that I believe ... not" (emphasis added).

As Hobbes turns to his treatment of Scripture in chapter 33, he makes clear that a challenge to the absolute authority of the sovereign arises not only from false latter-day prophets, but potentially from Scripture itself. For

by the Books of Holy Scripture are understood those which ought to be the canon (that is to say, the rules) of Christian life. And because all rules of life which men are in conscience bound to observe are laws, the question of Scripture is the question of what is law throughout Christendom, both natural and civil. (33.1)

For God is the "sovereign of all sovereigns," and when God speaks He of course must be obeyed. That is not in question, but instead "when and what God hath said." Now, the books of the Bible are said to contain, if not consist entirely of, prophecy. But, as Hobbes has already made plain, in believing the Bible to be prophetical, we believe not God, but those human beings who make the claim. We cannot, by natural reason, determine "who were the original writers of the several Books of Holy Scripture," but at best only the "not unuseful" knowledge of when they were written. Believing the Bible to be prophetical, then, cannot even mean believing the honesty of the authors, who are unknown and whose honesty therefore cannot be judged. And so we are left to trust the church, who first collected the books of the Bible as Holy Scripture – in particular the Council of Laodicea. But that council did its work 364 years after Christ, was teeming with ambition, and "endeavored to pass their doctrine, not for council and information, as preachers, but for laws, as absolute governors, and thought such frauds as tended to make the people the more obedient to Christian doctrine to be pious" (33.20). The question of Scripture emphatically concerns civil authority.

And yet, despite such intentions on the part of those who established the Christian canon, Hobbes says that he sees no "reason to doubt but that the Old and New Testament, as we have them now, are the true registers of those things which were done and said by the prophets and apostles" (33.20). What leads Hobbes to this startling non sequitur? His most adequate explanation appears not in the immediate context, but near the opening of the chapter. Without the benefit of direct supernatural revelation

> when and what God hath said ... cannot be known but by natural reason which guided them, for the obtaining of peace and justice, to obey the authority of their several commonwealths (that is to say, of their lawful sovereigns). *According to this obligation*, I can acknowledge no other books of the Old Testament to be Holy Scripture but those which have been commanded to be acknowledged for such by the authority of the Church of England... As for the Books of the New Testament, they are equally acknowledged for canon by all Christian churches. (33.1, 2; emphasis added)

Reason dictates that "we so speak as (by lawful authority) we are commanded" (33.4), though we disbelieve what we say. By stating explicitly that his "acknowledgement" is based on his obligation to obey the command of his sovereign, Hobbes comes as close as his principles allow (he must "forbear contradiction" [32.4; cf. Appendix 2.35–36]) to admitting that it is *not* based on belief. Too few interpreters of Hobbes have noted how this principle of his makes the task of interpreting his utterances on religion more difficult than it might otherwise be. For those who disbelieve, reason instructs hypocrisy for the sake of peace, and Hobbes writes under the authority of the Church of England.

Thus Hobbes's "acknowledgement" of the books of the Bible as prophetic is based on natural reason – but not because reason can lead to knowledge that they are prophetic. On the contrary, "it is manifest that none can know they are God's word (though all true Christians believe it) but those to whom God hath revealed it supernaturally" (33.21). But supernatural revelation is a miracle and "miracles now cease" (32.9). Without either natural or supernatural knowledge that the Scriptures are the word of God, one is not obligated to believe those human beings who claim that they are, and hence "not obliged to obey [the Scriptures] by any authority but his whose commands have already the force of law," that is, the sovereign's (33.24). The authentic word of God is, of course, higher than the sovereign's word. But since the authentic word of God is radically unknowable, what is "acknowledged" as the word of God is determined by the earthly sovereign. The only alternative is to take the word of private men, in which case it would be "impossible that any divine law should be acknowledged" (33.24). But the acknowledgment of a law as divine is in fact only the acknowledgment of the human authority of the sovereign, which we ourselves grant for the sake of peace.[9] This, then, is how the acknowledgment of the revelation of Scripture is grounded in reason: all obedience to the sovereign is grounded in reason.

Hobbes's treatment of prophecy in chapter 36 follows suit. There Hobbes asserts that God always spoke to the prophets of the Bible "no otherwise than from their dreams and visions, that is to say from the imaginations which they had in their sleep or in an ecstasy" (36.11). He allows that Moses was unique among the prophets, but only in that his was "a more clear vision than was given to other prophets" (3.11). But such imaginations may proceed from God either through supernatural revelation or "by his natural operation and mediation of second causes" (36.19). To draw from elsewhere in *Leviathan*, "ignorance of second causes" is one of "the natural seeds of religion" (12.11); and the nature of sight and therefore of imagination, dreams, and visions was "never discovered by the ancient pretenders to natural knowledge (much less by those that consider not things so remote as that knowledge is from their present use)" (45.2). Therefore, in the ignorance of ancient times, "it was hard for men to conceive of those images in the fancy and in the senses otherwise than of things really without us," though they be only imaginations originating within us. (Here we see why knowledge of *when* the Bible was written is "not unuseful.") Thus

men had need to be very circumspect and wary in obeying the voice of man that, pretending himself to be a prophet, requires us follow him on the way to eternal salvation. For he that pretends to teach men the way of so great felicity pretends to govern them (that is to say, to rule and reign over them), which is a thing that all men naturally desire, and is therefore worthy to be suspected of ambition and imposture, and consequently, ought to be examined and tried by every man before he yield them obedience (unless he have yielded it them already, in the institution of a commonwealth, as when the prophet is the civil sovereign, or by the civil sovereign authorized). (36.19, Latin version)

Hobbes makes a point of insisting that Biblical prophecy not be exempted from this suspicion: "Seeing, then, there was in the time of the Old Testament such quarrels amongst the visionary prophets ... and such controversies in the New Testament amongst the spiritual prophets, every man then was, *and now is* bound to make use of his natural reason, to ally to *all prophecy* those rules which God hath given us, to discern the true

---

[9] Hood begins his study of *Leviathan* with the assertion that "Hobbes professed to accord to Scripture, and only to Scripture, unquestionable authority over his mind" (1964, 1). Hood does not relate what in Hobbes's writings led him to this conclusion. He does not notice Hobbes's express statement of the basis of Scriptural authority in general and for himself, which has nothing whatever to do with authority over the mind.

from the false" (36.20, emphasis added). The conclusion to which Hobbes means to move us is made clear in his conclusion: only the sovereign is to be taken as God's prophet – even Christian subjects are to accept only their sovereign, whether he be Christian or not – or else risk destroying the commonwealth and reverting to a state of war. In other words, no genuine prophet is left standing; the sovereign is left as sole "prophet" only for the sake of peace.

We can now see more clearly than before a basic puzzle of Hobbes's civil religion. Hobbes's argument for sovereign authority to determine what is revelation depends on casting all claims to revelation in doubt. Without that doubt, those claims would enjoy an authority higher than the sovereign's. But Hobbes's procedure also casts doubt on the sovereign's claim. Sovereign authority over religion is built upon the ruins of *all* distinctly religious authority, of all authority *de Jure Divino*, which leaves in place only the otherwise lower authority *de Jure Civili* (cf. 42.71). Hobbesian Christianity is not only compatible with hypocrisy on the part of skeptics; it appears to have no other basis.

Hobbesian Christianity, then, seems to undermine itself, or to make itself unnecessary, and this is surely a powerful reason to suspect that Hobbes did not mean it as a serious proposal. Indeed, surely more than a few readers must be struck by how implausible, and at times even ludicrous, Hobbes's attempts to shoehorn Scripture and Christian doctrine into his own doctrine are – how transparent the attempt and often with a wink to the reader. Could Hobbes have seriously expected anyone to swallow his "new wine in a new cask" (R&C 14)? Has anyone ever swallowed it? For example, are we expected to take seriously Hobbes's claim that the authority of the Mosaic Law over the Israelites was grounded on their consent? And that their consent established Moses, not God, as their sovereign (40.6)? Are we expected to take seriously the claim that the central teaching of Biblical prophecy is to obey your sovereign in all things, including idolatry (43.23)? Are we to take seriously the claim that when Jesus said to his disciples, "Receive the Holy Spirit," he was breathing on them and referring to his breath (*pneuma*, which means most basically "wind" or "breath") as a metaphor (44.25)? Even or especially with regard to the most elementary teaching of Hobbesian Christianity: could Hobbes have expected any sincere believer to accept the central tenet of religion as he presents it – obey the sovereign commands regarding religion whatever they may be, including idolatry? In an apparent attempt to defend his bona fides as a good Anglican, Hobbes wrote: "There is nothing in [*Leviathan*] against episcopacy. I cannot therefore imagine what reason any episcopal man can have to speak of me, as I hear some of them do, as of an atheist or man of no religion, *unless it be for making the authority of the church wholly dependent upon the regal power*" ("Seven Philosophical Problems," emphasis added). As John Dewey pointed out in commenting on this passage, Hobbes not only fails to offer an adequate defense, he even draws attention to the core problem (Dewey 1974, 11–12).

In considering this question, it will be helpful to look at the tenets of Hobbesian Christianity more closely. If the sovereign does choose to establish Christianity, the required doctrines as Hobbes presents them prove to be slight. In the Christian commonwealth, there are two things necessary to enter "the Kingdom of Heaven," only one of which is a matter of belief in a theological doctrine: "All that is necessary to salvation is contained in two virtues: faith in Christ, and obedience to laws" (43.3). Hobbes at first speaks of obedience to "God's laws," which "if it were perfect, were enough to us" for salvation. Since none have obeyed God's laws perfectly, faith in Christ is needed. Despite Hobbes's quasi-Pauline introduction, he proves not to have in mind the Mosaic Law, which he insists was authoritative only for the ancient Hebrews under Moses' (not God's) sovereign authority. As for Jesus, he gave no laws, but only "counsel to observe those we are subject to" (43.5). The laws of God prove to be not revealed divine law, but the "law" of nature, which instructs us "to obey our civil sovereign." And so the generically worded requirement of "obedience to laws" turns out to mean (lo and behold!) obedience to the civil laws. Even the precepts of the Bible, Hobbes reminds us, "are only law where the civil sovereign hath made it so" (43.5).

As for "faith in Christ," Hobbes at first makes this requirement apparently impossible. For "it is impossible to believe any person before we know what he saith," and it is therefore necessary that "he be the one we have heard speak" (43.6). Thus it is the apostles, not we, who are able to have faith in Jesus. It is not even clear that we can have faith in the apostles. Rather, those that Christians have heard speak are their pastors; and "so the faith of Christians ever since our Saviour's time hath had for its foundation, first, the reputation of their pastors," and after them, Christian sovereigns, our "supreme pastors," who alone have authority to make the Bible "the rule of faith" (43.6).[10]

---

[10] The way Hobbes has ordered these two foundations of Christian faith is noteworthy, since the sovereign authority in establishing Christianity is dependent on or derivative of a prior faith in the pastors. This is an apparent departure for Hobbes's usual procedure of

Since faith in Christ is strictly speaking impossible, Hobbes restates that requirement to mean faith (in our pastors' declaration) that "Jesus is the Christ." Indeed, the "only necessary article of the Christian faith" is that "Jesus is the Christ," that is, "the king which God had before promised, by the prophets of the Old Testament, to send into the world to reign (over the Jews and over such of other nations as should believe in him [i.e., not all nations or all mankind]) under himself eternally and to give them that eternal life which was lost by the sin of Adam" (43.11). Hobbes does not mention Jesus' resurrection or divinity.[11]

One of Hobbes's proofs that this is the only necessary article of Christian faith is that there are places in Scripture that declare salvation to be easy: "For if an inward assent of the mind to all the doctrines concerning Christian faith now taught (whereof the greatest part are disputed) were necessary to salvation, there would be nothing in the world so hard as to be a Christian" (43.14). Nothing is harder to believe than these doctrines, whereas the eye of the needle of Hobbesian Christianity is plenty big for a camel (cf. Matthew 19:24). But Hobbes admits that he has avoided or ignored those parts of Scripture that "are of obscure or controverted interpretation" (43.24), for otherwise nothing could be derived clearly. And although it is true that other articles of faith may be implicit in this one, some are harder to deduce than others. Hobbes spares us the demonstrations, and even the complete lists of consequent articles of faith, which is presumably a matter of dispute,[12] asserting only that those who believe the one necessary article of faith also believe in those others "implicitly," "though he have not skill enough to discern the consequence" (43.18).[13] If someone "holdeth this foundation,

---

    making sovereign authority dependent only on the prior consent of the people, and even then not for the content of established religion. One possible interpretation of this departure is that, in Christian commonwealths, Christianity is a fact that the sovereigns of greatest concern to Hobbes inherit, regardless of whether it would be the best religion to establish if it were possible to start from scratch. Hobbes too inherits Christianity. More on this later.

[11] Hobbes's summary of the Gospel of Matthew ends, like Jefferson's expurgated gospel, with Jesus' death (43.11).

[12] Hobbes does here mention for the first time the (implied) necessity to believe that "Jesus Christ is risen." It is implied because "a dead man cannot exercise the office of king" (43.18).

[13] Hobbes does not follow the same principle when it comes to implied atheism: "For it is very difficult to judge the consequences of words. Therefore, if an accused person has said something against the letter of the law [professing atheism], because he did not know how to reason well, and has not harmed anyone, his ignorance will excuse him... The only ground on which [an atheist] can be accused is something he has said, either orally or in

Jesus is the Christ," whatever that may mean, he must be presumed to hold also "everything which can be inferred from it," whatever those things may be, "whether he understands the force of the inference or not" (43.18, Latin version). In this way, Hobbes signals his aim of avoiding disputation on the finer points of Christian theology, much of which, as Hobbes has told us repeatedly, is nonsense anyway. And though the sovereign's appointed priests or bishops may advise the sovereign on the laws regarding religion, Hobbes warns them that if they seek their every religious opinion "though obscure and unnecessary to salvation, to be law, there will be clashings innumerable, not only of laws but also of swords" (*English Works* 4:364–65).

Thus Hobbesian Christianity, despite its emphasis on civil authority over religion, seems to allow for broad theological disagreement. By keeping the theological essentials to a minimum – indeed it is hard to see how he could have reduced them further while remaining somehow distinctly Christian – Hobbes's prescription appears compatible with a broad religious pluralism, provided all defer to the civil authority. Even if the civil authority establishes a Christian commonwealth as Hobbes has described it, he will require very little besides outward civil obedience. Indeed, if he has civil obedience, it is not clear why he should require any religious practices or professions at all. Thus the line between the illiberal civil authority over religion that Hobbes grants and our liberal separation of church and state is more porous than it at first appears. Although the U.S. Constitution allows for a broad diversity of religions, it, like Hobbes, insists that the civil authority is supreme. The final court of appeal is the Supreme Court of the state, and the state's tolerance is based on and essentially limited by that fact.

So, too, the Hobbesian state is more open to religious toleration than it at first appears. As we noted previously, the sovereign has the authority to establish any religion he sees fit, or to establish no religion at all: "Where many sorts of worship be allowed, proceeding from the different religions of private men, it cannot be said there is any public worship, nor that the commonwealth is of any religion at all" (31.37). Part III of *Leviathan* indicates the best sort of Christian commonwealth possible, that is, the best if Christian public worship is required. But is it best to require any public worship at all?

writing, viz. *if he has straightforwardly denied that God exists*" (*Leviathan* appendix 2. 38, 36; emphasis added). Cf. Leo Strauss's reference to *De Cive* 15.14 together with *English Works* IV, p. 349 (Strauss 1953, 199 n. 43).

Hobbes provides his clearest indication that it would not be best to require public worship in the final chapter of *Leviathan*. At the same time, he indicates that this best case will not be feasible until the people are enlightened. As Hobbes says elsewhere, "The multitude [*vulgus*] is educated little by little" (*Opera Philosophica* 2:128). His opponents in the final chapter of *Leviathan* are those believers (exemplified, but not limited to, Roman Catholics) who "pretend the kingdom of God to be of this world, and thereby to have a power [i.e., a power over the affairs of this world] therein distinct from that of the civil state" (47.34). But the effects of this politically pernicious doctrine cannot be eliminated easily or quickly. The prosperity of these enemies of civil order, "together with their ambition, [has grown] to such a height as the violence thereof openeth the eyes which the wariness of their predecessors had before sealed up, and makes men by too much grasping let go all (as Peter's net was broken by the struggling of too great a multitude of fishes), *whereas the impatience of those that strive to resist such encroachment before their subjects' eyes were opened did but increase the power they resisted*" (emphasis added.) The "knot[s] upon [the people's] liberty" were tied over several hundred years and must be unraveled one step at a time, until

we are reduced to the independency of the primitive Christians, to follow Paul, or Cephas, or Apollos, every man as he liketh best. Which, if it be without contention, and without measuring the doctrine of Christ by our affection to the person of his minister ... is perhaps the best. First, because there ought to be no power over the consciences of men but of the Word itself, working faith in every one, not always according to the purpose of them that plant and water, but of God himself, that giveth the increase. And secondly, because it is unreasonable (in them who teach there is such danger in every little error) to require of a man endued with reason of his own, to follow the reason of any other man, or of the most voices of many other men (which is little better than to venture his salvation at cross and pile).[14] (47.20)

Hobbesian principles are flexible enough to permit a prudent concession to the need for public religion – flexible enough to allow for a Christian commonwealth.

This line of interpretation opens up an alternative view of Hobbesian Christianity, namely, that he meant it seriously to be adopted, but not

---

[14] "Cross and pile" was the English version of "heads or tails." Readers unfamiliar with the game may be more struck by Hobbes's choice of words than a contemporary reader, although also more likely to miss the joke.

as part of the ultimate solution. Instead, Hobbes's religious teaching may have been meant to be transitional, making timely concessions to accepted opinions of the present with a view to moving public opinion in a more enlightened direction, a direction that would in time see elements of that teaching dropped. Surely Hobbes's comment on the need of a gradual process of enlightenment ("little by little") suggests some transitional elements of his teaching. At the same time, this suggestion makes it still more difficult to say with any confidence what the end point of that process would be. More specifically in this context, we are forced to wonder how much worship (i.e., the attempt to appease invisible powers), even of a private sort, one would find among a people that has had its eyes opened by Hobbes. For when Hobbes observes in Christianity "such diversity of ways in running to the same mark, felicity," he takes it as a sign that "we are ... yet in the dark" (44.2). Religious pluralism – some following Paul, some Cephas, some Apollos – is ipso facto evidence of a lack of enlightenment. What of those who are enlightened? What of those who have been educated according to those Hobbesian principles that the sovereign commands to be disseminated and thus follow the principles of nature? Those who worship according to the principles of nature do not do so to please God. For, Hobbes tells us at the end of part II, "God hath no ends," and so has no reason to "wish himself to be worshipped" (31.13, English and Latin versions). According to nature, "the worship we do him proceeds from our duty, and is directed according to our capacity, by those rules of honour that reason dictateth to be done by the weak to the more potent *men*, in hope of benefit, for fear of damage, or in thankfulness for good already received *from them*" (emphasis added). Worship by nature is for the sake of pleasing not God, but more powerful human beings who dictate that we worship. If the sovereign dictates no worship, the enlightened human being has no cause to worship at all. Yet if such were the case, what we would find would not be a pluralism of private religion, but an enlightened (irreligious or unreligious) consensus. Could this be why Hobbes says that toleration of a private religious pluralism is "perhaps" the best? Would better still be the disappearance of all appeasement of invisible powers, all fear of invisible powers, leaving only fear of the sovereign?

Adding to these considerations, we note that in his chapter "Of Religion," Hobbes presents us with an example of a political regime that was tolerant of a great variety of religions, provided their adherents obeyed the civil law: "The Romans, that had conquered the greatest part of the then known world, made no scruple of tolerating any religion whatsoever in the city of Rome itself, unless it had something in it that could not consist with their civil government." Why not then Rome as a model? Rome's toleration was almost universal, but the exception is crucial. Hobbes continues, "Nor do we read that any religion was there forbidden but that of the Jews, who (being the peculiar kingdom of God) thought it unlawful to acknowledge to any mortal kind or state whatsoever." Since it is impossible to believe Hobbes's implicit assertion of ignorance of Roman persecution of Christians, suffice it to say that he sees in Christianity something from its inception that resists a civil policy of toleration. Hobbes seems not to have blamed Rome, whose policy in religious matters aimed "only to keep the people in obedience and peace."

It is difficult to answer the question of Hobbes's ultimate practical aim regarding religion. That difficulty is made particularly frustrating when we consider that he is renowned for the clarity of his thought and that religion was the principal difficulty he sought to solve. It is safe to conclude that the ideal solution (if we may speak of ideals in connection to Hobbes) would be the elimination of religion altogether. Beyond what we have mentioned, the strongest evidence supporting this conclusion is the trajectory of Hobbes's argument as a whole, which leads in the direction of the elimination of religion as the only truly stable solution to the political problem. In Hobbes's account "Of Man" in part I of *Leviathan*, human nature is presented to us as radically needy, but our natural needs are strictly temporal. Religion grows out of, and is intelligible strictly in light of, temporal needs. Hobbes presents human nature as devoid of any distinctly spiritual or religious need. Even "natural religion," opinion of the eternal first cause, is rooted in our temporal concerns (11.24). Moreover, the way out of our natural condition of war is intelligible without reference to religion, as the refutation of the Fool is meant to show. Of parts I and II, Hobbes says, "I have derived the rights of sovereign power, and the duty of subjects, hitherto from the principles of nature only" (32.1). What follows beginning in part III, which "dependeth much upon the supernatural revelations of the will of God," will supplement and support, but will not alter or add fundamentally to the principles discernable in nature alone. The argument from nature stands on its own and is therefore sufficient for anyone capable of being guided solely by his or her natural reason. Religion, then, is at best an inessential support, and at worst a terrible problem, for the leviathan state. And even if the fear of invisible powers can be used as a support for the sovereign, it remains in its nature a loose cannon that may turn against the sovereign. Does Hobbes's argument not lead us to raise the question, even if he himself does not: if human beings have no natural need of religion, or if the natural needs that lead to religion can be sufficiently met by human means, does not the surest solution to the political problem require its elimination?

It would not be long before Pierre Bayle, a great admirer of Hobbes, would make explicit this radical possibility: that a society of atheists, a society without religion, is possible. Bayle presents the argument that belief in God is not necessary for the level of moral virtue needed for political society. Bayle said of Hobbes, "Of all the moral virtues, there are hardly any but religion that was a problematic matter in the person of Hobbes" (1969:8, 166). One might even venture to say that moral virtue itself as traditionally understood, as requiring the subordination of self-interest, is not necessary: Human beings are driven by self-love, and earthly rewards and punishments are sufficient to make them adhere to basic moral rules. Moreover, atheism allows for better citizenship than "paganism," that is, superstitious religion. Bayle even goes so far as to use Christian examples to illustrate the problematic character of paganism, thus pointing to the question of whether a society of atheists is not only possible, but best. In each of these steps, Bayle follows Hobbes's principles, whether or not he draws the same conclusions from those principles. Commenting on *De Cive*, Bayle wrote, "Hobbes made many enemies on account of that work; but he made the most clear-sighted admit that no one ever penetrated the foundations of politics so well" (1969:8, 163).[15]

On the other hand, even if the trajectory of Hobbes's argument does lead in the direction of eliminating religion altogether, perhaps we have merely been put in a position to see what would, as we have said, be ideal, and of course Hobbes is no idealist. Hobbes might have supposed a world without religion would be the best imaginable, but too much to hope for – hope being "appetite with an opinion of attaining" (6.14).

The natural seeds of religious indifference

The clearest textual evidence suggesting that Hobbes could not have seriously hoped for the elimination of religion appears at the beginning of the passage discussed earlier on the causes of change in religion. There he says that the seeds of religion (here quoting the Latin version)

---

[15] Robert Bartlett (2001 3, n. 5) notes that Bayle's *Dictionnaire* was among the one hundred books Jefferson chose as the basis of the Library of Congress.

"can never be so abolished out of human nature but that new religions will spring from them, if suitable cultivators exist." Those seeds, we recall, are anxiety about the future combined with ignorance of natural causation. The seeds of religion, if not religion itself, seem to be natural.

Yet this statement by Hobbes is ambiguous. He does not say that religion can never be removed from human nature, but rather the *seeds* of religion. Indeed, he does not even quite say that. The seeds of religion "can never be *so abolished* out of human nature, but that new religions may again be made to spring out of them by the culture of such men as for such purpose are in reputation" (12.23, emphasis added). Hobbes seems to allow that the seeds of religion can be abolished to some degree.[16] Human beings will, of course, remain naturally anxious about their future. They will remain intensely self-centered. Their appetite for mundane goods, which aims not only at creature comforts but also at gratifying their vanity, will remain insatiable. Consider further the intense desire for preservation and thus the concern with sickness, accidents, and surely some violent crime, to say nothing of international war – such phenomena as no state could reasonably be expected to eradicate – and we may well expect to find the natural seeds of religion germinating. But Hobbes might have supposed that a vigilant gardener can keep his garden free of weeds without supposing that he can eradicate them once and for all.

We note that the causes of religion overlap with the causes of the leviathan state. The state will focus energies on both ignorance of natural causation and the gnawing anxiety about the future. The state is to educate the people and secure their lives. Hobbes does not understand religion to be rooted in anything essentially different from what the leviathan state can secure. If, thanks to the commonwealth, human beings find themselves safe and secure, comfortable and prospering – or at least with the hope of prospering through their own industry – might Hobbes have expected them not to turn to religion in the first place? With a *visible* power (the "mortal god" of the state) in place and doing its job, who needs to invent invisible powers?

In observing this aspect of Hobbes's teaching, we note the difference between Hobbes's account of the transition from an unreligious state of

---

[16] Hobbes does everything possible to cast doubt on the reputation of all potential cultivators, with the possible exception of himself. Cf. the altered wording of the Latin version quoted previously. Of course, Hobbes did not enjoy a great reputation, certainly not as a divine.

nature to the leviathan state and the actual condition of mankind that
Hobbes faced, a condition permeated by religion. In the former scenario,
one perhaps may not expect religion ever to arise in the first place. But in
the transition from the current condition to the leviathan state, what
would one expect? Although Bayle spoke of the possibility of a society
of atheists, he does seem to have expected such a society to come
into being, distinguishing between "practical atheists" – those "who live
without fear of God though not without belief in his existence" – and
speculative or theoretical atheists – those who have subjected theism to
a theoretical critique, "as for example Diagoras, Vanini, Spinoza, etc."
(2000, 317). Surely Hobbes was as aware as Bayle that theoretical human
beings of any sort are rare.

   Might Hobbes have hoped for something like what Bayle calls practical
atheism? Not unbelief, but a radical reorientation of human concerns
to the goods of this life. Not unbelief, but very little thought of belief.
Not unbelief, but indifference. From Hobbes's point of view, this might
mean tolerating a certain degree of confusion and superstition, so long
as they were sufficiently impotent not to disrupt sound worldly calculations. Indeed, theoretical wisdom disappears altogether from Hobbes's
teaching, as the standard for enlightenment is lowered. There are no
pointers to higher or deeper needs than the ones the leviathan state
can help to meet. In a society made secure by Hobbesian political science,
the "rationality" of the indifferent is sufficient.

3

Locke and the political theology of toleration

Heaven being our great business and interest, the knowledge which may direct us thither is certainly so, too; so that without peradventure the study which ought to take up the first and chiefest place in our thoughts. ("Of Study," p. 411)

Since then the Precepts of Natural Religion are plain and very intelligible to all Mankind, and seldom come to be controverted; and other revealed Truths, which are conveyed to us by Books and Languages, are liable to the common and natural obscurities and difficulties incident to Words, methinks it would become us to be more careful and diligent in observing the former, and less magisterial, positive, and imperious, in imposing our own sense and interpretations of the latter. (*Essay Concerning Human Understanding*, III.9.23)

The knowledge we acquire in this world I am apt to think extends not beyond the limits of this life. The beatific vision of the other life needs not the help of this dim twilight; but be that as it will, this I'm sure, the principal end why we are to get knowledge here is to make use of it for the benefit of ourselves and others in the world. ("Of Study," p. 412)

I.

With Hobbes we remain rather far from the American arrangement. The Hobbesian approach was, in one of its elements or another, almost universally reviled.[1] It was, moreover, subjected to a powerful critique by the philosopher who exerted the greatest influence on Jefferson and the American Founding: John Locke. Locke made concessions that Hobbes refused to make to a human attachment to liberty, one that is not unambiguously reducible to the desire for preservation. Whereas Hobbes was concerned that the call to "Liberty!" could be easily manipulated into a rallying cry of rebellion against the sovereign authority, Locke appealed emphatically to liberty, to the point of defending a right of revolution.[2] Not coincidentally, Locke seems to have made concessions that Hobbes refused to make to the place of religion in human life, as is evidenced in the shift from a purely political absolutism over religion to a policy of religious toleration.

As we saw in the previous chapter, Hobbes's argument for the sovereign's authority over religion is strictly one of *Jure Civili* and is based upon a radical critique of all *Jure Divino*. The sovereign authority over religion is so far from being a religious authority that its premise is a critique of religious authority, and indeed of religion itself. As Robert Kraynak characterizes it, Hobbes's "secular absolutism depends on a kind of enlightened cynicism" (1980, 60). In a passage from the *Letter Concerning Toleration* cited in the previous chapter, Locke makes a similar point after accusing the clergy of hypocrisy in the ease with

[1] Jonathan Israel writes that later Enlightenment figures had "a deep-seated aversion to Hobbes's anti-libertarianism, anti-republicanism, and scorn for democracy" (2006, 225). Despite this aversion, many viewed him "in a curiously equivocal, even paradoxical way, hardly ever disowning him and his system, and often betraying an unmistakable sympathy for elements of his thought ... Hobbes was a key stimulus to the kind of 'anti-Scripturalism,' materialism, and atheism which writers such as Bayle, Collins, and Diderot saw as integral to the radical attitudes they strove to propagate" (226–27).

Cf. also Macaulay's account of the prevailing spirit shortly after the Restoration of Charles II: "Ethical philosophy had recently taken a form well suited to please a generation equally devoted to monarchy and to vice. Thomas Hobbes had, in language more precise and luminous than has ever by employed by any metaphysical writer, maintained that the will of the prince was the standard of right and wrong, and that every subject ought to be ready to profess Popery, Mahometanism, or Paganism at the royal command. Thousands who were incompetent to appreciate what was really valuable in his speculations, eagerly welcomed a theory which, while it exalted the kingly office, relaxed the obligations of morality, and degraded religion into a mere affair of state. Hobbism soon became an almost essential part of the character of the fine gentleman" (134–35). Cf. Macaulay's description of Charles II, Hobbes's one-time pupil, at page 126.

[2] This is not to deny that Locke justifies freedom and the right of revolution in terms of preservation. Freedom from the arbitrary and absolute power of another "is the only security of my Preservation" (§17, cf. 23 and 137). Cf. Locke's defense of the right of revolution, §§208–09, 222–25; cf. 42–44 on the importance of property for preservation.

which they "change their Decrees, their Articles of Faith, their form of Worship, everything, according to the inclination of those Kings and Queens ... of such different minds, in point of religion" (1983, 38). He continues: "No man in his Wits (I had almost said none but an Atheist) will presume to say that any sincere and upright Worshipper of God could, with a safe Conscience, obey their several Decrees." The clergy, of course, whatever their deeds, did not *say* such things, but Hobbes, who was certainly not out of his wits, did. Surely Locke is correct to doubt that sincere and upright believers will change their articles of faith, form of worship, everything, whenever a new sovereign takes the throne. Now, of course, Hobbes may also have doubted it, which is why Kraynak says that his solution depends on "a kind of enlightened cynicism." In other words, as we have been compelled to conjecture more than once, perhaps Hobbes wished to do away with sincere and upright belief. Locke's more precise critique of Hobbes, then, appears to lie in questioning whether or the degree to which a political solution based on such "enlightened cynicism" is possible.

It would appear to be evident, then, that Locke's political agenda with respect to religion is more moderate than Hobbes's. And though we must ever distinguish the practical agenda or project from its theoretical basis, the difference in their agenda is necessarily linked to a theoretical disagreement. Locke's turn to toleration would seem to suggest a disagreement with Hobbes about how deeply entrenched religion is in human nature. This disagreement would seem to be linked to the disagreement regarding the appeal to liberty. In the case of both the religious and the political, Locke seems to appeal to a part of human nature that desires something more or higher than comfortable preservation and power. Thus to some degree, man or mankind seems to be both more religious and more political by nature for Locke than for Hobbes. Our judgment must, however, remain tentative, lest we lose sight of the fact that Locke's state of nature is as apolitical as Hobbes's.

Now, we might expect a transformative agenda from the more authoritarian Hobbes before we would expect it from the more tolerant Locke, since it would seem that to seek transformation is not to tolerate. Yet Locke spends far more time over the course of his writings on his ambitious transformative project than Hobbes does on his. That effort on Locke's part is evidence of his estimation of the magnitude or depth of transformation required in order to make religion suitably tolerant. What is particularly striking, moreover, as we shall see later, is the extent to which the more tolerant Locke's transformative agenda follows in the tracks laid by more the authoritarian Hobbes: The substance of Lockean Christianity closely resembles that of Hobbesian Christianity. Or should we say "lack of substance," owing to their similarly minimal theology aiming at the broadest possible inclusiveness? Locke also follows Hobbes by arriving at that minimalism through a sustained radical critique of claims to religious knowledge, above all divinely revealed knowledge, beyond the rationally demonstrated existence of "a God." Whereas the critique of religious knowledge in Hobbes leads to sovereign authority over religion, in Locke it leads in the opposite direction of toleration. In other words, fundamentally similar transformations of religion are meant to support seemingly opposite political policies.[3]

The relation between Hobbes and Locke is a matter of considerable controversy, particularly on the subject of religion. Only a handful of scholars accept Hobbes's professions of faith to be sincere, while the majority today (as in his own day) see them as a thin veil covering irreligion or extreme heterodoxy. The controversy centers on the interpretation of the place of religion in Locke's thought. Locke's religiosity has been deeply controversial from the start, and he frequently had to defend himself against the charge of veiling his own irreligion or extreme heterodoxy and (what amounts to the same thing) his debt to Hobbes and Spinoza. Moreover, Locke came under suspicion on account of his admirers as well as some of his intimate associates. Stuart Brown reports that "Locke was apparently warned by the anti-deist Francis Gastrell that he was highly regarded and much quoted by 'the Socinians, deists, Atheists, and freethinkers in the country' and that he ought to take steps to disavow them. He seems not to have been strenuous enough in distancing himself from radicals and indeed made Collins one of his executors" (1996, 224). (Anthony Collins was a prominent "freethinker" whom Voltaire called "one of the most terrible enemies of the Christian

---

[3] Interest in Locke's views on religion has increased markedly in recent years, with the majority of scholars arguing that Locke's teachings rest ultimately on a theological basis. See, e.g. Spellman 1988, Marshall, 1994, McClure 1996, Waldron, 2002, Forster, 2005. Paul Sigmund speaks of Locke's *Paraphrase and Notes on the Epistles of St. Paul* in connection with his "almost obsessive interest in religion in the final years of his life" (2005, 410), which he, along with Spellman, takes as evidence of Locke's devout faith, making Locke's profound debt to Hobbes "difficult to maintain" (412). Although it is obviously difficult to say whether a keen interest in religion does in fact evidence devout faith, it is clear that Locke's interest in religion was (like Hobbes's) at least partly linked to his aim of transforming religion, which is our main concern here. As for Locke's debt to Hobbes's approach to religion, the impressive resemblance between Hobbesian Christianity and Lockean Christianity suggests that Sigmund's conclusion is premature.

religion" and of whom Locke said: "A generation of such young men to come upon the stage as the old drop off would give a new life to the age" (Israel 2001, 614; cf. Owen 2010). According to Brown, the view of Locke as a metaphysical materialist, a view associated with Hobbes and Spinoza, was dominant among both his disciples and his critics in the eighteenth century.[4]

The trend of recent scholarship on Locke is, however, increasingly to dissociate him from radicals such as Hobbes and Spinoza and to view him as a devout Christian, although perhaps unorthodox in certain respects. Paul Sigmund calls this the "religious turn" in Locke scholarship, claiming that this scholarly trend together with the publication of some previously obscure writings of Locke make the claim that Locke was a "crypto-Hobbesian" (a claim associated today mainly with Leo Strauss and his students) increasingly "difficult to maintain" (2005, 412).[5] Discerning the private thoughts of any author is difficult, and the task is made especially difficult in the case of Locke. For, as his biographer Maurice Cranston notes, he "is an elusive subject ... because he was an extremely secretive man. He modified a system of shorthand for the purposes of concealment; he employed all sorts of curious little cyphers; he cut signatures and other identifiable names from letters he preserved; at one time he used invisible ink" (1957, xi). We do note, however, the testimony of the Third Earl of Shaftesbury, a philosopher of considerable rank himself, whose education Locke personally oversaw for many years. Shaftesbury confirms Locke's sincere Christianity even while associating his ideas with both the freethinkers and especially Hobbes:

In general truly it has happened, that all those they call free writers now-a-days, have espoused those principles [of philosophy and theology], which Mr. Hobbes set afoot in this last age. Mr. Locke, as much as I honour him on account of other writings (viz. on government, policy, trade coin, education, toleration, etc.) and as well as I knew him, and can answer for his sincerity as a most zealous Christian and believer, did however go in the self same track, and is followed by the Tindals, and all the other ingenious free authors of our time. 'Twas Mr. Locke

---

[4] Isabel Rivers notes that all of the leading "freethinkers in different ways were associated with Locke" (2000, 13).

[5] Sigmund evidently does not have in mind here the publication of Locke's long-lost early *Two Tracts on Government*. See Kraynak 1980 on Locke's early Hobbesian case against toleration. The claim that Locke was secretly a Spinozist was recently revived by the Dutch Spinoza scholar Wim Klever in "Locke's Disguised Spinozism" (http://www.benedictus-despinoza.nl/lit/Locke's_Disguised_Spinozism.pdf). Cf. "Locke as Secret 'Spinozist': The Perspective of William Carroll" (Brown 1994), for an account of a similar claim by one of Locke's contemporaries.

that struck the homeblow ... Hence Hobbes, Locke, etc. still the same man, same genus, at bottom. (1746, 31–32; 1914, 104; cf. Aronson 1959)

Shaftesbury's comments raise more questions than they answer. Nevertheless, having refrained from criticizing Locke during Locke's lifetime, Shaftesbury makes plain that his teacher's association with Hobbes and the freethinkers was substantial.

Yet we do not claim that Locke was a "crypto-Hobbesian": Locke's disagreements with Hobbes were real and momentous, as Jefferson's love of Locke and animosity to Hobbes attest. But Locke does follow Hobbes more closely and fundamentally than he would admit, as the similarities between Hobbesian Christianity and Lockean Christianity help to indicate. Even on the question of toleration, Locke's early affinity for Hobbes's teaching is obvious. That Locke changed his mind on the question of toleration means that he somehow moved away from Hobbes on the question of religion, even as he continued to hew closely to Hobbes's approach to religion in other respects.

A *Letter Concerning Toleration*

Locke's case for toleration in the *Letter* is by far his most famous and the most influential one of the Enlightenment.[6] Locke presents an array of arguments in a work that, as Ingrid Creppell points out, "may be interpreted as a political tract rather than a more strictly philosophical text" (1996, 219). Being chiefly a polemic, the *Letter* has a theoretical basis that is not altogether clear; nor is it clear which arguments are most fundamental. In recent years, a number of scholars have argued that the core of Locke's case is his contention that belief cannot be coerced.[7] Locke, however, is forced to go well beyond this contention. For, if one

---

[6] On Jefferson's debt to Locke's *Letter*, see Sandler 1960; Kessler 1983; Nadon 2006.

[7] Joshua Mitchell argues that "the cornerstone of Locke's call for toleration" is "the distinction between the interior realm of faith and the exterior realm of power," that is, the "separation of the political and spiritual realms," which is an "essentially theological" position (1990, 64–65). Jeremy Waldron has argued that Locke's theological arguments are "insufficiently general," since they speak only to Christian rulers rather than to the "state as such" (1988, 63). Waldron finds the general argument he wants in the claim that intolerance is irrational, since belief cannot be coerced. We note that Mitchell and Waldron identify the same claim as central (belief cannot be coerced), though the one believes that the basis of the claim is theological and the other that it is non-theological. To decide whether it is theological or not in Locke's own view, we would need to understand his teaching on what degree of theological knowledge is available to us, which further points to the theoretically foundational role of the *Essay Concerning Human Understanding*.

is confident in the true way to salvation, it does not follow that the propagation of false teachings should be tolerated simply because belief cannot be coerced. For one might wish to limit the spread and influence of harmful teachings. Locke thus goes on to attack confidence in the way to salvation. The deeper "ground of toleration" is, as G. A. J. Rogers observes, "the argument from ignorance" (1998, 113).[8] Let us trace the importance of that argument more carefully.

Near the end of the *Letter* (but not until near the end), Locke emphasizes the great importance of salvation, that is, our eternal happiness after death, for each of us as human beings. There Locke states that the "highest obligation of Mankind ... ought to be in the Search and Performance of" whichever things "are necessary to the obtaining of God's favour" and thus to obtaining eternal happiness (47). For no goods of this world can compare to eternal happiness. But this premise alone does not clearly point to toleration and might in fact point in the opposite direction, since the stakes may be thought too high to permit error to persist and spread. Locke allows that "the greatest Duty of a Christian" is to "employ as many Exhortations and Arguments as he pleases" in "affectionate Endeavors to reduce Men from Errors," an assertion that, if taken out of context, may lead us to suppose that Locke will argue for toleration on grounds akin to what we saw laid out by Backus, namely, that religion should be tolerated to permit the free evangelism of the true gospel for the salvation of souls. Instead, Locke's statement on "the greatest duty of the Christian" proves to be in tension with his main point in the paragraph: "The care of each Mans Salvation belongs only to himself." How can we have a duty to exhort others, if the care of their souls belongs to them only? Earlier Locke had praised those who, in their religion, "mind only their own business" (34). He had then made the following comparison:

In private domestick Affairs, in the managemenet of Estates, in the conservation of Bodily Health, every man may consider what suits his own conveniency, and follow what course he likes best. No man complains of the ill management of his Neighbor's Affairs. No man is angry with another for an Error in sowing his Land, or in marrying his Daughter. No body corrects a Spendthrift for consuming his Substance in Taverns. But if any man do not frequent Church, if he do not there conform his Behaviour exactly to the accustomed Ceremonies, or this or the other Congregation; this immediately causes an Uproar. The Neighborhood is filled with Noise and Clamour. Every one is ready to avenge so great a Crime. (34)

---

[8] Cf. Biddle 1977.

Here the greatest duty of a Christian does not appear so attractive, as again Locke concludes that the care "of every man's Soul belongs unto himself, and is to be left unto himself" (35). As Locke makes clear in the later passage, this applies not only to things that are not considered crucial to salvation, things "indifferent," but also to those that are necessary to salvation, whatever they may be.

Why should we tolerate others' persisting in errors that will lead to their damnation? Because "one Man does not violate the rights of another, by his Erroneous Opinions, and undue Manner of Worship, nor is his Perdition any prejudice to another Man" (47). And again: "because no body else is concerned in it, nor can receive any prejudice from his Conduct therein." Here the tension with our "greatest duty as a Christian" grows. The care of your neighbor's soul should be left to him alone, because his eternal damnation does you no harm. (Witness Jefferson's debt to Locke.) But how is the fact that his damnation does not hurt one relevant in light of one's "greatest duty as a Christian"? Christian charity means seeking the good of others, not protecting oneself against harm.

For help in sorting out this muddle, let us turn from near the end to near the beginning of the *Letter*, where Locke defines what a church is: "A Church then I take to be a voluntary Society of Men, joining themselves together of their own accord, in order to the publick worshipping of God, in such a manner as they judge acceptable to him, and effectual to the Salvation of their Souls" (28). Here too Locke speaks of salvation as a concern each has *for himself*: "The hopes of salvation ... can be the only cause" of entering the communion of a church. There are a variety of churches (not one universal church), each holding to certain beliefs and practices that its members think necessary for salvation. (Later on, Locke will treat each sect as a distinct religion, in effect defining away schism and heresy [56–58].) The hope of salvation is "the only cause of ... entrance" into "any particular Church or Sect" (28). Here we approach the problem regarding the things necessary for salvation. It is one thing to say that what is indifferent with regard to salvation should be tolerated. But the reason there are different churches is that there is disagreement over what things are necessary and what things are indifferent: "Every Church is Orthodox to itself; to others Erroneous or Heretical" (32, cf. 23). The observation regarding different opinions on what's necessary to salvation in itself does not point to toleration. Of course each church believes itself to be right. That much is obvious. Should sin and error be tolerated simply because they do not recognize themselves as such and thus doubly err?

This, however, is not Locke's argument. Locke's case for toleration depends instead on the more radical premise that the way to salvation is unknown. Speaking specifically of Armenians and Calvinists as an example of his general point, he states: "The Controversie between these Churches about the Truth of their Doctrines and the Purity of their Worship, is on both sides equal; nor is there any Judge, either at Constantinople, or elsewhere on Earth, by whose Sentence it can be determined" (32). Locke does not simply mean to state the obvious point that there is no one whose judgment all parties would accept. In stating that every church is orthodox to itself, Locke denies to every church the claim to orthodoxy. And to deny every church the claim to orthodoxy is tantamount to denying that there is in fact an orthodox church (cf. Kateb 2009, 1017).

Locke's more radical premise becomes sufficiently evident as the *Letter* continues. Immediately after reiterating that care for our salvation belongs to each alone, Locke raises the possibility that there are "several ways that lead" to heaven (35). This possibility will be denied "especially by those that plead for compelling men into this or that Way." For if there is one way to heaven – if there are things truly necessary to salvation – the case for toleration is weakened. Locke implies that only zealots would insist that theirs is the only way. He drops the suggestion of multiple paths and grants "unto these Zealots" that "there is only one of these which is the true way to Eternal Happiness" (36). Locke responds: "But in this great variety of ways that men follow, it is still doubted which is this right one." He draws the following analogy: "I have a weak Body, sunk under a languishing Disease, for which (I suppose) there is only one Remedy, but that unknown. Does it therefore belong unto the Magistrate to prescribe me a Remedy, because there is but one, and because it is unknown?" Locke thus makes plain, if not explicit, his premise: not, in fact, that there are many ways to salvation, but that the way or ways to salvation are unknown.

Locke's point extends not only to the magistrate, since the remedy is apparently unknown to anyone. What then becomes of the claims of the various churches? Of one's own church? Are they not as uncertain as any claim of the magistrate? Toleration should extend to things necessary to salvation, because it is unknown what is necessary to salvation. Indeed, to push Locke's analogy as far as it will permit, if the remedy is unknown, it cannot be known that there is a remedy at all. Those who claim that there is only one way to heaven are zealots, *because* they claim to know what is unknown. They bicker and struggle and fight with other zealots who also claim to know what is unknown. Locke ridicules the basis of such disputes: "Why am I beaten and ill used by others, because, perhaps, I wear not Buskins; because my Hair is not of the right Cut; because perhaps I have not be dip't in the right Fashion" (35). Their disputes concern "for the most part ... such frivolous things as these" (36). Locke does not tell us what serious things may be disputed, apparently because they are disputed without any basis in knowledge. He will later compare differences between the churches, and thus disagreement over the way to salvation, to differences in the color of eyes and hair (52).

The tenor of the *Letter* is to ridicule disputes over what is necessary to salvation, the disagreements that divide not only one church from another but one religion from another, as foolish. Intolerance is not the result of a genuine concern for the salvation of others; it is the result of a boastful ambition or some other base motive. Because the way to salvation is unknown, the "true church" is not defined by correct doctrine (orthodoxy) or worship, and therefore not by what those entering a church are in search of with a view to salvation, but by toleration. The *Letter*'s opening sentence declares "toleration to be the chief Characterstical Mark of the True Church" (23). The "true church" is true, not owing to the truth of its doctrine or the correctness of its worship. Churches fundamentally at odds on these points can still be labeled "true" so long as they tolerate one another. Lockean Christianity is ultimately about the promotion of a peaceable morality, not religious truth.

The most basic stratum of Locke's case for toleration, then, is radical theological doubt, particularly regarding the principal reason by his own account for church membership: salvation. The grounds of intolerance are thus to be undermined. And though "any one may employ as many Exhortations and Arguments as he pleases, towards the promoting of another man's Salvation" (we note Locke's language, "as he pleases," does not imply a duty), it is far from clear why anyone deeply affected by Locke's *Letter* would be inclined to do so. For those who feel compelled to exhort and argue with others over the way to salvation suppose that they know what they do not know. They are zealots. (Here we see the vast difference between Lockean Enlightenment and Backus's New Light evangelicalism.) In quelling zealotry, Locke would, it seems, quell even "charitable Endeavors to reduce Men from Errors," unless the error in question is the belief that one knows the way to salvation, in which case it is Locke who has undertaken such a charitable endeavor with respect to the error of intolerant zealots. In that way, he has fulfilled his "greatest obligation as a Christian."

Religious dispute is a waste of time, and in any case human life has given us more immediate matters to attend to. For

> besides their souls, which are Immortal, Men have also their Temporal Lives here upon the Earth; the State whereof being frail and fleeting, and the duration uncertain; they have need of several outward Conveniences to the support thereof, which are to be procured or preserved by Pains and industry. For those things that are necessary to the comfortable support of our Lives are not the spontaneous Products of Nature, nor do offer themselves fit and prepared for our use. This part therefore draws on another care, and necessarily gives another Imployment. (47)

Whatever goods human beings can acquire through their labor is precarious, owing to the "pravity of Mankind," who therefore enter into society. But "men thus entering into Societies, grounded upon their mutual Compacts of Assistance, for the Defence of their Temporal Goods, may nevertheless be deprived of them, either by Rapine and Fraud of their Fellow-Citizens, or by the hostile Violence of Forreigners" (47–48). Perhaps alluding to the passage discussed previously in which salvation was analogous to a remedy, Locke adds, "the Remedy of this Evil consists in Arms, Riches, and Multitude of Citizens; the Remedy of the other in Laws" (48). Unlike the remedy for the security of one's soul in the next life, which is not known, the remedy for the security of one's property in this life is known (cf. Owen 2001, 157–60).

We leave our section on the *Letter* with two significant difficulties. The first is that, in other works of his, Locke does in fact present a doctrine – or, rather, more than one doctrine – on the way to salvation. The *Letter* is obviously a polemical work, and it is possible that the theological uncertainty of Locke's doctrine does not extend quite as far as it seems to do on the basis of the *Letter* alone. But this question highlights another problem in the *Letter*. Those of us rooting for toleration may be likely not to notice that Locke's *Letter* fails to offer any argument whatever in support of the assertion that the way to salvation is unknown. For the foundation of the arguments of the *Letter Concerning Toleration*, we must turn to the work of his devoted to the limits of human knowledge: the *Essay Concerning Human Understanding*.[9]

---

[9] "Locke's argument would have been buttressed by a convincing argument of men's irreducible fallibility in religion, of men's limitation to faith and not knowledge in religious affairs in such a way that it could never be evident that anyone held the true religion... We have seen [that Locke was] contemporaneously committed to the necessary

An Essay Concerning Human Understanding

A common argument today for religious toleration is clearly heir to what we have just seen in Locke's *Letter*. It says that it is wrong to impose one's religion on others because no one truly knows which (if any) religion is the true one. Religious intolerance, according to the argument, stems from fanaticism – "zealotry," in Locke's language – which is identified by the certainty that one's opinions about the ultimate truth are correct. But the ultimate truth is unknowable. Offering a version of this argument, Bill Clinton addressed an audience at Harvard two months after the attacks of September 11, 2001: "The Taliban and bin Laden, like fundamentalist fanatics today and everywhere and throughout time immemorial, believe they have the truth. They have it, the whole truth ... We believe the limits of the human condition prevent anyone from having the absolute truth."[10] Clinton did not proceed to argue in support of this view of the human condition, which is presented almost as a creed. Clinton can be forgiven for not launching into a lecture on epistemology, but unless something like his account of "the limits of the human condition" can be demonstrated, he merely opposes what "fanatics ... believe" with what "we believe": belief versus belief. Without such a demonstration, we risk undermining the distinction between the reasonable liberal and the fanatic. The study of the limits of human understanding, which may appear to be essentially apolitical, is in fact fundamental to a prominent strand of the politics of toleration. This is no less the case if few defenders of toleration have noticed their implicit dependence on this notoriously thorny study or entered into it (cf. Owen 2001, 40–41, 36–39).

John Locke entered into this thorny study in his *Essay Concerning Human Understanding*, but the connection between the *Essay* and Locke's doctrine of toleration has been neglected. Although the *Essay* is Locke's most famous work and by far the most influential of the works that he published in his own name, its relation to his political philosophy, for which he is also justly famous, has been a perennial puzzle for scholars. Peter Laslett threw up his hands in despair of reconciling the two, concluding that Locke the philosopher must be interpreted separately from Locke the political theorist (1960, 79–92). Although

---

fallibility of almost all men in many religious issues ... The *Epistola*, however, does not expand in these directions" (Marshall 1994, 364). Cf. Kateb 2009 on the quietness of Locke's true agenda in the *Letter Concerning Toleration*: "The key theological text is the *Essay*" (1008).

[10] Bill Clinton, speech at Harvard University, November 19, 2001, http://clintonpresidentialcenter.org.

not all interpreters have agreed, most, like Laslett, have exerted their energies on the relation between the *Essay* and the *Two Treatises of Government*, focusing in particular on the puzzle of Locke's natural law doctrine.[11] Although that question is indeed indispensable to a full interpretation of Locke, we here will take a different approach to uncovering the political significance of the *Essay* by relating it to the *Letter Concerning Toleration*, where Locke builds his doctrine of religious toleration on the ruins of theological certainty.[12]

The link between the arguments of these two works also sheds light on the political character of the *Essay*. In a more painstaking theoretical fashion than the *Letter*, the *Essay* attempts to promote human welfare in this world by demonstrating that the most contentious and divisive theological or otherworldly questions are ultimately unknowable for human beings. In his Epistle to the Reader, Locke writes that he is working "as an Under-Labourer in cleaning Ground a little, and removing some of the Rubbish, that lies in the way to Knowledge." This famous expression of the aim of the *Essay* is reformulated in a more

---

[11] One notable exception is Grant 1987, which uses the *Essay* as a guide to understanding the precise sort of knowledge sought in the *Two Treatises*. Grant also provides a useful summary of the debate on Locke's natural law doctrine. See also Waldron 2002, which grapples with the problem of establishing human equality on the basis of the *Essay*. Waldron resolves this tension by turning to Locke's natural theology. Grant (1987, 29–30) and Myers (1998, 52–55) had suggested alternative solutions to the same problem.

[12] Although most of the scholarly discussion has centered on the question of natural law, the link between Locke's program of toleration and the *Essay* has been noted by a few scholars in recent years. Yet his argumentative strategy of the *Essay* in relation to toleration has not been explored in detail. Myers and Josephson stress the link between toleration and Locke's critique of enthusiasm, which will also be pivotal to the present study (Myers 1998, 46 and Josephson 2002, 254–56). Cf. Myers 1998, 125–27; Josephson 2002, 262–63, 272–73. Moore explores Locke's doctrine of assent in the *Essay* in its connection to the case for toleration in the *Letter* (1978). Jolley comments on the potential link between the "anti-voluntarist theory of belief" of the *Essay* and toleration, although that theory is "pressed into the service of a case for religious liberty" only in the *Letter* (1999, 192). Nevertheless, Jolley contends, the spirit of religious liberty is plain in the final sections of the *Essay*.

The most extensive treatment of the *Essay* as a political work is Neal Wood's *The Politics of Locke's Philosophy* (1983). Wood treats the *Essay* as an exercise in Baconian philosophy that aimed to reorient scientific inquiry in the direction of the "useful arts," while promoting "the ideal of the rational man" as a "social hero" (5–7, 82). The *Essay* was thus "a weapon of the socially progressive 'moderns' in their intellectual conflict with the conservative 'ancients'" (5). The present study does not quarrel with Wood's general assessment, which also recognizes the importance of toleration for the modern camp. Wood does not go so far, however, as to consider the foundation of the *Essay* to be its theology.

revealing way in a later passage. Having in mind chiefly theological disputes, Locke writes: "Our knowledge being so narrow, as I have shew'd, it will, perhaps, give us some Light in to the present State of our minds, if we look a little in to the dark side, and take a view of our Ignorance: which being infinitely larger than our Knowledge, may serve much to the quieting of Disputes, and Improvement of useful Knowledge" (IV.3.22). The argument of the *Essay* supports a policy of toleration. Yet toleration for Locke does not mean simply to live and let live. It marks a reorientation of human concerns: toleration and peace – the quieting of vain disputes – are the necessary conditions for concretely useful human endeavors: industry and invention aided by the practicality of the new natural science. But first the ground must be cleared of theological rubbish.

The *Essay* is thus more concerned with theology, as well as with politics, than is typically supposed.[13] Indeed the *Essay*'s theological concern is related to its political concern. In the *Essay*, Locke seeks to establish a relatively solid, but limited and uncontroversial theology rooted in and guided by reason. Accordingly, the theology of the *Essay* leans heavily in the direction of natural, as opposed to revealed theology. Locke, of course, never repudiates revealed religion in the *Essay*, and he appeals to it often, if selectively, in other works. But in the *Essay*, he seeks to diminish the authority of revealed religion insofar as it extends beyond or contradicts the principles of natural theology or reason. For precisely insofar as it strays from rational demonstration and depends on what is essentially mysterious, revealed religion is *inherently* prone to contention and thus potentially troublesome for political society, whose work in any case is properly limited to securing *mundane* goods. Needless to say, however, the movement away from the plane of that controversy in the movement from revealed religion toward natural religion – or, more basically, the establishment of reason as our "last Judge and Guide in Every thing" – is itself deeply controversial. Accordingly, the judicious Locke proceeds with the utmost care.

---

[13] Wolterstorff is correct to claim that "the center of gravity is Book IV" and not book II as "the traditional school-book interpretation of Locke" would have it (1996, xiv). Both Wolsterstorff and Spellman read the *Essay* as driven in large part by socio-theological concerns. Although my reading of the *Essay* differs markedly from theirs, I am sympathetic to Spellman's claim that the main concern of the *Essay* was "the problem of authority in religious and moral experience ... primarily because [Locke] was convinced that conflicting claims to authority in these two areas had in large measure penetrated the social and political instability of his own day" (1997, 1).

One sign of the *Essay*'s orientation toward natural rather than revealed theology is the fact that, despite its many theological discussions and references, it contains few references to the Bible and only a single allusion to Jesus. Indeed, Locke makes no explicit references to Jesus, Christ, or Messiah in the *Essay*, and only three references to the Holy Ghost or Holy Spirit (all in his chapter criticizing "enthusiasm," IV.19.10, 13, 16). To judge by appearances at least, the *Essay* is the least Christian (although not the least theological) of Locke's major works.[14] This is not to say that Locke supposed that theology as a whole could be simply natural,[15] or that his theological doctrine is not supplemented and perhaps completed in his other, more obviously theological works. But those works must be understood, as they typically today are not, in light of the theology, or theologically relevant arguments, of the *Essay*, since the precise status of their more emphatic appeals to revealed religion must be interpreted in light of the treatment of revealed religion in the *Essay*.

What we can know of (a) God

The *Essay* concerns what human beings can know and how they come to know. It is therefore concerned with what human beings cannot know, or the limits of human knowledge. Locke's *Essay* aims to show us how and about what we "may arrive at Certainty" (I.2.1), but it nevertheless leads us to "discover an huge Abyss of Ignorance" (IV.3.24). What we can know of the material world is negligible, limited to the existence, though not the substance, of particular beings present to our senses. Our knowledge of spiritual things is even more limited. Some theological truths, in particular the existence of a God, can be demonstrated by unassisted human reason. But "almost the whole intellectual world, is conceal[ed] from us in an impenetrable obscurity" (IV.3.27). By the "intellectual world" Locke means the spiritual world, and his approach to the spiritual world is indicated in this terminology. The spiritual world resides for human beings on the plane of ideas, the "intellectual world" or the mind. Its objective existence and substance – its reality outside the mind – is

---

[14] Other recent attempts to explore the *Essay*'s theological concerns are Yolton, 2004, Waldron 2002, and Nuovo 2003 – the last of these claiming that "Locke came to regard his great work [the *Essay*] as a natural theology" (141). On the priority of natural to revealed theology in Locke, see Forde 2001 and 2004. Cf. Zuckert 2002, 147–68; Myers 1998 180–90.

[15] Cf. the beginning of the *Reasonableness of Christianity*.

inaccessible to human understanding. Our knowledge "comes ... short of the reality of things" (IV.3.6). Even a "clear distinct [idea] of substance, which is the Foundation of all the rest, is concealed from us" (IV.3.23). Most of what passes for metaphysics and theology is groundless conjecture.

In order to determine what can be known, Locke aims to proceed from the ground up. Human beings by nature and to begin have no knowledge or awareness of any kind. There are no "innate ideas," of either beings or practical (which for Locke includes moral) principles. The mind begins as "white Paper" (II.1.2). We have no innate sense of right and wrong and no innate notion of God, however basic. There are no moral rules that enjoy universal assent, a lack that Locke takes to be evidence that morality is not innate. Likewise there are no universal opinions about God. Indeed, Locke tells us, there are whole nations with no notion of God or religion (I.4.8). Even in Christian nations, one finds "that many ... have no very strong, and clear Impressions of a Deity upon their minds." Atheism is more widespread than it may appear owing to political and social intolerance. Only "some profligate Wretches" openly deny the being of a God at present. Those unbelievers that are not profligate wretches conceal their unbelief: "Fear of the Magistrate's Sword, or their Neighbor's Censure, tie up People's Tongues" (cf. 1983, 51).

Locke's *Essay* is emphatically not atheistic. Although there is no innate "Idea of God" (I.4.8), "the Notion of a God" is "agreeable to the common light of Reason, and naturally deducible from every part of our Knowledge" (I.4.9). Nor does the *Essay* deny the possibility of moral knowledge: "Moral Principles require Reasoning and Discourse, and some Exercise of the Mind, to discover the certainty of their Truth" (I.3.1). Both moral principles and the existence of a God are "knowable by the light of Nature; i.e. without the help of positive Revelation" (I.3.13). Natural theology, however limited, is possible.

Locke thus makes a clear distinction early in the *Essay* between what is knowable by the light of nature, that is, by reason, and revelation. Later he will refer to reason as "natural Revelation" (IV.19.4; cf. IV.7.11, *1st Treatise* §86), but natural revelation remains essentially different from positive or supernatural revelation, however much they may agree on many points. Locke typically, however, refers to supernatural revelation simply as revelation, and here we will follow his more typical usage. Natural religion is based on reason, and Locke seeks to establish reason as "the last Judge and Guide in everything" – even, as we will see, with respect to revelation (IV.19.14; cf. IV.17.24, *1st Treatise* §58).[16] Whatever place revealed religion retains for Locke, it is to be tethered to and moderated by the dictates of reason.[17]

There are two "Fountains of Knowledge" for human beings: sense perception and reflection – the latter being "the Perception of the Operation of our own Minds within us" (II.1.2–4). According to Locke, "all our Knowledge is founded" on these two sources. Reflection provides two kinds of knowledge: intuition and demonstration. Demonstrated truths are inherently less certain and clear than intuition, since, among other reasons, the fact that something was in need of demonstration means that it was capable of being doubted. Whatever falls short of intuition and demonstration regarding general truths "is but Faith, or Opinion, but not Knowledge" (IV.2.14). Whatever status faith may prove to have later in book IV, it is inferior to knowledge.

Locke does not address revelation as a distinct source of knowledge in book II; nor does he explain where it would fit into his classification. Reflection works with ideas already in our possession, whereas revelation enters from the outside. Perhaps revelation would be what Locke calls sensitive knowledge – so that a prophet would know of God through the senses, as he knows of any human he has met. The decisive difficulty with this suggestion, however, is that Locke states simply that knowledge of the existence of a God is demonstrative (IV.3.21). Though we must wait for Locke's explicit treatment of revelation in book IV, at this stage, he seems implicitly to deny that human beings have knowledge of God through supernatural revelation.[18]

Locke's demonstration of God's existence in his official treatment of that subject (IV.10) proceeds in three main stages: the proof that there is an eternal being, the proof that this being is all-powerful, and the proof that this being is all-knowing. From the last proof, Locke asserts, God's

---

[16] In the "Epistle to the Reader," Locke informs us that the *Essay* was written following a discussion among friends "on a subject very remote from that of the *Essay*" (p. 7). The *Essay* was an attempt to follow a different course in seeking "a resolution to those doubts which perplexed us." For some reason, Locke does not tell us what that remote subject was, what their doubts were, or whether this new course succeeded in removing those doubts. A friend who was present notes two subjects that were discussed: "the principles of morality and revealed religion" (Locke 1975, xix). Of these two, only revealed religion could plausibly be described as a remote subject.

[17] Cf. Forde 2001.

[18] Cf. II.1.5. However they may be related, knowledge of the existence of a God is not to be confused with our idea of God. An idea does not imply knowledge. Cf. II.23.32–36 with II.22.2.

providence "and all his other Attributes necessarily follow." Locke's demonstration is notoriously thin, and apparently out of proportion to the certainty he had claimed for it up to that point.[19] Locke, for example, does not explain what he means here by providence, what these other unnamed attributes are, or how they follow from the argument. More directly relevant to our purpose here, is the God whose existence reason can demonstrate the God of revelation? This cannot be taken for granted. What should we make of the fact that Locke speaks repeatedly of our capacity to know of or demonstrate the existence of "a God," consistently using the indefinite article "a," while in other contexts he speaks simply of "God"?[20] The status of revealed religion remains highly uncertain.

Revelation

Although the question of revelation has been at issue all along in the background, Locke's most direct treatment of the subject begins near the end of the *Essay* in book IV, chapters 18 and 19. Because of the import-ance of this often neglected portion of the *Essay* for my interpretation, it is worth considering it in some detail.[21] Locke had written at the end of each of the previous two chapters that faith and reason, in the proper usage of those words, should agree (IV.16.14 and 17.24). Faith most basically means assent of the mind – what one believes – and "he governs his Assent right, and places it as he should, who in any Case or Matter whatsoever, believes or disbelieves, according as Reason directs him" (IV.17.24). In the chapter "Faith and Reason," however, Locke speaks of faith in its more commonplace, but improper usage, "as it is ordinarily placed, in contradistinction to Reason; though in Truth, it be nothing else but an Assent founded on the highest Reason" (IV.16.14). Whoever does place reason and faith in contradistinction to one another, or in other words, whoever bases his faith on something *other than* reason, Locke tells us in chapter 17, "transgresses against his own Light," "which God has given him," thus violating his "duty as a rational Creature"

---

[19] Ashcraft complains of being "overwhelmed by repetitious, dogmatic assertions" about Locke's confidence in his demonstration (1969, 203–04). Cf. Pangle 1988, 198–203; Josephson 2002, 93–96.

[20] For Locke's use of the indefinite article, see I.4.9, 12, 17, 18, 23; IV.3.27; IV.10 title, 1, 6, 7, 13, 18; IV.11.1; IV.12.11; IV.17.2. Cf. II.17.20, II.17.17 with II.22.2. Cf. also Dunn 1969 and Zuckert 2004, 7–8, 141–42.

[21] Paul Helm (1973) lamented the neglect of this part of the *Essay* more than thirty years ago, to little avail. One exception at the time was Ashcraft 1969; since then, Snyder 1986. See also Josephson 2002, 85–92.

(IV.17.24; cf. I.3.13 and *Works* III:482). This is "faith" for those persons he will discuss in chapter 18, which deals with (supernatural) revelation.[22] Yet, although this qualification casts its shadow over chapters 18 and 19, Locke nevertheless suggests the possibility in principle of a rational assent to revelation. What, if anything, does that possibility yield?

Locke frames his discussion of faith and reason in chapter 18 in terms of laying down "the Measures and Boundaries between Faith and Reason" (IV.18.1), implying the erroneous meaning of faith as something set in contradistinction to reason. Locke suggests that what is at stake in marking this boundary is the cause of "great Disputes," which take place "in vain," and which Locke will help us avoid.[23] Again toleration is somehow at stake, and we are reminded of Locke's statement in the *Letter* in which he attributes much strife to a failure to demarcate the boundary between church and state (1983, 26). In the present context, he defines reason and faith as follows:

> Reason therefore here, *as contradistinguished to Faith*, I take to be the discovery of the Certainty or Probability of such Propositions or Truths, which the Mind arrives at by Deductions made from such Ideas, which it has got by the use of its natural Faculties, viz. by Sensation or Reflection. Faith, on the other side, is the Assent to any Proposition, not thus made out by the Deductions of Reason; but upon the credit of the proposer, as coming from God, in some extraordinary way of communication. This way of discovering Truths to Men we call Revelation. (IV.18.2, emphasis added)

At this point it appears that faith in contradistinction to reason (faith in the erroneous sense) means faith based on revelation. But note Locke's crucial move here of defining faith as belief in the claims of other human beings as opposed to faith in God. It is not necessarily impious to doubt the claims of human beings.

Locke divides these claims of revelation into three categories in relation to reason. Some alleged revelation accords with reason, some contradicts reason, and some does neither. Faith, as Locke treats it in chapter 18, concerns only the last of these varieties. With claims that accord with reason, "there is little need or use of Revelation, God having furnished us with natural, and surer means to arrive at the Knowledge of them" (IV.18.4). We can, for example, know that the angles of a triangle add up to 180° with more certainty by reason than by faith in someone else's

---

[22] Neither Ashcraft 1969 nor Helm 1973 nor Snyder 1986 notes Locke's qualification of his usage of "faith" in their discussions of chapter 18.

[23] Cf. Locke's journal entry of August 24, 1676, reproduced at Locke 1954, 275.

claim to have received this truth from God. Locke tells us in the next chapter that whatever is *known* to be true must be known through reason; and whoever knows something to be true by reason "in vain supposes it to be a Revelation" (IV.19.11). Locke seems, then, to indicate that faith properly understood (as grounded in reason, IV.16.14 and 17.24) does not depend on revelation. As regards claims that contradict reason – above all, intuitive knowledge – these too must be rejected as frauds. Even if we suppose ourselves to be the direct recipient of revelation that contradicts reason, we must reject it. For we can never be as sure that the revelation is genuine as we are of what is knowable through reason – all of which leaves us with claimed revelation concerning what neither accords with nor contradicts reason. Locke labels such claims "above reason." Such claims are neither rationally knowable nor refutable, for instance, "that part of the Angels rebelled against God, and thereby lost their happy state; and that the dead shall rise, and live again" (IV.18.7).

Here, in those claims that are above reason, we find the potential objects of faith, including perhaps revelation. As we noted previously, the ground of faith is inferior to the ground of knowledge. But this does not mean that the ground of faith is *necessarily* left in the dark, or that the alternative to knowledge is simply ignorance. On the contrary, Locke says that "most of the Propositions we think, reason, discourse, nay act upon, are such, as we cannot have undoubted Knowledge of their Truth: yet some of them border so near upon Certainty, that we make no doubt at all about them" (IV.15.2). There are "degrees herein, from the very neighborhood of Certainty and Demonstration, quite down to Improbability and Unlikeliness, even to the confines of Impossibility; and also degrees of Assent from full Assurance and Confidence, quite down to Conjecture, Doubt, and Distrust." These statements appear in Locke's chapter on probability: probability is "to supply the defect of our Knowledge, and to guide us where that fails" (IV.15.4).

To say, then, that the ground of revealed religion is "but faith, or opinion, but not knowledge," is not in itself tantamount to declaring ignorance. Revelation, being above reason and a potential object of faith, ought to be assessed according to probability, "if it will proceed rationally" (IV.15.5). The degree of assent, or faith in revelation, "can reach no higher than an Assurance or Diffidence, arising from the more, or less apparent Probability of the Proofs" that it is in fact revelation (IV.16.14). But, as we have seen, for most human beings faith is not based on reason: it is not probability that typically guides religious belief. It is instead "the Opinion of others" on which "men ... pin their faith more than any thing else," leading them to be "Heathens in Japan, Mahumetans in Turkey, Papists in Spain, Protestants in England, and Lutherans in Sueden" (IV.15.6). No religion is believed, by and large, on the basis of its probable truth.

How can we apply the standard of probability to Locke's treatment of revelation in IV.18? To attempt to put these passages together: Without revelation, a proposition contrary to probability is *against* reason; with revelation, it is *above* reason.[24] That is, where God has revealed something, reason's assessment of probability must be subordinated: "Since God in giving us the light of Reason has not therefore tied up his Hands from affording us, when he thinks fit, the light of Revelation in any of those matters, wherein our natural faculties are able to give a probable determination, revelation, where God has been pleased to give it, must carry it, against the probable Conjecture of Reason" (IV.18.8). That God is able to reveal truths directly and supernaturally to human beings "cannot be denied" (IV.19.5).[25]

We thus arrive at a possibility for which Locke has nowhere in the *Essay* prepared us: assenting to something as true that we do not understand according to reason, as either certain or probable. Would this not mean opening up the possibility of *not* taking reason as our last judge and guide in everything, even or precisely in matters of greatest importance to us? Here, however, the importance of Locke's emphasizing the *human* role in revelation emerges. What God reveals must certainly be true, of course, but every revelation is revealed to some human being and is therefore encountered as a human claim. Before consenting to the truth contained in God's revelation, we first must be certain that it truly is from God. God, of course, is *capable* of supernatural revelation, but how can we know when or whether He has done it? The question becomes

---

[24] By the strict standard of reason, still in the context of IV.17, "above reason" refers to "such propositions whose truth *or probability* we cannot by reason derive" (IV.17.23, my emphasis). Sometimes, however, "above reason" also refers only to what we cannot determine with certainty – a much broader category than what cannot be determined even with probability. It is in this sense that Locke speaks of "above reason" in relation to revelation in chapter 18. Locke says, "In that larger sense also, contrary to reason is, I suppose, sometimes taken." That is, what is contrary to probability may also be said to be contrary to reason.

[25] Cf. p. 162. Cf. also Zuckert's comments on the relevance of the limitations of *Essay* IV.10 (2002, 140–42).

how to assess whether a claimed revelation is genuine, determining which would require one to set aside what would otherwise be a rational (though not certain) judgment of the content of revelation based on probability:

Because the Mind, not being certain of the Truth of that it does not evidently know, but only yielding to the Probability of what appears in it, is bound to give up its Assent to such a Testimony, which, it is satisfied, comes from one, who cannot err, and will not deceive. But yet, it belongs to Reason, to judge of the Truth of its being a Revelation, and of the signification of the Words, wherein it is delivered. (IV.18.8)

Reason may subordinate its judgment to revelation, but only where reason determines the revelation is real. Perhaps this would enable Locke to maintain consistently that reason should be our last judge and guide in everything. For reason would then remain the judge of revelation – not of the *content* of revelation, to which reason must bow, but of the *fact* of revelation. Once reason has determined the fact of revelation, it must step aside.

However one might settle that question, the prior question is whether it is possible for the claim of a human being to have received supernatural revelation to pass muster with reason.[26] Here we see how important epistemology is for Locke's approach to theology. Locke sets a high standard for rational assent to revelation, especially where the grounds of assessment must be in terms of probability: it must be "an *evident* Revelation," "*clear* Revelation" (IV.18.9, my emphasis). In order reasonably to accept a revelation as genuine, one must be satisfied, Locke says, that the (human) testimony to it "comes from one, who cannot err, and will not deceive." But he soon tells us that "all men are liable to error, and most men are in many points, by passion or interest, under temptation of it" (IV.20.17). Moreover:

Immediate Revelation being a much easier way for Men to establish their Opinions, and regulate their Conduct, than the tedious and not always successful Labour of strict Reasoning, it is no wonder, that some have been very apt to pretend to Revelation, and to persuade themselves, that they are under the peculiar guidance of Heaven in their Actions and Opinions, especially in those of them, which they cannot account for by the ordinary Methods of Knowledge and Principles of Reason. (IV.19.5)

---

[26] Cf. Jolley 1999, 189; Snyder 1986, 206–07; and Helm 1973, 58–63, which provides an effective critique of Ashcraft 1969.

To summarize: reason is to judge what is and is not revelation, and it judges according to probability. Not only is the content of what is claimed improbable (otherwise it would not be "above reason"), but the fact of revelation itself is an extraordinary event and therefore also improbable. The temptation to *pretend* to revelation, on the other hand, is not extraordinary; bogus revelation is "no wonder." If we follow Locke's reasoning, we are forced to ask whether, in any given instance of a claimed revelation, it is not *probable* that the (human) claim is false.

But Locke does distinguish between "original revelation" and "traditional revelation," and we have been discussing chiefly the latter. Original revelation is the direct communication of God to a human being. Traditional revelation is the report of original revelation passed from human beings to one another. Faith as Locke had defined it in IV.18.2 concerns traditional revelation. Perhaps if it cannot be clear and evident to others that a revelation is genuine on the basis of mere testimony, it can be clear and evident to the recipient of revelation. As we noted, Locke claims that putatively original revelation cannot supersede rational knowledge, because "we cannot have an assurance of the Truth of its being a divine Revelation, greater than our own Knowledge" (IV.18.5). Yet in chapter 19, "On Enthusiasm," Locke acknowledges that for some, the experience of what is believed to be divine illumination is as clear "as the Sun at Noon." For them "'tis clear and visible, like the Light of bright Sunshine shows itself and needs no other Proof, but its own Evidence," and this in comparison with "the twilight of Reason" (IV.19.8). Yet Locke contends that the supposition that such an experience actually is from God "is at most but belief and assurance" (IV.19.10) and not knowledge. More than this, "if strength of Persuasion be the Light, which must guide; I ask how shall any one distinguish between the delusions of Satan, and the inspirations of the Holy Ghost?" (IV.19.13). Locke here allows for no reasoned assessment of probability short of knowledge: "If I know not this, how great soever the Assurance is, that I am possess'd with, it is *groundless*; whatever Light I pretend to, it is but Enthusiasm" (IV.19.10, emphasis added).

Scripture

But what of that traditional revelation called Scripture? To this point, Locke has by and large avoided raising the obvious question of whether the doubts raised throughout the *Essay* must not also apply to Scripture. Can Scripture retain its authority in Locke's epistemology? Locke began with the mind as "white paper" and so with no innate awareness of God. Our knowledge of God is gained from demonstration, and revelation possesses at best an epistemological status inferior to that of reason. Traditional revelation, Locke tells us, is conveyed "by the Tradition of Writings, or Word of Mouth," and whether "such or such a Proposition, to be found in such or such a Book, is of Divine Inspiration" can only be determined by reason *by each of us*, without our own revelation. When Locke does allude to Scripture in his treatment of traditional revelation, it is to assert that the assurance that the stories reported in the Bible are true can never be as great as our assurance regarding what we see for ourselves. We can never be as certain, according to Locke's example, that there was in fact a great flood based on Scripture as we would be if we witnessed it ourselves. We can be assured that the story "is writ in the Book supposed writ by Moses inspired;" but we cannot have "so great an assurance, that Moses writ that Book," or "of its being a Revelation" (IV.18.4). Moreover, as Locke had asserted not long before, in the context of his treatment of probability: "A credible Man vouching his knowledge of [a thing] is a good proof: But if another equally credible, do witness it from his Report, the Testimony is weaker; and a third that attests the Hear-say of an Hear-say, is yet less considerable. So *that in traditional truths, each remove weakens the force of the proof*" (IV.16.10; emphasis in the original). And yet the opposite principle is more often followed. So that "some Men ... look on Opinions to gain force by growing older; and what a thousand years since would not, to a rational Man, contemporary with the Voucher, have appeared at all probable, is now urged as certain beyond all question."

It was not until the late addition of IV.19, "Of Enthusiasm," to the fourth edition of the *Essay*, that Locke laid out a clear way to salvage Scriptural authority: miracles.[27] Locke tells us that "the holy Men of old,

---

[27] Even this appears quite late in the argument of IV.19, at the end of a relentless attack on enthusiasm, which Locke comes close to defining simply as the belief that one has been inspired by God. Some commentators have claimed that Locke's targets in this chapter are contemporary Protestant Christians who supposed themselves recipients of some supernatural divine enlightenment. Locke doubtless does have such people in mind, reporting, it seems, from experience "the way of talking of these men" (IV.19.9). And yet as plausible as that inference may be, not only does Locke never so limit the scope of his discussion for his reader, but there is no apparent basis in his argument for doing so. So far is Locke from limiting his discussion to his contemporaries that his only example of an enthusiast is St. Paul – albeit as Saul, prior to his conversion (IV.19.12).

who had Revelation from God, had something else besides that internal Light of assurance in their own Minds, to testify to them, that it was from God; they had ... outward Signs to convince them of the author of those Revelations" (IV.19.15). Inner assurance is in no case adequate, even in the case of Biblical prophecy. These holy men of old had their inner assurance confirmed by miracles. Moses not only heard a voice, but saw the burning bush – evidence that the voice was God's. Locke concludes from this and other examples that the biblical prophets agreed that "an inward seeing or perswasion of their own Minds without any other Proof [is not] a sufficient Evidence that it was from God," although he immediately adds that "the Scripture does not every where mention their demanding or having such Proofs" (IV.19.15). The authority of at least some portion of Scripture, then, might be salvaged. Locke does not specify or draw any conclusions for us about those Biblical prophecies that are not said to have been supported by such proofs. Nor does he return to the question of how confident we can be, how probable it is, that miracles reported in the Bible actually occurred (recall his example of the flood), to say nothing of the questions of what miracles are and how they can be known as such – the sort of questions the *Essay* has surely prepared the reader to ask. The only other reference to miracles in the *Essay* appears in IV.16.13. There, too, miracles are presented as giving credit "to other Truths, which need such Confirmation," a clear allusion to the requisite confirmation of revelation that Locke demands in IV.19. In IV.16, miracles are defined simply as

Cf. Locke's comments on St. Paul in his *Paraphrase and Notes* (1987), where Locke tells us that Paul believed the Christian religion to be "derived intirely from divine revelation wherein humane abilities had noe thing to doe" (182). Paul believed that "all other wisdom ... of the world was foolishness" (184), including "the humane arts and sciences" (177). Paul was evidently far from Lockean. Locke paraphrases Paul's belief thus: "I who renounceing all humane learning and knowledge in the case take all that I preach from divine revelation alone I am sure that there in I have the mind of Christ" (177). Locke describes the mammoth undertaking, apparently unique in Christian history, of drawing out the plain and intelligible meaning of Paul's letters: "It requires so much more Pains, Judgment, and Application, to find the Coherence of obscure and abstruse Writings, and makes them so much more unfit to serve Prejudice and Pre-occupation when found, that it is not to be wondered that St. Paul's Epistles have with many passed rather for disjointed, loose pious discourses, full of Warmth and Zeal, and Overflows of Light, rather than for calm strong coherent Reasonings, that carried a Thread of Argument and Consistency all through them" (110). As for Locke's own procedure, he leaves it to "some very sober judicious Christians" to "judge whether I proceeded rationally" (109). In light of the *Essay*, Locke's judgment of Paul is hard to mistake.

"supernatural Events," contrary to "common Experience, and the ordinary Course of Things," although they must be "well attested."

Locke does take up the question at some length in a separate work, the "Discourse on Miracles," which he did not publish, although he did grant permission for its publication after his death (Cranston 1957, 478). In it he reiterates that "to know that any revelation is from God, it is necessary that the messenger that delivers it is sent from God, and that cannot be known but by some credential given him by God himself" (Locke 1958, 80). The question of the discourse is whether miracles "in my sense, be not such credentials, and will not *infallibly* direct us right in the search of divine revelation" (emphasis added). A miracle, he says, is "a sensible operation, which, being above the comprehension of the spectator, and in his opinion, contrary to the established course of nature, is taken by him to be divine" (79). Of Scripture he says, "I think the most scrupulous or skeptical cannot from miracles raise the least doubt against the divine revelation of the gospel" (81). He does allow, however, that "everyone being able to judge of those laws [of Nature] only by his own acquaintance with Nature, and notion of its force (which are different in different men) it is unavoidable that that should be a miracle to one, which is not so to another" (80). Moreover, "what is the uttermost power of natural agents or created beings, men of the greatest reach cannot discover" (84), who therefore also cannot discover "what operations can be performed by none but a divine power, and require the immediate hand of the Almighty" (85). Miracles as such, it seems, are not knowable infallibly and therefore cannot serve as infallible credentials.[28]

Although his discussion in the *Essay* omits these crucial questions, Locke does affirm the reasoned acceptance of Scripture as the revealed word of God. Yet he also insists, as we recall, that reason guide us not only in judging the fact of revelation, but also "the signification of the Words" (IV.18.8). Reason stands judge over not only the fact but the meaning of revelation. Here a new wave of difficulties and uncertainties enter, owing to the "imperfection of Words," especially "moral Words,"

---

[28] Cf. *Leviathan* ch. 38; Rabieh 1991, 950–51; and Myers 1998, 44–45. According to Ayers, the *Discourse on Miracles* has a "less orthodox face" than the *Essay*, yet "the argument of the *Essay* is at least capable of bearing an interpretation which makes it compatible with that of the *Discourse on Miracles*: which is not, of course, to allow [the claim of miracles] much force" (1991, 120). Cf. also the *Third Letter on Toleration*: "but that [miracles] were not sufficient to make all that saw them effectually to receive and embrace the gospel, I think is evident"; "even miracles themselves did not effect upon all eye-witnesses" (*Works* 5:438, 455).

such as "Honour, Faith, Grace, Religion, Church, etc.," which refer to "mixed Modes." For most human beings, these words "are little more than bare Sounds; and when they have any [meaning], 'tis for the most part but a very loose and undetermined, and consequently obscure and confused signification." Even from those who are capable of speaking clearly, such words are doubtful, thus only showing "how uncertain the Names of mixed Modes naturally are." It is for this reason that there can never be a definitive interpretation of laws, whether those laws are divine or human.

One confronts the same difficulty in determining the "meaning of a text of Scripture" itself. Indeed, the problem is only compounded in the case of "the Writings of Men, who have lived in some remote Ages, and different Countries" (III.9.10). These writers "had very different Notions, Tempers, Customs, Ornaments, and Figures of Speech, etc. every one of which influenced the signification of their Words" (III.9.22). The problem of interpreting old, foreign books becomes urgent in the case of books like Scripture "that contain either Truths we are required to believe, or Laws we are to obey, and draw inconveniences on us when we mistake or transgress" (III.9.10). Unfortunately, precisely that urgency increases their obscurity: "In Discourses of Religion, Law, and Morality, as they are matters of the highest concernment, so there will be the greatest difficulty" (III.9.22). Darkness unavoidably shrouds the meaning of Biblical revelation, as well as all commentaries on it.

Though everything said in the Text be infallibly true, yet the Reader may, nay cannot but chuse but be very fallible in the understanding of it. Nor is it to be wondered, that the Will of God, when clothed in Words, should be liable to that doubt and uncertainty, which unavoidably attends that sort of Conveyance, when even his Son, whilst clothed in Flesh, was subject to all the Frailties and Inconveniencies of human Nature, Sin excepted.

That is, the words of Christ are no exception.

Locke concludes from the uncertain meaning of Scripture that "it would become us to be charitable one to another in our Interpretations or Misunderstandings of those ancient Writings" (III.9.22). Revelation is subject to natural limitations; it cannot overcome "common and natural obscurities and difficulties."

Since then the Precepts of Natural Religion are plain and very intelligible to all Mankind, and seldom come to be controverted; and other revealed Truths, which are conveyed to us by books and languages, are liable to the common and natural obscurities and difficulties incident to Words, methinks it would become us to be more careful and diligent in observing the former, and less magisterial, positive, and imperious, in imposing our own sense and interpretations of the latter. (III.9.23)

Locke has obviously not repudiated the authority of Scripture, but rather of our merely human ability to understand Scripture. The effect, however, is similar. One's "interpretation or misunderstanding" is one's own, but as a consequence God's revelation is unavoidably hidden or supplanted by human interpretation. Because an interpretation is mine, that is, merely human, and so uncertain, it has no authority over others. Revealed religion is demoted in favor of natural religion, or religion insofar as it is intelligible to reason alone.[29]

The Reasonableness of Christianity

Yet to say that Locke demotes revealed religion is not to say that he does away with it altogether. It is true that Locke says that "reason must be our last Judge and Guide in everything" and that he declares, even more strongly, reason to be "our only star and compass" (*Essay* IV.19.14; *1st Treatise* §58). It is true, moreover, that it is no easier on the basis of Locke's epistemology than on Hobbes's to see how revealed religion could ever reasonably rise to the level of credibility. Yet also like Hobbes, Locke does not limit himself to a critical assault, but elaborates at great length his own version of the Christian religion. But, as with Hobbesian Christianity, Lockean Christianity must be approached ever mindful of his epistemology, or else his religious teaching will lose any semblance of coherence. Most relevant to us here, in the *Reasonableness of Christianity*, Locke presents a doctrine on the way to salvation, despite his assertion in the *Letter* (supported by the epistemology of the *Essay*) that the way is unknown.

Hobbes, too, as we recall, had presented a doctrine of Christian salvation. The requirements of salvation were obedience to God's law and, because obedience is never perfect, faith in Christ. God's law proved to mean natural law rather than revealed law, and natural law proved to require obedience to civil law. Faith in Christ proved to mean belief that Jesus was the Messiah – the king promised in Old Testament prophecy to

---

[29] Cf. Ayers 1991, 121: "Yet what is so effusively given to the 'evidence' of revelation is at once taken away. Because 'we must be sure that it be a divine revelation and that we understand it right,' all this security is rapidly reduced to probability … Locke is really arguing that nothing is, in his usual sense, 'evident' about revelation, apart from the platitude that what God has revealed is true." Cf. also Locke's journal entry of August 26, 1676, reproduced at Locke 1954, 279–80.

rule over the Jews and other nations that believed in him "and to give them that eternal life that was lost by the sin of Adam" (*Leviathan* 43.11). While the saved enjoy eternal life, the unsaved are not damned to hell for eternity, but suffer eternal death. Hobbes hedges on whether belief in Christ's resurrection is necessary for salvation and more generally eschews all finer points that are difficult to comprehend and would thus lead to controversy and make Christianity less credible. His procedure, as he claims, is to stick to those parts of Scripture whose "sense is most plain and agreeable to the harmony and scope of the whole Bible" (43.24). On these basic points, Locke follows Hobbes closely. And to the extent that we noticed common elements in Hobbesian and Jeffersonian Christianity, Locke provides the link: We know from Jefferson's notes that he studied the *Reasonableness of Christianity* carefully. And yet Lockean Christianity does not seem to undermine itself in the way that Hobbesian (and perhaps Jeffersonian) Christianity does. There seems clearly to remain a need for belief in revelation. But how does such a need fit with reason's being our only star and compass?

Locke begins by telling us that Jesus was sent into the world to restore the eternal life that was lost with Adam (§2). The Bible is clear that "death came on all men by Adam's sin," but it is far from clear that death here means "deserved endless torment in hell-fire." Such punishment would mean that a man would not "lose his life, but be kept alive in perpetual exquisite torments" (§3). And so "by death here, I can understand nothing but a ceasing to be, the losing of all actions of life and sense" (§4). Locke's interpretation of the biblical teaching on the afterlife thus follows Hobbes's.[30] Eternal life is gained through resurrection, or "recovery" from death, which could be had from obedience to God's law, if obedience were perfect. But obedience is never perfect, and so there must be a law of faith alongside the law of works. God's law means, in the first place, the law of Moses, including or in addition to the "law of nature, knowable by reason" (§19). For us, however, in contrast to the ancient Hebrews, God's law means "not the ceremonial or political part ..., but the moral part of Moses's law, or the moral law (which is everywhere the same, the eternal rule of right)" (§§22–23). As for the

---

[30] Cf. *Leviathan*, ch. 38. In *The Decline of Hell*, D. P. Walker observes that the belief that the unsaved were not damned but were merely annihilated was generally considered a heresy in the seventeenth century, generating suspicions of depravity and atheism: "This is the reason why nearly all discussions of hell until well into the 18th century are veiled by a mist of secrecy and dishonesty. The peculiar dangers attached to any discussion of the eternity of hell were such that they produced a theory of double truth" (1964, 5).

law of faith, what God requires us to believe has changed over time: what was required of Abraham is not what is required of us. "What we are now required to believe to obtain eternal life, is plainly set down in the gospel" (§26). Locke quotes John 3:36: "He that believeth on the Son, hath eternal life; and he that believeth not the Son, shall not see life." He omits the conclusion of the sentence: "but the wrath of God abides on him." We are to "believe on the Son," which means "believing that Jesus was [sic] the Messiah; giving credit to the miracles he did, and the professions he made of himself" (§27). The Messiah was "the promised Deliverer" for those that would "receive him for their King and Ruler" (§178). As for Christ's resurrection, Locke, like Hobbes, equivocates, seeming to have noticed some ambiguity in the historical record of the apostle's preaching: it "was also *commonly* required to be believed as a necessary article, and *sometimes* solely insisted on" (§32, emphasis added). Locke arrives at this interpretation of Scripture by seeking only "the necessary points, to be understood in the plain and direct meaning of the words and phrases ... without learned, artificial, and forced systems of divinity" (§1, cf. p. 96).

And so we see how much Lockean Christianity resembles Hobbesian Christianity. Yet crucial differences remain. As suggested in the previous chapter, there are reasons to wonder whether Hobbes thought Christianity, or any religion – specifically any revealed religion – a permanent necessity for political life, to say nothing of private life. In the *Reasonableness of Christianity*, Locke seems clearly to indicate both that mankind is in permanent need of revelation and that Christianity meets that need. *The Reasonableness of Christianity* would then preclude the possibility, which we saw opened in Hobbes's approach, of doing away with religion altogether. Reason, Locke teaches, is insufficient for the moral guidance of mankind, since "the greatest part cannot know, and therefore they must believe" (§243). We thus return to the portrayal of Locke as a moderate in comparison to Hobbes, by not only being more accommodating of religion through his doctrine of toleration, but also affirming the needed benefit to mankind of belief in revealed religion.

An examination of Locke's argument on behalf of Christianity's benefit to mankind, however, leads us to place an asterisk beside this claim of moderation. Revelation – to be more precise, belief in revelation – is necessary owing to the limited rational capacities of "the vulgar," who constitute "the bulk of mankind." The rational few do not share that need. It is therefore not clear that Locke's theoretical view of revealed religion, as opposed to his practical view of its utility, is less radical than Hobbes's.

It is "the greater part" of mankind that "cannot know, and therefore they must believe." Locke tells us that "whatsoever should ... be universally useful, as a standard to which men should conform their manners, must have its authority either from reason or revelation" (§242). There is, however, a problem with reason in regard to its universal utility. "The greatest part of mankind want leisure or capacity for demonstration, nor can carry a train of proofs" (§243; cf. ECHU IV.20). Reason may suffice for a few, but revelation or belief in revelation is necessary for the vast majority. Locke tells us on page 1 that he approaches the New Testament as "a collection of writings, designed by God, for the instruction of the illiterate bulk of mankind, in the way to salvation" (§1). It is in this book that we find Locke's doctrine of Christian salvation.

Locke highlights two areas where Christian revelation has made available to mankind at large what had been a preserve of the small "rational and thinking part of mankind" (§238), that is, the philosophers: knowledge of the one true God and knowledge of our moral duties. Concerning the former, some ancient philosophers appear to have been able through reason alone to discover "the one, supreme, invisible God." Yet it is difficult to say what their private thoughts on the matter may actually have been, since they kept them secret. Outwardly, they conformed to the pagan religion of their society: "Whatsoever Plato, and the soberest of the philosophers thought of the nature and being of the one God, they were fain, in their outward worship, to go with the herd, and keep the religion established by law" (§238). Philosophers are not above such dissembling, and Locke does not blame them.[31] It was Jesus' "clear revelation" that "made the one invisible true God known to the world," that is, to the bulk of mankind who could not reason their way to knowledge (§239).

---

[31] Locke's young friend and admirer John Toland wrote that "it was the common practice of all the ancient philosophers" to employ both an "external and internal doctrine": "the one Popular, accommodated to the Prejudices of the vulgar, and to the receiv'd Customs or Religions; the other Philosophical, comfortable to the nature of things and consequently to Truth; which, with doors fast shut and under all other precautions, they communicated onely to friends of known probity, prudence, and capacity" (1720, 69, 65–66). Plato "furnish'd large materials for fables to the Platonics [i.e., Platonists] falsely so call'd; for night is not more unlike to day, than the modern to the primitive Platonics" (75). Toland laments that, although Christians should be devoted wholly to the truth, rancor among the sects has led to "circumstances [that] cannot fail to beget the woful effects of insincerity [and] dissumultion" (67). "The External and Internal Doctrine are as much now in use as ever" (94), and indeed commonplace. To prove his point, Toland goes so far as to recount a conversation involving Locke's longtime sponsor and intimate friend the First Earl of Shaftesbury. Cf. Owen 2010.

The situation was similar, but only similar, concerning morality, and interpreting Locke's teaching here becomes decidedly more difficult. Before Jesus, "a clear knowledge of their duty was wanting to mankind. This part of knowledge, though cultivated with some care by some of the heathen philosophers, yet got little footing among the people" (§241). Yet knowledge of morality was, it seems, rather more precarious than knowledge of God, even for the philosophers: "'Tis plain in fact, that human reason unassisted, failed men in its great and proper business of morality." Locke makes clear that he means morality in the full and strict sense, "a *complete* morality that may be to mankind the *unquestionable* rule of life and manners" (§242, emphasis added). Unassisted reason "never, from *unquestionable* principles, by clear deductions, made out an entire body of the law of Nature" (241, emphasis added). Now, it was evident prior to the Christian revelation which civil laws "conduce to the prosperity and temporal happiness of any people" (§243) – laws lying within a more limited range than would be found in complete morality. But, though rationally discernable, these "were looked upon as bonds of society, and conveniences of common life, and laudable practices," that is, not as law in the proper sense. Here is the central problem: They "could not be" viewed as law in the proper sense "without knowledge and acknowledgement of the law-maker, and the great rewards *and punishments*, for those that would or would not obey him" (emphasis added). Locke thus follows his systematic treatment of law in the *Essay*, to which we will turn in a moment. Reason can recognize certain moral rules as socially useful and even necessary, but it is far from clear that it can discern that those rules have been commanded by a divine lawgiver who supports them with rewards and punishments.

Yet despite indicating such limitations of reason even for the philosophers, Locke emphasizes the advantage of the Christian revelation for the "vulgar" in particular:

> It should seem, by the little that has hitherto been done in it, that 'tis too hard a task for unassisted reason, to establish morality, in all its parts, upon its true foundation, with a clear and convincing light. And 'tis at least a surer and shorter way to the apprehensions of the vulgar, and mass of mankind, that one manifestly sent from God, and coming with visible authority from him, should as King and lawmaker tell them their duties and require their obedience than leave it to the long and sometimes intricate deductions of reason. (§241)

Locke does, it is true, tell us along the way that Jesus' title as Messiah was not at the time altogether manifest and was even controversial among his disciples, some of whom left him over the question (§28). Jesus, moreover, concealed his true mission, even from his remaining disciples, until after his resurrection (§§61 ff.), when he revealed it only to them. We now see that Jefferson's unflattering view of the disciples (ch. 1) follows Locke's: According to Locke, our testimony of Jesus' mission is "from the mouths of a company of illiterate men" (§243) that followed him while ignorant of that mission, leaving Locke to wonder aloud "whether twelve other men, of quicker parts, and of a station of breeding, which might have given them any opinion of their own abilities, would have been so easily kept from meddling beyond just what was prescribed to them, in a matter they had so much interest in" (§142). Nevertheless, the fact that the miraculous events reported in that testimony could only come about by supernatural power is something that lies "level to the ordinariest apprehension" (§243). And so, even if the moral law could be rationally demonstrated, the gospels present a better vehicle for the instruction of the people in moral precepts. The gospels are, indeed, more suited to the ignorant than to the wise: "The learned scribe, the disputer or wise of this world" who expects subtle and abstract truths is "rather shut out from the simplicity of the gospel, to make way for those poor, ignorant, illiterate, who heard and believed the promises of a deliverer, and believed Jesus to be him; who could conceive a man dead and made alive again, and, believe that he should, at the end of the world, come again, and pass sentence on all man, according to their deeds" (§252).

Thus we arrive at "the reasonableness of Christianity," which is not due to the comprehensibility of every aspect of its teaching to unassisted reason – not to "the rationality of Christianity" – but to its being "a religion suited to vulgar capacities and the state of mankind in this world" (§252). As such, properly interpreted or transformed, it is suitable to the requirements of social life.

Locke's account of the utility of belief in revealed law – law in the full sense, with a lawgiver and sanctions – draws our attention to a passage early in the *Essay* that may at first be overlooked as a curious aside in the course of arguing that moral principles, which he classifies as practical principles, are not innate. For however much agreement there may be about certain social rules – Locke's example is "that Men should keep their Compacts" – there is disagreement about the reason, or principle, underlying such rules. The Christian, the Hobbist, and the heathen philosopher disagree. (The Hobbist is not a Christian.) This disagreement shows that moral or practical principles are not "imprinted on our Minds immediately by the Hand of God" (I.3.6). Locke writes:

It must be allowed, That several Moral Rules, may receive, from Mankind, a very general Approbation, without either knowing, or admitting, the true ground of Morality; which can only be the Will and Law of a God, who sees Men in the dark, has in his Hand Rewards and Punishments, and Power enough to call to account the Proudest Offender. For God, having by an inseparable connexion, joined Virtue and publick Happiness together; and made the Practice thereof, necessary to the preservation of Society, and visibly beneficial to all with whom the Virtuous Man has to do; it is no wonder that every one should, not only allow, but recommend, and magnifie those Rules to others, from whose observance of them, he is sure to reap advantage to himself. He may, out of Interest, as well as Conviction, cry up that for Sacred; which if once trampled on, and prophaned, he himself could not be safe or secure. (I.3.6)

One need not know the true ground of morality, which "can only be" a lawgiving God that rewards and punishes, in order to recognize the social utility, and particularly the benefit to oneself, of the general public adherence to "several Moral Rules." As we have already noted, those several moral rules that are socially useful are perhaps not the whole of morality. Moreover, their benefit is evident in their possession by others, in particular. This is why they are praised, indeed praised as divinely ordained, and in this way supported by public opinion. Even among those who do not know these moral rules to be grounded in divine will, there is a strong incentive to affirm publicly that they are.[32]

And yet, however much this reading of Locke may help to resolve certain tensions in Locke's teaching regarding religion, his teaching in another respect now appears to be in profound tension with itself. On the one hand, the true ground of morality – a complete moral law in the proper sense – requires a God who is a known lawgiver, a God who punishes and rewards in an afterlife. Even if the required knowledge cannot be widespread, Christianity can at least provide widespread confidence in the way to salvation, making it therefore a reasonable religion to support and affirm. On the other hand, Locke exerts considerable effort attempting to demonstrate the severe limits of human knowledge, in large

---

[32] When Locke addresses those who, after his demonstration, still doubt the existence of an omniscient god whose wisdom rules the universe, he asks the doubters to consider a passage from Cicero "at their leisure" (IV.10.6). The rhetorical question cited is introduced by Cicero as "what we must persuade our citizens" of: for "who will deny that such beliefs are useful when he remembers how often oaths are used to confirm agreements, how important to our well-being is the sanctity of treaties, how many persons are deterred from crime by fear of divine punishment, and how sacred an association of citizens becomes when the immortal gods are made members of it, either as judges or as witnesses" (*Laws*, II.vii.16).

part in order to quiet disputes over the way to salvation and promote toleration. In the course of that effort, he goes so far as to deny that the way to salvation is known. And insofar as he undermines the doctrine of hell in the *Reasonableness of Christianity*, he undermines belief in the great punishment of the lawgiver. Do not these two strands of Locke's teaching pull in different directions? Is not Locke's defense of toleration tantamount to an assault on the true grounds of morality? It is necessary to return to the *Essay* for Locke's systematic account of moral law.

II.

The true ground of morality

Locke states early in the *Essay* that true morality requires a providential God, a God who supernaturally supports morality through rewards and punishments, including "the Hell he has ordain'd for the punishment of those that transgress" (I.3.6). And again in the chapter "Of Power": "It is certain that Morality, established upon its true Foundations, cannot but determine the Choice in any one, that will but consider: and he that will not be so far a rational Creature, as to reflect seriously upon infinite Happiness and Misery, must needs condemn himself, as not making that use of his Understanding he should" (II.21.70). Let us turn briefly, then, to Locke's moral science in order to see why true morality entails the prospect of "infinite happiness and misery."

Locke's moral science begins with the premise that human beings are moved by pleasure and pain. We are motivated constantly by the "pursuit of happiness," which "in its full extent [is] the utmost pleasure we are capable of" (II.21.43 and 42).[33] Or "The greatest Happiness consists, in the having of those things, which produce the greatest Pleasure; and in the absence of those, which cause any disturbance, any pain" (IV.21.55). Good and evil most basically are not moral terms, according to Locke. Good and evil "are nothing but pleasure or pain, or that which occasions or procures pleasure or pain to us" (II.28.5). Moreover, what is pleasant or painful to one may not be so to another. The differences between human beings with respect to good and evil are tantamount to a difference of taste. And, also like taste, what is good and evil for an individual may change from day to day. Thus, although at one point Locke seems,

---

[33] Jefferson's famous amendment of Locke's phrase "life, liberty, and estate" (with which he elaborates the term "property") to "life, liberty, and the pursuit of happiness" in the Declaration of Independence thus remains fully within the Lockean frame.

however obscurely, to identify rewards in an afterlife with our summum bonum as human beings (IV.12.11), in Locke's systematic treatment of happiness, he denies there is a summum bonum: "Hence it was, I think, that the Philosophers of old did in vain enquire, whether summum bonum consisted in riches, or in bodily Delights, or Virtue, or Contemplation: And they might have as reasonably disputed, whether the best Relish were to be found in Apples, Plumbs, or Nuts; and have divided themselves into Sects upon it" (II.21.55).[34]

This does not mean that human beings are slaves to immediate pleasures and pains. We can weigh immediate pleasures and pains against future ones. The capacity for self-control, which Locke praises, is merely the capacity to control one's desire for immediate pleasure and pain with a view to later pleasure and pain. Pleasure and pain remain determinate. As for what is pleasant and painful itself, what is good or evil for me, the only measure is my own pleasure and pain: "As to present happiness and misery, when that alone comes to consideration, and the consequences are quite removed, a man never chooses amiss; he knows what best pleases him, and that he actually prefers" (II.21.58). Locke is aware of the implications for morality as it is thought of universally. There is no such thing as virtue and vice as those terms are "pretended and supposed everywhere to mean," namely, "actions in their own nature right and wrong" (II.28.10). No action is intrinsically good or evil, morally or otherwise, though it may carry with it future pleasures or pains quite naturally as a consequence. The pleasure (good) of drunkenness may lead to the pain (evil) of a hangover. Whether it does or not is irrelevant to the pleasure (goodness) of the act itself.[35]

---

[34] Cf. Hobbes, *Leviathan* (11.1): "For there is no such *Finis Ultimus* (utmost aim) nor *Summum Bonum* (greatest good) as is spoken of in the books of the old moral philosophers." Locke's denial of a summum bonum is a reformulation of a statement in the previous section that includes a proviso: "Were all the Concerns of Man terminated in this Life, why one followed Study and Knowledge, and another Hawking and Hunting; why one chose Luxury and Debauchery, and another Sobriety and Riches, would not be, because every one of these did not aim at his own happiness; but because their Happiness was placed in different things" (II.21.54). The proviso "were all the concerns of man terminated in this life" is replaced in the second formulation with "I think."

[35] Cf. Hobbes, *Leviathan* (6.7): "But whatsoever is the object of any man's appetite or desire that is it which he for his part calleth good; the object of his hate or aversion, evil ... For these words, good [and] evil ... are ever used in relation to the person that useth them, there being nothing simply and absolutely so, nor any common rule of good and evil to be taken from the nature of the objects themselves."

Moral good and evil enter only with the introduction of some law. "moral good and evil ... is only the conformity or disagreement of our voluntary actions to some law, whereby good and evil [pleasure and pain] are drawn on us from the will and power of the law-maker" (II.28.5). The pleasure and pain that follow from our actions in the case of moral good and evil are "not the natural product and consequence of the action itself" (II.28.6): not a hangover, but jail for public intoxication. Human beings under a law, including those acting in accordance with true morality, are still moved solely by pleasure and pain (and thus good and evil still refer only to pleasure and pain), but their judgment of what conduces to their pleasure and pain has been altered by the lawmaker, in particular by the sanctions attached to the law: "Since it would be utterly in vain, to suppose a Rule set to the free actions of Man, without annexing to it some Enforcement of Good and Evil, to determine his Will, we must, where-ever we suppose a Law, suppose also some Reward or Punishment annexed to that Law" (II.28.6). Thus morality, even in the full and proper sense, does not involve better or nobler intentions – more "moral" intentions – since it is still based on a calculation of one's own pleasure and pain: "Moral laws are set as a curb and restraint to ... exorbitant desires, which they cannot be but by rewards and punishments that will over-balance the satisfaction anyone shall propose to himself in the breach of the law" (I.3.13). Law thus depends crucially on evident and reliable enforcement, without which it is "utterly in vain."[36] Locke says that "this, if I mistake not, is the true nature of all Law, properly so called" (II.28.6).[37] So too the law itself must be clearly known to those under it. And a law cannot "be known or supposed without a law-maker" (I.3.12).[38]

---

[36] Interpreters often fail to appreciate that moral law for Locke operates, and can only operate, by appealing to private interest. McClure, for example, expunges private interest altogether, claiming that for Locke an action subject to moral law "recognize[s] an objective moral duty independent of one's preferences or this-worldly considerations of private advantage" (1996, 69–70).

[37] Since law, properly so called, requires sanctions that are "not the natural product and consequence of the Action itself," it is hard to see how Natural Law could be law properly so called. Cf. Hobbes, *Leviathan* (26.8): "For the laws of nature, which consist of equity, justice, gratitude, and other moral virtues on these depending, in the condition of mere nature ... are not properly laws, but qualities that dispose men to peace and obedience." (Thus Hobbes removes the equivocation of 15.41, on which Warrender bases his interpretation.)

[38] Cf. Hobbes, *Leviathan* (26.16).

Now that we have a clearer sense of what Locke means by the true ground of morality, we return to our puzzle. If morality for "the greatest part of mankind" and therefore society as a whole requires belief in not only God's revelation, but also his providence – those "great rewards and punishments" – Locke himself emphasizes at some length in the *Essay* a difficulty with this requirement, in the course of demonstrating that moral principles are not innate. For morality to be innate, all human beings would have to know the moral law clearly, knowledge that would mean also knowing the Lawmaker *and His enforcement* clearly. But human beings lack such clear knowledge.

If therefore anything be imprinted on the mind of all men as a law, all men must have a certain and unavoidable knowledge that certain and unavoidable punishment will attend the breach of it ... it being impossible that men should, without shame or fear, confidently and serenely break a rule which they could not but evidently know that God had set up and would certainly punish the breach of (which they must if it were innate) to a degree to make it a very ill bargain to the transgressor. *Without such a knowledge as this, a man can never be certain that any thing is his duty.* Ignorance *or doubt* of the law; hopes to escape the knowledge or power of the law-maker, or the like, may make men give way to a present appetite. But let any one see the fault, and the rod by it, and with the transgression a fire ready to punish it, a pleasure tempting, and the hand of the Almighty visibly held up, and prepared to take vengeance (for this must be the case where any duty is imprinted on the mind). (I.3.13; emphasis added)

Without certainty in moral sanctions, we can never be certain that anything is our duty, and hence that there is morality in the full sense. So far as this world is concerned, those sanctions are far from certain. Evident in all ages, however, as Locke tells us in the *Reasonableness of Christianity*, are "the pains and hardships of those who stuck firm to their duties, and suffered for the testimony of a good conscience. The portion of the righteous *has always been in all ages taken notice of* to be pretty scanty in this world: virtue and prosperity do not often accompany one another, and therefore virtue seldom had many followers" (§245, emphasis added). If, then, God's reliable providence (the rod by the fault) is evidently lacking in this world, it would appear to be all the more important for morality that it be confidently anticipated in the next. But, as we have seen, Locke's argument in the *Essay* aims to shake whatever certainty we might have supposed we had about the spiritual realm, and he seems to deny punishments after death in the *Reasonableness of Christianity*.

Our tour of Locke's moral science, however, is not yet over. Divine sanctions are not the only, nor are they the surest, support of morality. To be more precise, divine law is not the only law; there are also civil law and the "law of opinion or reputation." The civil law is the "rule set by the commonwealth" (II.28.9). Unlike the divine law, "this law nobody overlooks: the rewards and punishments being ready at hand and suitable to the power that makes it." That is, civil law is more effective than divine law, more effective than the "true ground of morality," the sanctions of which are less evident and therefore more readily ignored. Though more effective than divine law, civil law is also more limited in scope. It is not the complete morality that reason has been unable to discern. Civil law is not concerned with the soul's health or future state. The commonwealth is "engaged to protect the lives, liberties, and possessions of those who live according to its laws" and is thus concerned with those laudable practices that are beneficial to society and intelligible as such to unassisted reason.

Yet the effectiveness of civic sanctions, though surer than that of divine sanctions, is also limited: "Men frequently flatter themselves with the hopes of impunity" from civil law (II.28.12). More effective than either divine law or civil law is the law of opinion or reputation, "wherein everyone finds his advantage." The effectiveness of each type of law is inversely related to its rank or elevation. But the law of reputation is largely "coincident with the divine law." Divine law is, then, effective in a manner, but not *as* divine law. Divine law is not respected as divine, but as "fashion," and the penalty feared is not damnation, but a bad reputation with those in one's society. Hence: "I think there is nobody so brutish as to deny [the divine law]" (II.28.8) – except, of course, those "profligate wretches" mentioned in book I.[39] (We will see a similar account in Tocqueville of American religion's basis in popular opinion.)

Now, the fact that "perhaps most men seldom seriously reflect on" the "penalties that attend the breach of God's laws" need not mean that most men do not believe in those penalties, however unreflectively. Still, Locke's account of the three types of law suggests that divine sanctions

---

[39] "It is commonly suggested that Lockean man is not only self-directing but self-sufficient, owing nothing to society for the development of his person and capacities. This is, however, in certain important respects misleading ... Far from owing nothing to others, Locke constantly reiterates that ordinarily the bulk of men's ideas and attitudes are derived from others... As children they imbibe propositions, especially about religion, from parents and teachers, and when adults they come to regard these propositions as 'sacred things' which not only may not be questioned, but serve themselves as the standards of truth...The love of reputation is what moves most men. They desire to stand well in the opinion of others, which they are most likely to do if the conduct themselves as others do... [Tradition and fashion are] effective in a way which neither the laws of the state nor even the laws of nature commonly are" (Geraint 1978, 44–45).

in an afterlife, which become increasingly obscure in Locke's teaching, are not so crucial a support of at least the socially useful part of morality as they may appear. We thus confront the possibility that society can function well without morality in the full sense or placed on its true foundations. The earthly goods that are society's aim can be secured using earthly and humanly enforced sanctions.

   Compare here Locke's *Thoughts Concerning Education*, in which he instructs the reader on the theological doctrine suitable to a child: "There ought very early to be imprinted on his mind a true notion of God, as of the independent Supreme Being, Author and Maker of all things, from whom we receive all our good, who loves us, and gives us all things" (§136). That is, belief in God is instilled for the sake of virtue. But for children, at least, the notion of a providential God is allowed only warily. Children should hear "only ... upon occasion" that "God made and governs all things, hears and sees everything, and does all manner of good to those that love and obey him." Such notions should be rarely mentioned lest their thoughts become distracted "with curious enquiries into [God's] inscrutable essence and being." Locke does not mention teaching children of a God who legislates or punishes – the "true ground of Morality" (*Essay* I.3.6), including divine and natural law.[40] It is perhaps for this reason that Locke speaks of "a true notion of God" as the foundation of virtue rather than of morality, and it is not clear that Locke uses the terms interchangeably. To be still more precise, such belief lays "the first foundations of virtue in a child" (§139). "As he grows up, the tendency of his natural inclination must be observed" and corrected through habituation. Accordingly, "the great principle and foundation of all virtue and worth is plac'd in this: that a man is able to deny and cross his own inclinations, and purely follow what reason directs as best, tho' the appetite lean the other way" (§33; cf. §§38, 45, 143, 200). The "true principle of virtue and industry" is "this habit ... the true foundation of future ability and happiness" (§38). Indeed, "virtue itself [is] valued only as conducing to our happiness," "the happiness that all men pursue consisting in pleasure" (§139). Whereas virtue is more likely to be spoken of as self-control through habituation in Locke's treatise on education, morality is more likely to be spoken of in relation to religion (§§116, 146, 159, 185, 200).

---

[40] Cf. Tarcov 1984, 186–91.

The idea that curious theological inquiries, even those related to our salvation, might prove a distraction points us in the direction of the moral transformation Locke sought to effect as part of or alongside the religious one. The morality Locke seeks to defend is less in need of the traditional Christian support because the morality he seeks to defend is not traditional Christian morality. Indeed, it is not enough to say that an active, providential God is unnecessary to Lockean "morality"; it is a hindrance to it.

Religious transformation and the new morality

In the *Essay*, Locke says that those who hold religious opinions with the most unwavering assurance are those "who have least examined them" (IV.16.3). It is precisely such strong assurance that Locke means to weaken if not destroy in the *Essay*. Locke does not point to some new assurance, but rather to the "blindness we are in" (IV.16.4). On account of this blindness, "it would ... become all Men to maintain Peace, and the common Offices of Humanity, and Friendship, in the diversity of Opinions." "We should," Locke says, "do well to commiserate *our mutual Ignorance*, and endeavor to remove it in all the gentle and fair ways of Information; and not instantly treat others ill, as obstinate and perverse, because they will not renounce their own, and receive our Opinions, or at least those we would force upon them" (emphasis added). From here we can see that the main thrust of Locke's theological epistemology is not in the positive work of grounding religious belief – even the tenets of natural religion. Rather, its chief work is negative, in its attempt to demonstrate the "blindness we are in."

Yet this negative work in theology is for the sake of a positive agenda that is not essentially theological. Or, to put the matter more cautiously, according to Locke God has not provided us with faculties suited to theological speculation (beyond, perhaps, knowledge of the existence of a God). We can deduce God's intention for us from observing what our faculties are instead suited to do, and our faculties are suited to addressing practical, earthly ends. Locke indicates this positive agenda in chapter 12 of book IV of the *Essay*: "Of the Improvement of Our Knowledge." That improvement requires turning away from vain speculation, both metaphysical and theological, and turning to useful inquiry – above all moral science and "the useful arts" directed toward "the Conveniences of Life" and "Plenty" for "common use of humane Life ... in this World." Inquiry should not be directed toward metaphysics or "separate Spirits in this World" (to say nothing of other worlds), which we could know "only from Revelation." "Rational men" seek instead "real Improvements" in this world, improvements that modern natural science at last affords thanks to "those, who in this latter Age have taken another Course and have trod out to us, though not an easier way to learned Ignorance, yet a surer way to profitable Knowledge" (IV.12.11–12). While natural theology takes precedence over revealed theology, our main concern ought to be (as it at bottom, in fact, already is) this life.[41] As Locke states plainly in his neglected essay "Of Study": "The knowledge we acquire in this world I am apt to think extends not beyond the limits of this life. The beatific vision of the other life needs not the help of this dim twilight; but be that as it will, this I'm sure, the principal end why we are to get knowledge here is to make use of it for the benefit of ourselves and others in the world" (Locke 1968, 412).

Thus our speaking of Locke's political theology is misleading to the extent that he aims to enervate theological speculation, though he does so with a political aim. So far as natural theology is concerned, what we can know is very limited. There is little to discuss and still less to fight over. Locke, of course, praises the study of theology.[42] We therefore exaggerate, but nevertheless capture something of the spirit of Locke's epistemology, to say that it is ultimately antitheological. Even when considering the much-discussed limitations of toleration presented in the *Letter* (Locke's alleged intolerance of Catholics and atheists), Locke argues on the basis of civil concerns, not a concern for correct theology or salvation. This applies both to those who join a church that delivers them "up to the Protection and Service of another Prince" and to those "who deny the Being of a God" (1983, 50–51; cf. *Essay*, I.4.8, II.28.8 and 10). Locke's guiding principle is set with a view to the worldly ends of government: "No Opinions contrary to human Society, or to those rules which are necessary to the preservation of Society, are to be tolerated by the Magistrate" (49). The beliefs of a Roman Catholic unrelated to the preservation of society do "no injury thereby to his Neighbor" and ought not to be forbidden (46).[43] Even idolaters are to be tolerated. A key to the spirit

---

[41] Cf. IV.11.8 on the sufficiency of our knowledge and Pangle 1988, 207–09.

[42] See, for example, Locke's brief comments on theology in the *Conduct of the Understanding*, §23, which consists of praise for "that noble study [which] everyone that can be called a rational creature is capable of," and, on the basis of that nobility, a call for toleration and an end to the "strife, faction, malignity, and narrow imposition" occasioned by the study of theology. Note the context provided by §§22 and 24.

[43] The passage cited indicates that Locke's intolerance of Catholics is not as clear-cut as many readers have made it out to be. Even the intolerance of atheists attributed to Locke

of the *Essay* in this regard is found in the opening sentence of the *Letter*, where Locke asserts that "toleration is the chief Characteristical Mark of the True Church" (23). The question of true theology is replaced by toleration.

One aspect, then, of the transformation Locke sought to effect is the fundamental change in orientation, the turn away from the mysterious, supernatural, otherworldly and to the goods of this world and this life. A more traditional Christian morality than Locke's is also, of course, concerned with providing earthly goods to a certain extent, such as aiding the poor and the sick. The morality Locke promotes, however, departs decisively from what Christians have considered "the great monuments of exemplary charity." It does so in part through a certain kind of natural science, one directed toward increasing human know-how:

> If rightly directed, [the study of nature] may be of greater benefit to mankind than the monuments of exemplary charity that have at so great charge been raised by the founders of hospitals and alms-houses. He that first invented printing; discovered the use of the compass, or made public the virtue and right use of kin kina [quinine] did more for the propagation of knowledge, for the supplying and increase of useful commodities, and saved more from the grave than those who build colleges, work-houses, and hospitals. (IV.12.12).

A more fundamental departure from traditional Christian morality, however, is found in the fact that the human discoveries and inventions that Locke would have us make our business are not simply, indeed not primarily, pursued by individuals for the good of others. Locke says that those who pursue such knowledge do so for both "the common use of humane life, *and* their own particular subsistence in this world" (emphasis added). That is, Lockean morality, and hence Lockean religion, does not demand the subordination of one's own interests – a subordination Lockean psychology denies is possible. Rather, one's own interest is united with the common interest of

---

must be qualified. In the *Letter*, Locke would deny toleration to those who "deny the being of a God," on the grounds that the bonds of society can have no hold on an atheist. Yet, as we have seen, in the *Essay* Locke suggests that even atheists can see the social necessity of certain moral rules for their own safety and may defend them as sacred out of interest, if not out of moral conviction. These do not, as do the atheists denied toleration in the *Letter*, "undermine and destroy all religion" (51), but on the contrary defend it as a support of those moral rules necessary for society. (Cf. *Democracy in America*, 286–87 and Chapter 4.) Recall that in the *Essay*, Locke says that "only some profligate wretches" admit to atheism "now"; "yet, perhaps, we should hear, more than we do, of it, from others, did not the fear of the magistrates sword, or their neighbor's censure, tie up people's tongues" (I.4.8). Cf. Nadon 2006.

mankind, or rather the common interest of mankind is advanced through the pursuit of one's own interest.[44]

This union is evident, in the first place, in the case of those "several moral rules" discussed previously that are "visibly beneficial to all" and promoted chiefly out of self-concern. But Locke's emphasis on invention, useful commodities, and conveniences indicates a more novel way in which self-concern and benefaction may unite. Locke's clearest example is provided in the *Second Treatise of Government*'s chapter on property, with the crucial human invention of money. With the invention of money, human beings had for the first time an interest in producing more goods than they themselves could use, since the surplus could be sold rather than going to waste. This led to further inventions, in order to extract as much of use as possible from whatever natural resources were available. The common stock of goods was increased for all, more cheaply and efficiently. These productive benefactors of mankind need not be especially charitable. All the better if they are eager for gain. Lockean morality is thus strange from (but not only from) a traditional Christian point of view. Locke does not tell us that the poor are blessed, instruct us to give away our possessions, or warn us about how hard it is for a rich man to enter the kingdom of heaven (cf. Luke 6:20, 14:33; Mark 10:23; Matthew 19:21–24). Such moralism is counterproductive and must therefore be undone. He instructs us instead to acquire as much as we (prudently) can. The desire for unlimited acquisition benefits mankind and is thus justified and unleashed. Steve Jobs, Locke might say, benefited more human beings than a thousand Mother Teresas, and his wealth was tangible proof of that benefit. The entrepreneur and industrialist are far closer than Teresa to being the model of rationality and thus of Lockean morality and, it seems, religion. For, as Locke says in the chapter on property, God has given the earth to the producers of abundance, the "industrious and the rational" (§34).

Yet as the chapter on property proceeds, we are forced at least to wonder whether Locke's agenda regarding religion is simply transformative. He begins the chapter in a quite pious manner, appealing to revelation, quoting Scripture, telling us that "God has given the world to men in common," and speaking of the "plenty" God gave to men. Locke's famous doctrine is that human beings acquire property as they mix their labor with some part of this plenty – for example, picking an apple – provided there are as many and

---

[44] Cf. Chapter 4 on the doctrine of interest well understood in *Democracy in America*.

as good left for the rest. We are reminded of the early presentation of the benevolent state of nature, as we are presented with a benevolently given land of plenty. And just as in Locke's presentation of the state of nature, which we learn will quickly permanently degrade into a state of war, so too the story of the chapter on property likewise changes dramatically. The story shifts from one in which God has given us what we need in abundance to one in which nature provides raw material that is virtually worthless in itself and whatever we have of value results from human labor.[45] "Nature and the earth," he tells us, "provided only the almost worthless materials." It is "labour indeed that puts the difference in value on every thing" (§39), pushing the point more and more as the chapter proceeds. At first labor adds ten times the natural value of what nature has provided (§37). Later it is a hundred times (§§ 37 and 40), then a thousand times (§43), then a hundred thousand times (§43). Note also that the shift is not only one from plenty to penury. It is also a shift from what God has given to what nature has given. Locke mentions God sixteen times in the first eleven sections of the chapter and not once in the last sixteen sections. He does, however, speak of the "great art of government: and that prince, who shall be so wise and godlike, as by established laws of liberty to secure protection and encouragement to the honest industry of mankind" (§42).[46] As God disappears from the story, the role of man grows: "Man (by being master of himself, and proprieter of his own person, and the actions of labor of it) had still in himself the great foundation of property" (§44). There is no indication whatsoever of a fall from grace or of labor's being a curse, as we find in the book of Genesis. Returning to the *Essay*, we find Locke saying that the human being who first learned to make use of iron, "that contemptible mineral, may be truly styled the Father of the Arts, and Author of Plenty" (with which he immediately juxtaposes the Author of Nature; IV.12.11–12; cf. *2nd Treatise*, §28).

---

[45] Even amid the happy story of God's plenty at the beginning, Locke leaves a clue that something else is afoot. Speaking of the power of labor to make property out of God's plenty, Locke says: "By virtue thereof, what fish any one catches in the ocean, that great and still remaining common of mankind; or what ambergrise any one takes up here, is by the labour that removes it out of that common state nature left it in, made his property, who takes that pains about it." Fish out of an ocean teaming with others is one thing, but ambergris? That valuable, because exceedingly rare, substance? Another odd example from this early stage of supposed plenty mentions the labor of a servant. A servant? Another mentions iron ore. Why in this land of plenty are there servants and why would anyone mine ore?

[46] Cf. Hobbes, *Leviathan* (17.13).

This much is clear: man must be responsible for his own welfare. Might not a morality that depends on providence for support too easily pass mastery of human affairs to God, leaving it to God to supply our needs? The old piety hinders the new morality. In the gospel of Matthew, for example, Jesus says:

No one can serve two masters; for either he will hate the one and love the other, or he will hold to one and despise the other. You cannot serve God and mammon. For this reason I say to you, do not be anxious for your life, as to what you shall eat, or what you shall drink; nor for your body, as to what you shall put on ... Look at the birds of the air, that they no not sow, neither do they reap, nor gather into barns, and yet your heavenly Father feeds them. Are you not worth much more than they? ... And why are you anxious about clothing? Observe how the lilies of the field grow; they do not toil nor do they spin, yet I say to you that even Solomon in all his glory did not clothe himself like one of these. But if God so arrays the grass of the field, which is alive today and tomorrow is thrown into the furnace, will he not much more do so for you, O men of little faith? ... For all these things the Gentiles eagerly seek; for your heavenly Father knows you need all these things. But seek first His kingdom and His righteousness; and all these things shall be added to you. (Matthew 6:24–33)

In contrast, Locke's message, in the phrase made popular in America by Benjamin Franklin, is that God helps those that help themselves. He instructs us to accumulate "mammon," not despise it.

Morality that depends on providence, moreover, may too easily attribute hardships to God's providence, accepting them as deserved. But Locke stresses at the beginning of the *Reasonableness of Christianity* that the human condition, though hard, is no punishment: "Everyone's sin is charged upon himself only" (§4). Labor is not a punishment for original sin (Genesis 3:17–19), but the necessary means to alleviating or escaping the harsh conditions of nature, as directed by the "senses and reason," toward not just self-preservation, but "comfortable preservation" (*1st Treatise*, §§ 86–87). Similarly, for women, though Genesis 3:16 seems to suggest that God's punishment of Eve, and "in her ... all other women," subjected women to the authority of their husbands and to painful childbirth, Locke asserts that "there is here no more law to oblige a woman to such a subjection, if the circumstances either of her condition or contract with her husband should exempt her from it, than there is that she should bring forth her children in sorrow and pain, if there could be found a remedy for it, which is also part of the same curse upon her" (*1st Treatise*, §47). Humankind's harsh condition is attributable to nature, not to God. Locke's God is not a harsh God.

III.

We thus return to the promotion of a certain religious doubt, and therefore the importance of the *Essay*, as a part of Locke's political project.
Locke does not promote a thoroughgoing religious doubt, even with
regard to the supernatural. Christianity cannot be reduced to natural
religion. But Locke clearly does promote considerable uncertainty
regarding the supernatural, and even the spiritual, in general, for the sake
of promoting a peaceful toleration and turning attention in a more
tangibly productive direction. There are moral-political reasons to be
attracted to such doubt, despite or because of the fact that it introduces
uncertainty regarding what Locke calls our "greatest concern" as well.
But we must distinguish the place of that doubt in Locke's political project
from its place in his philosophy proper. An opinion may be politically
useful but false (or politically harmful but true). The question of whether
belief in the supernatural is conducive to material prosperity and a
peaceful political order is distinct from the question of whether that belief
is valid or not.

The core of Locke's theoretical case is epistemological, and in this too
he follows Hobbes. However great the doubts they mean to raise about
the supernatural in general, and revealed religion in particular, neither
attempts to refute their possibility. Although the chief objective of the
Essay is to make the case for reason as the sole guide of human life,
Locke does not deny, as we have observed, that revelation is possible.
Asserting, as he does, our insuperable ignorance of both the material and
spiritual worlds, he cannot *prove* its impossibility. Accordingly, Locke's
approach to the question of revealed religion appears to be defensive
rather than offensive. Serious reflection on human understanding compels us to admit that all claims to knowledge of spiritual things, even of
their existence, are radically dubious. The likelihood that any claimed
revelation is real is so remote that the willingness of anyone, even the
alleged recipient, to believe can never be based in a desire to know the
truth, but must rather be based in other "passions or interests," such as
the desire for "an authority of dictating to others" (IV.19.1–2). Locke
does grant various degrees of assent short of certain knowledge, and he
insists that the degree of assent depend upon the degree of evidence and
probability. Inner conviction, however strong, counts for nothing whatever in establishing evidence and probability. Locke's *argument* leads to
a conclusion that he himself does not state: Revelation is so improbable
as to be unbelievable.

Is that conclusion sound? Is unbelief in revealed religion warranted on these defensive epistemological grounds? It is helpful to turn for a moment to consider a slightly later Enlightenment thinker who, though a critic of Locke in other respects, follows suit in approaching religion by the standard of probability. In his *Inquiry Concerning Human Understanding* (the title of which signals its debt to Locke's *Essay*), David Hume argues against miracles and prophecy on the basis of their improbability: "A miracle is a violation of the laws of nature; and as a firm and unalterable experience has established these laws, the proof against a miracle, from the very nature of the fact, is as entire as any argument from experience can possibly be imagined ... And as a uniform experience amounts to a proof, there is here a direct and full proof, from the nature of the fact, against the existence of any miracle, nor can such a proof be destroyed or the miracle rendered credible but by an opposite proof which is superior" (122–23). This proof holds even in the face of many reputed witnesses: "And what have we to oppose such a cloud of witnesses but the absolute impossibility or miraculous nature of the events which they relate? And this, surely, in the eyes of all reasonable people, will alone be regarded as sufficient refutation" (133). Hume, writing a full generation further into the Age of Enlightenment,[47] makes explicit the obvious application to "the truth of the Christian religion" (117), going so far as to assert that "according to the principle here explained, this subtraction [of the supernatural] with regard to all popular religions amounts to an entire annihilation" (137). "What we have said of miracles," Hume states, "may be applied without any variation to prophecies" (140). All of which leads him to conclude:

So that, upon the whole, we may conclude that the Christian religion not only was at first attended with miracles, but even at this day cannot be believed by any reasonable person without one. Mere reason is insufficient to convince us of its veracity. And whoever is moved by faith to assent to it is conscious of a continued miracle in his own person which subverts all the principles of his understanding and gives him a determination to believe what is most contrary to custom and experience. (141)[48]

---

[47] Commenting on lessons historians have learned from the discovery of the clandestine literature of the early Enlightenment, Antony McKenna says, "The High Enlightenment was to be less a battle of philosophical ideas than a cultural battle for the wide diffusion of ideas that had hitherto circulated covertly" (2003, 251). But on Hume, cf. Russell 1993.

[48] It is worth noting that Hume begins his argument on miracles with the following claim: "Nothing is so convenient as a decisive argument ... which must at least silence the most

The boldness of Hume's application or extension of Locke's argument allows us better to see the vulnerability of its basis. A miracle, according to Hume, would be contrary to the "laws of nature." These laws are not established by obvious necessity – they are not, in Locke's terminology, intuitive. Rather they are established by a "firm and unalterable experience" of their regularity. Because that experience is firm and unalterable, claims of miracles are not believable, so that Hume is willing to equate "miraculous nature" with "absolute impossibility." That an event would be miraculous ipso facto is grounds for disbelief. But if there are, in fact, so many claimed miracles – "found in all history, sacred and profane" (118) – by what right does Hume claim that the laws of nature are based on firm and unalterable experience? How can he be sure that there are, in fact, inviolable "laws of nature" – necessities – and not rather mere regularities, without knowledge of the grounds of those regularities? He is, after all, forced to admit that "there may possibly be miracles or violations of the usual course of nature, of such a kind as to admit of proof from human testimony, though perhaps it will be impossible to find any such in all the records of history" (137). But should this ever happen, philosophers "ought to search for the causes whence it might be derived" (138), that is, natural causes, not God, whose attributes and actions it is impossible to know (139).[49]

Hume agrees with Locke (and Hobbes before him), moreover, that the importance of miracles lies in establishing prophecy: Prophecy, which instructs human beings how to behave, is the more fundamental question. Hume dismisses prophecy by considering it a type of miracle, which he has already dismissed. But not only is his dismissal of miracles hasty, surely prophecy is a special class of miracle, one particularly difficult to refute. For prophecy, and with it any form of divine illumination, may be chiefly an inner experience and therefore invisible to others. This more difficult case Hume sets aside with the joke about the "continued miracle in his own person" quoted previously.

Despite Hume's greater boldness in other respects, it is Locke who confronts prophecy and divine illumination more squarely. As we have already seen, he grants that in the experience of those claiming divine illumination, it is as clear "as the sun at noon." According to Locke, they

---

arrogant bigotry and superstition and free us from their impertinent solicitations. I flatter myself that I have discovered an argument of [such a] nature" (117–18).

[49] Cf. Owen 2001, 26–28 on Dewey's treatment of "mystical experience" in relation to the scientist and 182 n. 7.

say that "they see the light infused into their understandings, and cannot be mistaken; 'tis clear and visible there; like the light of bright sunshine shows itself and needs no other proof, but is its own evidence" (IV.19.8). Locke is evidently more impressed by the challenge than is Hume.

Locke, moreover, admits that "when a man says he sees or feels, no body can deny it him that he does so" (IV.19.10). Here Locke challenges:

This seeing, is it the perception of the truth of the proposition, or of this, that it is a revelation from God? This feeling, is it a perception of an inclination or fancy to do something, or of the spirit of God moving that inclination? These are two very different perceptions, and must be carefully distinguished if we would not impose upon ourselves ... But however it be called light and seeing, I suppose it is at most but belief and assurance ... And if I do not know [that God is the revealer of this to me], how great soever the assurance is that I am possessed with, it is groundless, and whatever light I pretend to, it is but enthusiasm. (IV.19.10)

Though it may seem to them as clear as the noonday sun, in comparison with "the twilight of reason" (IV.19.9), Locke "supposes" that it cannot be genuine knowledge. It cannot, Locke is convinced, be nearly so certain as intuitive knowledge, which cannot be doubted by a "mind that has its faculty of perception left to a degree capable of distinct ideas, no more than it can be a doubt to the eye, (that can distinctly see white and black) whether this ink and this paper be all of a color" (IV.2.5).

But, even granting that these things cannot be doubted by those who have the appropriate faculty of perception in a healthy condition, is it not conceivable that those claiming divine illumination have (or have been given) a faculty of perception that others, including Locke, lack? Consider the following passage from Jonathan Edwards, the great divine of colonial New England who was among the principal leaders of the Great Awakening that so profoundly affected Backus:

In those gracious exercises which are wrought in the minds of the saints, through the saving influences of the Spirit of God, there is a new inward perception or sensation of their minds, entirely different in its nature and kind, from anything that ever their minds were subjects of before they were sanctified. For doubtless if God by his mighty power produces something that is new, not only in degree and circumstances, but in its whole nature, and that which could be produced by no exalting, varying, or compounding of what was there before, or by adding of the like kind; I say, if God produces something new in a mind, that is a perceiving, thinking, conscious thing; then doubtless something entirely new is felt, or perceived, or thought; or which is the same thing, there is some new sensation or perception of the mind, which is entirely of a new sort, and which could be produced by no exalting, varying, or compounding of that kind of perceptions or sensations which the mind had before; or there is what some metaphysicians call a new simple idea. (1959, 205)

The principal "metaphysician" alluded to is surely Locke, whose *Essay* greatly impressed Edwards.[50] Simple ideas, according to Locke, result from either sensation or reflection and are "the materials of all our knowledge" (II.2.2). The mind does not have the power to invent simple ideas; they must originate outside the mind. A simple idea therefore cannot even be imagined by one who has never perceived it.

It is not in the power of most exalted wit, or enlarged understanding, by any quickness or variety of thought, to invent or frame one new simple idea in the mind ... I would have anyone fancy any taste which has never affected his palate; or frame the idea of a scent he had never smelt: And when he can do this, I will also conclude that a blind man hath ideas of colors, and a deaf man true distinct notions of sound ... we cannot believe it impossible for God to make a creature with other organs and more ways to convey into the understanding the notice of corporeal things than those five, as they are usually counted, he has given to man. (II.2.2–3).

If Locke wishes to take a lack of knowledge as a refutation, may he not be asked how he knows that he is not spiritually blind, incapable of perceiving, for whatever reason, certain "simple ideas" that are evident to others (including, perhaps, some who have read and admired the *Essay Concerning Human Understanding*)? Does Locke's case for the supreme guidance of reason ultimately rest on anything more solid than his own unbelief? Belief versus belief?

But Locke's approach is not simply defensive. We have already commented on how the spread through society of uncertainty and doubt regarding revealed religion aids Locke's socio-political agenda, insofar as they are linked to toleration and the redirection of human energies to the earthly goods of peace and prosperity. But such a spread, insofar as it is linked to a weakening of supernatural religion, could also be supposed to strengthen the theoretical case in favor of a strictly natural or rational account of things. For, Locke might say, the only potential evidence contradicting such an account – evidence that there is *not* necessity behind the apparent regularities of things, evidence of the supernatural – is found in claimed experiences of certain human beings. As we have seen, Locke

[50] A friend of Edwards wrote that when he first encountered Locke's *Essay*, Edwards reported that "he was as much engaged and had more satisfaction and pleasure studying it, than the most greedy miser in gathering up handsful of silver and gold from some new discovered treasure" (Hopkins 1810, 6).

cannot in every case deny the fact of those experiences, however much he may doubt what was experienced. Might not the widespread weakening – perhaps even the eventual disappearance – of supernatural religion also carry with it the ever-diminishing frequency of such claims? As Hume says, we will always have stories of the supernatural in "histories, sacred and profane," but perhaps fewer and fewer. Perhaps someday the spread of science and reason, supporting and supported by a preoccupation with material goods and comforts, will disenchant the world, and one will require histories to learn of such claims.[51] They would then pose no more of a theoretical challenge than do ancient tales of Zeus and Apollo. We would still not have a theoretical refutation in the full sense, but perhaps enough to put the question reasonably to rest.

We could understand such an approach as an adumbration of the Socratic approach – questions that could not be settled directly by theoretical science owing to its inherent limitations were approached in a "second sailing" by way of a dialectical movement of human opinions. If Locke's approach lacks the surgical precision of Socratic dialectic, could it make up for that shortcoming in its more ambitious sweep? Locke's socio-political project would thus be linked to his theoretical project in a way we have not considered. Rather than the theoretical arguments supporting the political project, the political project would form the foundation of the theoretical project, just as political philosophy is the core of Socratic philosophy.

This admittedly conjectural possibility raises many questions, not least of which is this: If (assuming he was in earnest) Locke is correct that a concern for our eternal fate is our greatest concern, regardless of whether we can gain knowledge about it, then would we not expect at least this essentially un-Hobbesian seed of supernatural religion to remain always a part of human life? In the next chapter, we will consider Tocqueville's analysis of religion in America. Tocqueville observes that American religion has, in a way Locke would have applauded, adopted an almost thoroughly this-worldly focus – consumed with material goods and suspicious of the supernatural. Yet this focus on material goods can only partly obscure something deeper at work in the soul: "Man did not give himself the taste for the infinite and the love of what is immortal. These sublime instincts are not born of a caprice of his will: they have their immovable foundation in his nature; they exist despite his efforts.

---

[51] Consider Keith Thomas, *Religion and the Decline of Magic* (1971); D. P. Walker, *The Decline of Hell* (1964).

He can hinder them and deform them, but not destroy them" (511). In democratic societies, one sees religion endangered less by disbelief than by distraction: "One sees the men who let the object of their dearest hopes escape almost by forgetting" (286). Tocqueville finds that democratic life, precisely in its Lockean preoccupation with material acquisition, is fundamentally unsatisfying for human beings, and that it is therefore not surprising to see human nature sometimes rebel, even amid America's radically democratic society, in the form of radically other-worldly religion (510–11).

And yet, despite his calling it our "greatest concern," Locke's teaching on the depth or naturalness of that concern for the eternal fate of our souls is far more ambiguous than Tocqueville's. In the penultimate chapter of the *Essay*, he confronts the question of why, if this is man's greatest concern, we find that the vast majority of human beings apparently give it little thought. The chief reason at first seems to be that "the greatest part of mankind" are consumed with meeting their immediate material needs. They lack leisure, being "given up to labour, and enslaved to the necessity of their mean condition" (IV.20.2). Our greatest concern need not be our most urgent concern. But Locke then says that "there are none so enslaved to the necessities of life who might not find vacancies that might be husbanded to advance their knowledge"; or at least this would be so *"were men as intent upon this as they are on things of lower concernment"* (IV.20.3, emphasis added). Urgent material needs do not explain the lack of attention to our eternal souls, which are evidently, *empirically*, of less concern than the lowly pleasures and pains of this world. Locke explains in his most fundamental chapter on human psychology, part II, chapter 21, entitled simply "Of Power":

In this life there are not many whose happiness reaches so far as to afford them a constant train of moderate mean pleasures without any mixture of uneasiness; and yet they could be content to stay here forever: Though they cannot deny, but that it is possible, that there may be a state of eternal durable joys after this life, far surpassing all the good that is to be found here. Nay they cannot but see that it is more possible than the attainment and continuation of that pittance of honour, riches, or pleasure which they pursue, and for which they neglect that eternal state: But in full view of this difference, satisfied of the possibility of a perfect, secure, and lasting happiness in a future state, and under a clear conviction, that it is not to be had here, whilst they bound their happiness within some little enjoyment or aim of this life, and exclude the joys of Heaven from making any necessary part of it, their desires are not moved by this greater apparent good, nor their wills determin'd to any action or endeavor for its attainment. (II.21.44).

The mundane goods of this world and not the sublime goods of the next, to say nothing of natural philosophy, are man's naturally greatest concern.

But what of the obvious fact – obvious to Locke and recently again made obvious to us his heirs – of those who fight and die in the name of their faith? What of the warring sects, the pacification of which is clearly central to Locke's political program? Turning back to book IV, to what is nearly Locke's last word in the *Essay*, we find the surprising claim that religious disagreement is not so great as it would appear, even in times of religious conflict. At the end of his chapter "Wrong Assent and Errour" (and confirming the extent to which religion has been on his mind all along), he argues that sectarian strife is not rooted in religious disagreement, at least not to the extent commonly supposed.

But notwithstanding the great noise is made in the world about errours and opinions, I must do mankind that right, as to say, There are not so many men in errours, and wrong opinions, as it is commonly supposed. Not that I think they embrace the truth; but indeed, because, concerning those doctrines they keep such a stir about, they have no thought, no opinion at all. For if anyone should a little catechize the greatest part of the the most partisan of most of the sects in the world, he would not find, concerning those matters they are so zealous for, that they have any opinions of their own: much less would he have reason to think that they took them upon the examination of arguments and appearance of probability. They are resolved to stick to a party, that education or interest has engaged them in; and there, like common soldiers of an army, shew their courage and warmth, as their leaders direct, without ever examining, or so much as knowing the cause they contend for. If a man's life shews that he has no serious regard to religion; for what reason should we think that he beats his head about the opinions of his church, and troubles himself to examine the grounds of this or that doctrine? 'Tis enough for him to obey his leaders, to have his hand and his tongue ready for the support of the common cause, and thereby approve himself to those who can give him credit, preferment, or protection in that society. Thus men become professors of, and combatants for those opinions, they were never convinced of, nor proselytes to; no, nor ever had so much as floating in their heads: And though one cannot say, there are fewer improbable or erroneous opinions in the world than there are; yet this is certain, there are fewer that actually assent to them and mistake them for truths than is imagined.

People align on the basis of interest and what they have been taught, following leaders and seeking approval of others where they see some advantage either in reputation or in protection. We are reminded of Locke's claim that the law of opinion is more powerful than the divine law.

We opened this chapter under the impression that Locke's promotion of toleration indicates a judgment that religion is more deeply rooted in human beings than Hobbes in his more combative stance had supposed. That impression was supported by Locke's suggestion in the *Letter* that the Hobbesian solution, presumably unlike his own, would require unbelief. It was also supported by the fact that Locke, despite also founding his political doctrine on an apolitical state of nature and the desire for preservation, seems to allow for something inherently political in human nature, as he appeals emphatically to liberty and even to a right of revolution, which would have been unthinkable for Hobbes. And as we observed in Hobbes and will observe soon in Tocqueville, there is somehow a link between the political and the religious. Yet so far as the religious is concerned, we are forced to admit at the end of this chapter that Locke's anthropology as he presents it in the *Essay* does not upon examination unambiguously support our initial impression.

Locke's account of what we might call natural religious indifference helps us interpret a passage near the end of the *Letter* where he addresses the concerns, not of those that seek religious establishment for the sake of saving souls, not the "zealots," but those that resist toleration saying that religious "Assemblies and Meetings endanger the Publick Peace, and threaten the Commonwealth" (51). He addresses, in other words, the Hobbesian concern (as well as his own concern at the time he composed the *Two Tracts*). To this Locke replies:

The Magistrate is afraid of other Churches, but not of his own; because he is kind and favourable to the one, but severe and cruel to the other. These he treats like Children, and indulges them even to Wantonness. Those he uses as Slaves; and how blamelessly soever they demean themselves, recompenses them no otherwise than by Gallies, Prisons, Confiscations, and Death. These he cherishes and defends: Those he continually scourges and oppresses. Let him turn the Tables: Or let those Dissenters enjoy but the same Privileges in Civils as his other Subjects, and he will quickly find that these Religious Meetings will no longer be dangerous. For if men enter into Seditious Conspiracies, 'tis not Religion that inspires them to it in their meetings; but their Sufferings and Oppressions that make them willing to ease them. (52)

Hobbes's mistake, Locke might say, is not that he fails to recognize how deeply rooted religion is, how vital a force in the human soul. On the contrary, Hobbes's mistake is to overestimate the inherent power of religion.

Suppose this Business of Religion were let alone, and that there were some other Distinction made between men and men, upon account of the different

Complexions, Shapes, and Features, so that those who have black Hair (for example) or gray Eyes, should not enjoy the same Privileges as other Citizens; that they should not be permitted to buy and sell, or live by their Callings; that Parents should not have the Government and Education of their own Children; that all should either be excluded from the Benefit of the Laws, or meet with partial Judges; can it be doubted but these Persons, thus distinguished from others by the Colour of their Hair and Eyes, and united together by one common Persecution, would be as dangerous to the Magistrate, as any other that had associated themselves merely upon the account of Religion? Some enter into Company for Trade and Profit: Others, for want of Business, have their Clubs for Clarret. Neighborhoods joyns some, and Religion others. But there is one only thing which gathers People into Seditious Commotions, and that is Oppression. (52)

Because he sees religious belief as smoldering embers that are ever ready to burst into flame, Hobbes supposes that the sovereign must be, at least, more diligent and if necessary assertive and restrictive. Locke's response is that such assertiveness, not nature, produces the heat in the first place.

4

Tocqueville on the democratization of American religion

> The philosophers of the eighteenth century explained the gradual
> weakening of beliefs in an altogether simple fashion. Religious zeal, they
> said, will be extinguished as freedom and enlightenment increase. It is
> unfortunate that the facts do not accord with this theory ... in America one
> sees one of the freest and most enlightened peoples in the world fulfill all the
> external duties of religion.
>
> *Democracy in America*, p. 282.

> Their passions, needs, education, circumstances – all in fact seem to
> cooperate in making the inhabitant of the United States incline toward the
> earth. Religion alone, from time to time, makes him raise passing, distracted
> glances toward Heaven.
>
> *Democracy in America*, p. 430.

A student of John Locke who turned to Tocqueville's *Democracy in
America* could be excused the temptation to view the people described in
its pages as a Lockean model. Tocqueville's Americans are practical and
innovative. They devote their energies to concrete goods, above all to
commerce and the production of wealth. They are, to use Locke's phrase,
industrious and rational. They are restless, being continually spurred to
new endeavors in the hope of acquiring wealth more quickly. In the terms
of Locke's *Essay*, they are driven by perpetual unease, yet engaged in
pursuit of ephemeral material delights that are never fully enjoyed
or capable of truly satisfying them: theirs is an endless "pursuit of
happiness" (in Locke's phrase) or material well-being (in Tocqueville's).
Tocqueville's Americans, moreover, adhere to a "philosophic method"
that bears more than a passing resemblance to the approach of Locke's

Essay, in that they turn "toward their own reason as the most visible and closest source of truth" and take "current facts only as a useful study for doing otherwise and better." They "seek the reason for things by themselves and in themselves alone" and "strive for a result without letting themselves be chained to the means." They do not take their bearings by tradition. They "see through the form to the foundation" (403–04).

Moreover, Tocqueville's Americans are morally decent, and in certain respects even morally strict. But theirs is not a morality of grand virtue and sacrifice, but rather, as they themselves freely acknowledge, of a more humble standard that is supportive of their material interests. Their "interest well understood" resembles the new Lockean morality discussed in the previous chapter. Tocqueville's Americans are deeply democratic and conceive "a lofty idea of political rights," though their "idea of rights is bound to the personal interest" (228).

Despite their preoccupation with material well-being, Tocqueville's Americans are religious, predominantly Protestant Christian, and their religion too seems somehow anticipated by Locke. The religion of the Americans professes belief in, but is not preoccupied with, the next life. It does not condemn, but instead supports their commercial passions. It is a practical religion that turns its attention "constantly ... back to the earth." American preachers, "to touch their listeners better, ... make them see daily how religious beliefs favor freedom and public order" (505–06). Accordingly, American religion is tolerant and private. There is a variety of sects, but the differences among them are not profound, or at least Americans are ever ready to turn away from doctrinal differences and emphasize instead a common socially useful morality. The sects unanimously support the separation of church and state, to which they attribute their peaceful coexistence.

None of this is say, however, that Tocqueville attributes these Lockean features to the influence of Locke or the Enlightenment more generally. Tocqueville suspects that "there is no country in the civilized world where they are less occupied with philosophy than the United States. The Americans have no philosophic school of their own, and they worry very little about all those that divide Europe; they hardly know their names" (403). Americans, nevertheless, according to Tocqueville, share the "philosophic method" mentioned previously with the Enlightenment. This shared method is practical and worldly and submits beliefs to be judged by each individual's reason. As we note similarities to Locke, the Frenchman Tocqueville notes the similarities to Descartes. Taking Descartes as the philosopher whose method exemplifies the one that has come to predominate in democracies, Tocqueville says that "America is ... the one country in the world where the precepts of Descartes are least studied and best followed." But "Americans do not read Descartes's works because their social state turns them away from speculative studies, and they follow his maxims because this same social state naturally disposes their minds to adopt them" (403). The Enlightenment approach is essentially democratic, and Tocqueville provides a careful account of how the features that we have described as Lockean arise "naturally" through the influence of democratic society.

Here we glimpse the puzzle of American religion in Tocqueville's analysis. Religion is a vital force in America. It was America's religious aspect that first struck Tocqueville's eye (282). It is not clear, however, that Tocqueville sees this so-called philosophic method that is common to American democracy and the Enlightenment as conducive to religion. For it not only erodes respect for tradition and forms, it also fosters "an almost invincible distaste for the supernatural" (404). This method, which places the seat of judging beliefs in the individual, has not always been and need not be applied to every belief. Tocqueville attributes the same method, applied ever more thoroughly, to Luther in the sixteenth century, to Descartes and Bacon in the seventeenth, and at last in the eighteenth century and in its most thorough application to Voltaire.[1] The question thus arises as to the compatibility of the approach to belief naturally fostered in democracies and religious belief in particular. This method "is followed more rigorously and applied more often by the French than by the Americans"; and it accordingly appears that America is the place in the world where Descartes's method is "*best* followed," precisely because it is not the country in the world where it is followed *most thoroughly*: "Christianity has preserved a great empire over the American mind, and . . . it reigns not only as a philosophy that is adopted after examination, but as a religion that is believed without discussion" (406). Indeed, the strong hold religion maintained in America served, for Tocqueville, to refute the expectation of the "philosophers of the eighteenth century," who

explained the gradual weakening of belief in an altogether simple fashion. Religious zeal, they said, will be extinguished as freedom and enlightenment increase. It is unfortunate that the facts do not accord with their theory. There is a certain population in Europe whose disbelief is equaled only by their brutishness and ignorance, whereas in America one sees one of the freest and most enlightened peoples in the world eagerly fulfill all the external duties of religion. (282)

---

[1] Tocqueville says that Descartes himself wanted "to make use of his method only in certain matters even though he had put it in such a way that it applied to all" (405).

Yet, as we shall see, the way in which American religion confounds the hopes of the philosophers of the eighteenth century proves to be ambiguous.

To say that Americans exempt religion from the application of the democratic philosophic method is not to say that American religion has been unaffected by democracy. On the contrary, Tocqueville shows American religion to have been profoundly *transformed* by democracy, and transformed in a direction of which Locke would approve. Tocqueville, too, of course, approves of American religion, but certain aspects of precisely the transformation that Locke would applaud cause Tocqueville concern, as we will consider more fully later. Tocqueville's account of American religion is thus paradoxical. Tocqueville holds up American religion as a vivid example that confounds the hopes of Enlightenment thinkers – "the philosophers of eighteenth century," at least, if not the philosophers of the seventeenth century. Religion retains a strong influence among Americans, despite their being among the most democratic and enlightened in the world. And yet American religion reveals itself as profoundly transformed and by the same force, democracy, that finds itself pitted against religion in Europe. At one moment Americans are described by Tocqueville as highly religious; the next moment they are said to concentrate their minds "in a singular manner on caring purely for material things" (430), driven especially by the "mother-passion" for wealth that religion dare not oppose (422).

Precisely in this paradoxical account, Tocqueville provides a frame for understanding what appears to be religion's stronghold within an enlightened democratic society that is fundamentally different from the Enlightenment view in either its radical or its moderate forms. Tocqueville has grave doubts that the way of life deemed most natural by both Hobbes and Locke, and pursued without parallel by Americans – the individual pursuit of comfortable preservation – is truly capable of satisfying the deepest needs of human nature. The clearest sign of the difference is that Tocqueville approaches otherworldly religion – as opposed to an enlightened, natural religion – as a vital good both for society and for the citizen as a human being, rather than as a political problem to be solved or contained. Religion is vital for every political society, but particularly for democratic society. Tocqueville thus presents us with an alternative strand of liberal thought, one that poses a profound challenge to the Enlightenment, even while befriending modern democracy.

The Puritan point of departure

The central importance of religion to Tocqueville's analysis of American democracy is evident from the central role of the Puritans at the start of *Democracy in America*. After a brief consideration of the "external configuration" of America, that is, its geography, he immediately turns to the "point of departure" of the society of "the Anglo-Americans." Just as the prejudices, habits, and passions of the adult are evident in the child, so too the fundamental character of a society is evident in its infancy. Moreover, "America is the only country where one has been able to witness the natural and tranquil developments of a society, and where it is possible to specify the influence exerted by the point of departure on the future of states" (28). Accordingly, Tocqueville claims that his chapter on American society's point of departure contains "the seed of what is to follow and the key to almost the whole work" (29).

American society, in fact, was never wholly new. The immigrants who founded American society were "all children of one and the same people," a very old people, the English.

Born of a country that the struggle of parties had agitated for centuries, and where factions had been obliged in their turn to place themselves under the protection of the laws, their political education had taken place in that rough school, and one saw more notion of rights, more principles of true freedom spread among them than in most of the peoples of Europe. In the period of the first emigrations, township government, that fertile seed of free institutions, had already entered profoundly into English habits, and with it the dogma of the sovereignty of the people was introduced in the very heart of Tudor society. (29)

The English, moreover, like the rest of the Christian world, had been caught up in religious quarrels, and the deeply Protestant Puritans had suffered persecution at the hands of a king who claimed spiritual powers akin to those claimed by the pope. These theologico-political struggles not only contributed a certain intellectual ingredient to the education of the Puritans, but also intensified religious passions and purified mores. Mores (*moeurs*) are of paramount importance for Tocqueville's political science: "The importance of mores is a common truth to which study and experience constantly lead back. It seems I have placed it in my mind as a central point; I perceive it at the end of all my ideas" (295). Tocqueville argues that mores are the principal cause of the maintenance of a democratic republic in America. So the mores that American society inherited from the English – those of the early *Anglo-Americans*, as Tocqueville repeatedly refers to them in this section – are the most important element of the point of departure.

The New England Puritans, for whom mores cannot be separated from religion, stand out as the most important of the English immigrants. For it was the principles of the settlers of New England that spread to penetrate "the entire confederation" and "exert their influence ... over the whole American world" (32). The first English settlers came to Virginia, and they came chiefly in pursuit of opportunities for wealth not available in the Old World: "No noble thought, no immaterial scheme presided at the foundation of the new settlements" of Virginia (31). The Puritans of New England, on the other hand, "belonged to the well-to-do classes of the mother country" (32). They did not immigrate to America "to improve their situation or to increase their wealth; they tore themselves away from the sweetness of their native country to obey a purely intellectual need; in exposing themselves to the inevitable miseries of exile, they wanted to make *an idea* triumph" (32, Tocqueville's emphasis).

What was this idea? Puritanism was in the first place a *religious* doctrine, characterized by principles so austere as to lead others to call "Puritans" those who called themselves "pilgrims." They were pilgrims not because they had left their homeland but rather, as Tocqueville quotes the Puritan historian Nathaniel Morton, because "they knew that they were pilgrims and strangers here below, and looked not much upon these things, but lifted up their eyes to heaven, their dearest country, where God hath prepared for them a city" (33–34). They were pilgrims owing to a radically *otherworldly* orientation.

But Puritanism "was *almost as much* a political theory as a religious doctrine" and "blended at several points with the most absolute and democratic and republican theories" (35, 32, emphasis added). This political theory contributed at least as much as the austerity of their religious doctrine to their being "persecuted by the government of their mother country" (32). Fleeing this persecution, they "sought a land so barbarous and so abandoned by the world that they might yet be permitted to live there in their manner and pray to God in freedom." They were uniformly middle class, exhibiting "an almost perfect equality in fortunes and still more in intelligence" (40). They governed themselves, moreover, in a decentralized manner that Tocqueville greatly admires – in independent townships, each naming its own magistrates, taxing itself, and treating "affairs that touch the interest of all ... in the public square and within the general assembly of citizens, as in Athens."

The Puritans thus bequeathed to Anglo-American civilization the ability to combine "two perfectly distinct elements that elsewhere have often made war with one another, but which, in America, they have succeeded in incorporating somehow into one another and combining marvelously. I mean to speak of the *spirit of religion* and the *spirit of freedom*" (43, Tocqueville's emphasis). By freedom here Tocqueville means not only the independence of republican townships, but freedom from "all political prejudices." The Puritans were "at once ardent sectarians and exalted innovators" in politics.

We will consider in a moment why Tocqueville was so impressed by the American capacity to combine religion with democratic and republican institutions, but we must first highlight what the later American combination that he admires did *not* inherit from the Puritans. For, although he clearly wishes to cast the connection to the Puritans in the best possible light, he is nevertheless sharply critical of Puritan laws and mores. He surveys the penal laws of Puritan Connecticut and finds them "bizarre and tyrannical" (39). "The legislators of Connecticut ... conceived the strange idea of drawing from sacred texts ... from the texts of Deuteronomy, Exodus, and Leviticus... They carried the legislation of a rude and half-civilized people into the heart of a society whose spirit was enlightened and mores mild" (38). The mildness of their mores meant that the death penalty was applied to few of the guilty, though "one never saw it laid down more profusely in the laws." The aim of such extreme laws was to maintain moral order and good mores, and thus the legislators sought to penetrate into the conscience by leaving almost no sin beyond the reach of the magistrate (38). Drunkenness and laziness were severely punishable. An indiscreet word and kiss were subject to a fine and reprimand. And "the mores were still more austere and puritanical than the laws. At the date of 1649," Tocqueville reports, "one sees a solemn association being formed in Boston having for its purpose to prevent the worldly luxury of long hair" (39). The Puritan, moreover, forgot "completely the great principles of religious liberty he himself demanded in Europe" by forcing "attendance at divine service by fear of fines" and by going "as far as to strike with severe penalties and often death, Christians who wish to worship God according to a form other than his" (39). The laws of Massachusetts, for example, not only would expel Catholic priests, but would punish by death those who returned after expulsion.

By the 1830s, America had long ceased to be Puritan. Tocqueville will still comment on "the great severity of mores" in the United States, mores that remain directed by religion (278). But he admires American mores of the 1830s, never hinting that they are "lapses" that "bring shame to the human mind" in their excess, as he says of Puritan mores (39). Gone were the "bizarre and tyrannical laws" drawn from the Pentateuch. Gone were the compelled worship and expulsion, let alone execution, of adherents to other sects. The citizens of the United States that Tocqueville met were no longer "ardent sectarians," having instead become religiously tolerant. Tocqueville found "an innumerable multitude of sects in the United States" (278) living peacefully side by side.

Tocqueville never comments directly on how much American religion had changed by the 1830s, but he does make it plain to see. More precisely, he makes it plain to see that Americans themselves had changed in their priorities and passions. As we noted earlier, the Puritans, according to Tocqueville, did not sail to America to improve their social situation or to acquire wealth, but rather to make an idea triumph – an essentially religious idea that oriented these pilgrims and strangers here below by the heavenly city of God. The Americans Tocqueville met, however, were moved most deeply by "commercial passions" (273). Or, as he puts it in volume 2, the "mother passion" of the Americans is love of material well-being, so powerful that "a religion that undertook to destroy [it] would in the end be destroyed by it" (422).

The question of the essential relation between democracy and religion

Tocqueville's goal in examining American democracy in such detail was to understand democracy as such, in the belief that it was sweeping the globe and would require unbiased guidance. He viewed the United States as more thoroughly democratic than any other country on earth, but this does not mean that America was an exhibit of democracy as such. As with every nation, some features of America are peculiar to it, and it is the task of the social scientist to sort the particular from the general. Accordingly, Tocqueville spends considerable effort distinguishing what is characteristic of America in particular – beginning with its "accidental or providential" features – from what is characteristic of democracy as such.

Tocqueville claims that while all societies benefit from religion, democracy stands especially in need of it. Yet this claim faced an obvious difficulty in the case of post-Revolutionary France. Among his countrymen and in Europe generally, religion had come to be intimately entwined with the old regime. The forces of democracy, which by definition opposed the old regime, thus found themselves in opposition to religion. There was indeed an antireligious spirit that permeated the French

Revolution, emanating from the radical Enlightenment.[2] But believers found themselves enemies of democracy, regardless of any political attachment to the old regime, and therefore on the losing side of a social struggle whose outcome is so inevitable that it could be called providential. This pervasive animosity between religion and democracy, Tocqueville argues, is the result of an accidental cause peculiar to Europe, namely, the intimate union between religion and the old regime. The power of religion in America, in the most democratic nation on earth, proves not only that religion and democracy are not necessarily opposed, but also how religion can positively benefit democracy.

And yet, as we have seen, America has its own accidental causes that help to sustain democracy, including the foundational role of a peculiar and persecuted Christian sect. We can, then, no more assume that the American situation reveals the essential relation between democracy and religion to be harmonious or mutually supportive than we can assume from the European situation that it is antagonistic. Tocqueville's teaching on the essential relation between democracy and religion is far from straightforward, and two apparently conflicting accounts can be gleaned from *Democracy in America*. We will take up each account in turn.

Democracy as a secularizing force

Despite an initial impression to the contrary, if one considers what Tocqueville says repeatedly throughout *Democracy in America* about the types of people that democracy tends to produce – their mental habits and preoccupations – a powerful case can be made that there is a fundamental tension, if not an opposition, between democracy and religion. Democracy is described as what today would be called a secularizing force, not only for political society, but above all for individuals, who become increasingly preoccupied with material goods, calculation of self-interest (understood in terms of material goods), and the here and now, as the proper transcendent objects of religion increasingly recede from human consciousness. Democracy, according to Tocqueville, draws people to a mentality that appears thoroughly worldly. Americans are far from immune to this influence. In his chapter on the "philosophic method of the Americans," Tocqueville describes a way of thinking that hardly seems drawn to religion:

As they see that they manage to resolve unaided all the little difficulties that practical life presents, they easily conclude that everything in the world is

[2] See chapter 2 of Tocqueville's *The Old Regime and the French Revolution* (1955).

explicable and that nothing exceeds the bounds of intelligence. Thus they willingly deny what they cannot comprehend: that gives them little faith in the extraordinary and an almost invincible distaste for the supernatural. (404)

This philosophic method seems to be not only thoroughly secular, but secularizing.

Now, these habits of thought are called "philosophic" despite the fact that Tocqueville attributes them wholly to the democratic social state and not to any American exposure to philosophy. This is democratic, not truly philosophic, thinking. Yet as we saw previously, the "method" fostered by democracy in America is essentially the same as that of the notoriously antireligious Voltaire: "Who does not see that Luther, Descartes, and Voltaire made use of the same method, and that they differ only in the greater or lesser use they claimed that one might make of it?" (405) Voltaire, then, and "the philosophers of the eighteenth century, finally generalizing the same principle, undertake to submit the objects of *all beliefs* to the individual examination of each man" (403–04, my emphasis). If Americans, like Luther, do not apply the method to all beliefs, this does not alter the fact that the thorough application of the method leads to Voltaire. The method of the philosophers of the eighteenth century is, then, not only essentially democratic, but the most thorough realization of an essentially democratic method. And Tocqueville associates the philosophy of the eighteenth century with a thoroughgoing secularism, and even a hostility to religion. "It is undeniable," Tocqueville would later write, "that our eighteenth century philosophers were fundamentally anti-religious" (1955, 6). We arrive at the notion that a thoroughgoing democracy would be somehow corrosive of religion and thoroughly secular.

We see further pointers in the same direction in Tocqueville's characterization of "our day" and "our century," phrases Tocqueville uses several times and that seem to indicate the dawning democratic age as a whole. In speaking of "our century" and "our day," the situation of religion is central for Tocqueville, and the trend is unmistakable. For Tocqueville suggests that we have left "centuries of religious fervor" behind and have passed into a "century of doubt" (180, 286). What is characteristic of our day is the weakening of "profound convictions" (234) and of "religions" generally (228), as well as the disappearance of "divine notions of right" (228). The democratic age is permeated by a spirit of doubt, which in Europe threatens religion, while in America the spirit of doubt extends to political theories and authorities but draws short of religion. Viewed in this light, American religion runs counter to the broader social and intellectual trends of democratic times. American religion serves as an example *precisely because* of the conditions that prevail "in our day."

The notion that democracy and religion lie somehow in essential tension with one another is further supported by Tocqueville's argument for why religion, necessary for any society, is of the greatest value to democratic society: "The greatest advantage of religions is to inspire *wholly contrary instincts*" to those democracy inspires (419, my emphasis). For "equality, which introduces great goods into the world, suggests to men very dangerous instincts . . .; it tends to isolate them from one another and to bring each of them to be occupied with himself alone. Democratic instincts, if left unchecked, lead to a demeaning materialism and spiritually unsatisfying pursuit of ephemeral goods; to a radical individual isolation from society and unawareness of society's needs; and to a destructive domination of individual interests. It is precisely because of Tocqueville's concerns about the deleterious effects of democracy that he hopes to see those effects opposed by the wholly contrary instincts of religion, which ought to draw the mind away from the tangible to the intangible, from the ephemeral to the eternal, from oneself as individually sufficient to one's radical incompleteness and dependence on what is higher than oneself. Tocqueville goes so far as to say that "religious peoples are . . . naturally strong in precisely the spot where democratic peoples are weak." Can then a people be simultaneously democratic and religious?

The account of the "secularizing" force of democracy pervades *Democracy in America* from start to finish. But, as we have also seen, Tocqueville uses the example of American religiosity to refute the "altogether simply way" that the philosophers of the eighteenth century expected religious zeal to fade away. We are led to conclude that while America is the most democratic nation on earth, it is not thoroughly democratic, *as precisely its religiosity demonstrates*. Religion, as Tocqueville will later describe it, is "the most precious inheritance from aristocratic centuries" (519), and he aims to "*preserve* [religion's] empire in the democratic centuries that we are entering" (419, my emphasis). We might, then, view democracy as a force that by its nature is not conducive to religion, but that is not *necessarily* destructive of it in the right circumstances.

What ought to be religion's natural state in our day
The evidence in support of the preceding interpretation is too powerful to be ignored, but it is in obvious tension with Tocqueville's suggestion that the separation of religion from politics in America allows for religion's

natural power to grow and that crucial aspects of American religion resemble what he describes as the "natural state of men with respect to religion in our day." Setting aside the puzzles of his speaking of what "ought to be" natural, and natural "in our day," Tocqueville seems to indicate that while the relation between democracy and religion in America may be exceptional, it is *not* accidental but revealing of their natural or essential relation, a relation that is not only harmonious but mutually supportive.

Tocqueville can claim that separating religion from politics is more natural because it removes the artificial support and potentially distorting influence of the state over religion. This change means an evident weakening of religion in some respects, indeed in the most obvious and visible respects, when compared to the old regime. But the removal of these artificial supports leads to an uncluttering that allows religion's natural power over the human soul to be strengthened. For the permanent and essential power of religion lies in the natural human dissatisfaction with the finitude of this mortal life.

The short space of sixty years will never confine the whole imagination of man; the incomplete joys of this world will never suffice for his heart. Alone among all the beings, man shows a natural disgust for existence and an immense desire to exist; he scorns life and fears nothingness. These different instincts constantly drive his soul toward contemplation of another world, and it is religion that guides it there. Religion is therefore only a particular form of hope, and it is as natural to the human heart as hope itself. Only by a kind of aberration of the intellect and with the aid of a sort of moral violence exercised on their own nature do men stray from religious beliefs; an invincible inclination leads them back to them. Disbelief is an accident; faith alone is the permanent state of humanity. (283–84)

We see clearly here that, for Tocqueville, religion is most essentially oriented to "another world" owing to a permanent human longing to transcend death.

Now, it cannot simply be the case that this natural power of religion is strengthened in democratic times, even setting aside the accidental opposition between democracy and religion in Europe. For, in framing his account of what ought to be the natural state of men with respect to religion in our day, Tocqueville reiterates the distinction between centuries of religious fervor and centuries of doubt, making plain that "our day" is one of doubt. But how can this be? How can the "real power" of religion be permanent, let alone strengthened, in a century of doubt? We must look more carefully at this "natural state" in "our day."

In framing his account of this natural state, Tocqueville identifies the two great threats to religion – schism and indifference – each characteristic of a different age. In centuries of fervor, religion is threatened by schism, as one religion or sect is threatened by another: "Faith changes its object, it does not die"; and although "beliefs differ, irreligion is unknown" (286). Our day belongs to a century of doubt, and in our day, religion is threatened not by schism but by indifference. Previously, we spoke of "indifference" as a state that is compatible with belief. For Tocqueville the word refers to a condition "when a religious belief is silently undermined by doctrines that I shall call negative, since in affirming the falseness of one religion they do not establish the truth of any other."

> Then prodigious revolutions are worked in the human mind without the apparent aid of man's passions and so to speak without his suspecting them. One sees men who let the object of their dearest hopes escape almost by forgetting. Carried along by an insensible current against which they do not have the courage to struggle and to which they nonetheless yield with regret, they abandon the faith they love to follow the doubt that leads them to despair. In the centuries we have just described, beliefs are abandoned in coldness rather than hate; they are not rejected, they leave you.

It is this coldness and quasi-forgetting that warrant the name "indifference."

Tocqueville takes for granted the indifferent doubter as a phenomenon of our day. As a doubter, he is an aberration or accident when considered in light of man's permanent nature (284), but part of what makes his case relatively healthy is the fact that he feels no animosity to faith. On the contrary, he regrets the loss because, "considering religious beliefs under a human aspect, he recognizes their empire over mores, their influence on laws. He understands how they can make men live in peace and prepare them gently for death" (286). Regretting the loss of faith in himself, he has no wish to see the faith of others undermined. He hides his unbelief while supporting belief. Unlike in Europe, where unbelief has become widespread and many "who still believe do not dare to say it" (287), in this natural state public opinion remains supportive of religion.

> With those who do not believe hiding their disbelief and those who believe showing their faith, a public opinion in favor of religion is produced; people love it, sustain it, and honor it, and one must penetrate to the bottom of their souls to discover the wounds that it has received. The mass of men, whom religious sentiments never abandons, see nothing, then, that turns them aside from established beliefs. The instinct for another life leads them without difficulty to the foot of altars and delivers their hearts to the precepts and consolation of faith. (287)

In what ought to be the natural state of men in the matter of religion in our day, religion continues to exercise its natural power over the majority and even over the minority of unbelievers insofar as they regret their loss of faith.[3]

Tocqueville's account of this "natural state" is clearly central to his teaching on democracy and religion, but it is also deeply puzzling for several reasons. To begin, we note that Tocqueville does not attribute the doubting indifference he describes to the worldly preoccupations fostered by life in democratic society, as we might expect, but instead to unspecified doctrines that undermine all religious belief – presumably, the irreligious doctrines of the philosophers of the eighteenth century (or their English predecessors [1955, 153; cf. XV, p. 696]). This does help to explain how this sort of doubt could be limited through concealment, since if it were the product of the general influence of democratic society, we would expect it to spread despite concealment. On the other hand, if doubt is not widespread, why would "our day," the time in which the state described would be "natural," deserve to be called a century of doubt? Even if religion had withdrawn from politics, would not the state he describes appear from the outside as universally religious, just as centuries of religious fervor appear to have been? Were there no hidden doubters in centuries of fervor?

We are further puzzled as to why Tocqueville does not explicitly identify this natural state with America. He contrasts this state explicitly with Europe, and to be sure its features closely resemble those he has

---

[3] Pierre Manent interprets Tocqueville as implying that religious doubt had become characteristic of the majority in America: "The religious situation in American democracy is thus ambiguous. It is universally professed; its precepts are even more observed there than elsewhere. But Americans profess it and accept it less by conviction and love of its truth than by conviction in its utility ... In the United States, the great mass of men hardly believe, but judge themselves obligated, like the patricians of yore, to save appearances. Each American citizen simultaneously assumes the role of patrician hypocrite and sincere plebeian ... American democracy has democratized the point of view of the Romans in matters of religion. That is why the weakening of religious faith does not issue into anarchy" (90, 92). Manent's reading is made more plausible by Tocqueville's letters to Louis Kergorlay, discussed later. Cf. Tocqueville 2000, 616 and Kessler 1994, 149.

   Achille Murat, a French contemporary of Tocqueville's who lived in America for many years, concluded in 1832 that religious skeptics were in the majority, a fact obscured by the prevalence of hypocrisy: "Everybody knows very well the degree of sincerity there is in the religion of his neighbor, but nobody likes to be the first to take off the mask ... The notion generally entertained of the strength of religious prejudices is much exaggerated ... The skeptical party has only to know its strength, to shake off entirely the yoke of superstition, and for some time it has been making immense progress toward that object" (Powell 1967, 55–56).

attributed to the United States. Are there features of this natural state that Tocqueville did not find in America? Or is something else found in America or Americans that moves outside what "ought to be" the natural state in our day? We will be in a better position to answer these questions after we have examined more closely Tocqueville's account of the power of religion in America.

The power of religion in America

As we have seen, Tocqueville suggests in volume 1 of *Democracy in America* that by separating religion from politics, the real power of religion – the power over the individual soul, rooted in the deep and permanent dissatisfaction with mortality – grows. Does the rest of the book bear out this claim?

In approaching this question, we begin by noting that Tocqueville's statement that the Americans, unlike the Europeans, separate religion and politics is subject to misunderstanding. For he examines at length the ways in which religion influences politics in America. So great is that influence that religion "should ... be considered as the first of their political institutions" (280). By the separation of religion and politics, he means that religion "never mixes directly in the government of society," in the ever-changing partisanship and policy changes. On one level, American politics, like all democratic politics, is characterized by continual change – in law, policy, and political fortunes. On a more fundamental level, however, there are an unaltering unanimity and consistency in American politics. All Americans take for granted democratic republican institutions and especially the sovereignty of the people. America thus does not have, as Europe does, what Tocqueville calls "great parties," which differ precisely on the fundamental questions of government and sovereignty. Or rather, America has only one great party, and it is not clear from Tocqueville's account that Americans separate religion from great party politics less than Europeans, for whom the great partisan struggle is not yet settled.

Tocqueville speaks of two kinds of influence of religion on politics: direct and indirect. The direct influence is linked to a universal tendency of the human mind to harmonize the regulation of religion with the regulation of political society, "to harmonize earth with Heaven" (275). Tocqueville points not only to the Puritan part of American society's origins, but also to the fact that the large majority of Americans have been Protestant. Having rejected the authority of the pope, they "brought to the New World a Christianity that I cannot depict better than to call it democratic and republican: this singularly favors the establishment of a republic and of democracy in affairs." Tocqueville initially speaks of this harmonization as the influence of religion over politics.

The case of American Protestants illustrates what Tocqueville means by religion's direct influence on politics – on the fundamental political questions disputed by great parties. But whereas a *majority* of Americans are Protestant, *all* Americans, Protestants and non-Protestants alike, wholeheartedly support democratic republican institutions. In considering religion's direct influence, Tocqueville spends far more time considering American Catholics, who profoundly disagree with Protestants (who in fact disagree among themselves) over the regulation of religion. If there exist fundamental differences among Americans on the question of regulating religion, why is there unanimity on the question of regulating political society?

Tocqueville answers that even religions that do not have the affinity with democratic and republican institutions that Protestantism generally has nevertheless come, through what he calls "hidden causes," to embrace those institutions. Catholicism's hierarchical ecclesiastical structure would suggest an affinity to aristocracy or kingship. Yet the priesthood is open to all regardless of social class, and "the priest alone is raised above the faithful: everything is equal below him" (276). Thus Catholicism is not as opposed to equality of conditions as it at first appears. Nevertheless, Catholics are not naturally drawn to democracy. The hidden cause of the Catholic embrace of democratic republicanism in the United States lies in their weak social position and small numbers, which cause Catholics "to embrace democratic and republican opinions ... as by a law."

Most Catholics are poor, and they need all citizens to govern in order to come to govern themselves. Catholics are a minority, and they need all rights to be respected to be assured of the free exercise of theirs. These two causes drive them *even without their knowing it* toward political doctrines that they would perhaps adopt with less eagerness if they were wealthy and predominant. (276, emphasis added)

There is, in fact, "an innumerable multitude of sects in the United States. All differ in the worship one must render to the Creator, but all agree on the duties of men toward one another" (278). Though the cause of the attachment to democratic institutions may be hidden, the attachment itself is overt, as Tocqueville demonstrates by quoting at length the prayer of a Polish-American priest (277). Thus, in this tendency to harmonize earth and heaven, it sometimes happens that "heaven" is under the influence of "earth," a fact whose importance becomes increasingly evident in Tocqueville's account of American religion as a whole.

What Tocqueville calls "the indirect action of religion on politics seems to [him] more powerful" than its direct action or influence. Religion influences politics indirectly by guiding mores, the single most important cause for maintaining a democratic republic in the United States. It is in this context that he calls religion the first political institution of the Americans. Religion facilitates the use of freedom by instilling "habits of restraint": "At the same time that the law permits the American people to do everything, religion prevents them from conceiving everything and forbids them to dare everything ... If it does not give them the taste for freedom, it singularly facilitates their use of it" (280). We see here more clearly the importance of the Puritans in Tocqueville's analysis, as it is precisely this restraint amid political freedom that he had emphasized early in the book when discussing what Americans inherited from the Puritans:

Before them fall the barriers that imprisoned society in whose bosom they were born; old opinions that have been directing the world for centuries vanish; an almost boundless course, a field without horizon, are discovered: the human mind rushes toward them; it traverses them in all directions; but, when it arrives at the limits of the political world, it halts; trembling, it leaves off the use of its most formidable faculties; it abjures doubt; it renounces the need to innovate; it even abstains from sweeping away the veil of the sanctuary; it bows with respect before truths that it accepts without discussion. Thus in the moral world, everything is classified, coordinated, foreseen, decided in advance. In the political world, everything is agitated, contested, uncertain; in the one, there is passive though voluntary obedience; in the other, there is independence, contempt for experience, and jealousy of every authority. Far from harming each other, these two tendencies [the spirit of religion and the spirit of freedom], apparently so opposed, advance in accord and seem to lend each other a mutual support. (43)

The Americans themselves see religion – in particular, Christianity – as necessary for the maintenance of their freedom and therefore as first among their political institutions. Tocqueville found that Americans "so completely confuse Christianity and freedom in their minds that it is almost impossible to have them conceive of one without the other" (280–81). Americans would send missionaries into the frontier, not only out of concern that religion might not be lost there, but also for the sake of freedom. Thus "religious zeal constantly warms itself at the hearth of patriotism" (281).

Years later, Tocqueville claimed never to have heard an American fail or even hesitate to affirm this opinion. In his book on the French Revolution, he reports:

I have sometimes asked Americans whom I chanced to meet in their own country or in Europe whether in their opinion religion contributes to the stability of the State and the maintenance of law and order. They always answered, without a moment's hesitation, that a civilized community, especially one that enjoys the benefits of freedom, cannot exist without religion. In fact, an American sees in religion the surest guarantee of the stability of the State and the safety of individuals. This much is evident even to those least versed in political science. (1955, 153)

So salient was the belief in the political necessity of religion that Tocqueville found it to be more universal among Americans than religious belief itself: "I do not know if all Americans have faith – for who can read the bottom of hearts? – but I am sure that they believe it necessary to the maintenance of republican institutions. This opinion does not belong only to one class of citizens or to one party, but to the entire nation; one finds it in all ranks" (280). Some Americans, Tocqueville supposed, adhere to religion more out of habit than conviction, and he suspected that religious hypocrisy was common (278). Nevertheless, the majority are religious – indeed, it is precisely for this reason that Tocqueville suspects hypocrisy among some – and America is "still the place in the world where the Christian religion has most preserved genuine power over souls."

Tocqueville agrees with Americans that religion is necessary for the maintenance of republican institutions, but their views differ in a crucial respect. Tocqueville and the Americans both prize religion as a support for the mores, or moral restraints, that help them not abuse the freedom of their political institutions. But whereas Tocqueville in large part is troubled by the preoccupation with material well-being fostered by democracy and hopes that religion will redirect and elevate the mind, the American prizes the stability produced by regular mores precisely with a view to material well-being and the accumulation of wealth:

The passions that agitate the Americans most profoundly are commercial passions and not political passions, or rather, they carry the habits of trade into politics. They love order, without which affairs cannot prosper, and they particularly prize regular mores, on which good houses [of business] are founded... One must go to America to understand what power material well-being exerts on political actions and even on opinions themselves, which ought to be subject only to reason. (273)

This truth, Tocqueville says, is most evident among emigrants from Europe, and he makes the connection between the power of material well-being and religious opinion in particular by telling the story of a French expatriate he encountered in a remote part of Pennsylvania. The Frenchman had fled France on account of his political views, having been "a great leveler and an ardent demagogue," as Tocqueville knew by reputation. The refugee had in America become a wealthy planter, and Tocqueville was surprised to hear him "discuss the right of property as an economist, I was almost going to say a property owner."

He spoke of the necessity of hierarchy that fortune establishes among men, of obedience to established law, of the influence of good mores in republics, and of the assistance that religious ideas lend to order and freedom: he even came, as if inadvertently, to cite the authority of Jesus Christ in support of one of his political opinions. (273)

Unlike the pilgrims who started with a religious idea, one that is bound secondarily to republicanism in politics, and one that is moreover oriented to another world and extraordinarily austere with respect to material well-being, the Americans Tocqueville met were moved most powerfully by the desire for material well-being. It was this desire, and the associated "passions that agitate the Americans most profoundly" (273), that led them to prize order, which led them to prize good mores, which led them to prize religion.

What we see unfolding through Tocqueville's account of the power of American religion is the transformation of religion at the hands of democracy, and hence the correction of an impression the reader might have received, to the effect that when religion is separated from politics in democratic society, and hence freed from the artificial distortions of religion imposed in the old regime, it becomes purer and its natural power stronger. Tocqueville had informed us on the first page that democracy "modifies everything it does not produce" (3), and his consistent teaching is that human beings are profoundly shaped by the social and political state, be it democratic or aristocratic.

The implications of this teaching for religion emerge most clearly early in volume 2 in a chapter entitled "How, in the United States, Religion Knows How to Make Use of Democratic Instincts." The meaning of the title is not at first clear, since the largest portion of the chapter is on the concessions religion must make to, or the ways in which it must be transformed by, democratic instincts if it is to survive. Considering his comments in volume 1 on the universal inclination to harmonize religion and political society, it is no surprise that this transformative influence is not unique to democracy:

> Men who are alike and equal readily conceive the notion of a single God imposing the same rules on each of them and granting them future happiness at the same price. The idea of the unity of the human race constantly leads them back to the idea of the unity of the Creator, whereas on the contrary, men very separate from one another and very unalike willingly come to make as many divinities as there are peoples, castes, classes and families, and to trace a thousand particular paths for going to Heaven. One cannot deny that Christianity itself has in some fashion come under the influence exerted over religious beliefs by the social and political state. (420)

Accordingly, Christianity, which was born amid the uniformity of the Roman Empire, adapted to the fragmentation that followed the empire: "Unable to divide the Divinity, [men] at least multiplied its agents beyond measure; the homage due to angels and saints became an almost idolatrous worship for most Christians, and one could fear a moment when the Christian religion would regress to the religions it had defeated" (421).

So, too, in democratic times, Christianity must adapt to the prevailing social and political state. Religion must, for example, minimize "forms" – ritual, ceremony, external practices, symbols. For democratic human beings, "symbols appear ... to be puerile artifices that are used to veil or adorn for their eyes truths it would be more natural to show to them altogether naked and in broad daylight; the sight of ceremonies leaves them cold, and they are naturally brought to attach only a secondary importance to the details of worship" (421). The same can be said of tradition, which Tocqueville had told us is taken "only as information," not as prescription. Above all religion must not oppose the love of material well-being, which "forms the salient and indelible feature of democratic ages" (422). This is a passion religion is incapable of overcoming: "One may believe that a religion that undertook to destroy this mother passion would in the end be destroyed by it." Instead religion should aim to "purify, regulate, and restrain" this "mother passion."

How, then, does this chapter follow its title's question of religion's making use of democratic instincts? Just as Tocqueville saw that in the fragmentation of medieval Europe, Christianity managed not to "lose sight of the principal ideas it had brought to light" (421), so he looks to religion's maintaining its core transcendent or otherworldly orientation without altogether opposing the unopposable desire for material well-being. He points to the example of American Catholic priests, who not only have conformed to democratic tastes in other respects, but also allow for "the goods of this world as important though secondary objects":

> If they do not associate with industry, they are at least interested in its progress and applaud it, and while constantly showing to the faithful the other world as the great object of their hopes and fears, they do not forbid them from honestly searching for well-being in this one. Far from bringing out how these two things are divided and contrary, they rather apply themselves to finding the spot at which they touch and are bound together. (423)

By showing how their otherworldly hopes, concern for which democracy of itself does not foster, can support those worldly hopes that democracy does foster, religion can make use of democratic instincts to preserve itself in what are potentially inhospitable democratic times.

And yet, as Tocqueville soon makes clear, American clergy have their work cut out for them. For, in addition to their highly democratic social state, "a thousand particular causes, of which I could make only the principal ones known, must have concentrated the American mind in a singular manner on caring for purely material things. Their passions, needs, education, circumstances – all in fact seem to cooperate in making the inhabitants of the United States incline toward the earth. Religion alone, from time to time, makes him raise passing distracted glances toward Heaven" (430).

The problem of individualism

To this point, we have focused on the inordinate love of material well-being as the problem Tocqueville hopes to address with religion. In volume 2, there emerges a related danger that is also inherent to the democratic age: what Tocqueville calls individualism. In the final footnote to *Democracy in America*, he says: "One cannot say in an absolute and general manner whether the great danger of our day is license or tyranny, anarchy or despotism. Both are equally to be feared and can as easily issue from one and the same cause, which is *general apathy*, the fruit of individualism" (704, Tocqueville's emphasis). We today may tend to understand by "individualism" precisely the capacity to withstand the tyranny of the majority. Not so for Tocqueville, who understood by individualism the tendency to fall into a narrow sphere of concern, bounded by one's daily interests and circle of friends and associates. One is attuned only to what and who are immediately before oneself, forgetful of any greater whole of which one is a part, on which one depends, and to which one owes some duty. What lies beyond is not a greater whole, but a mass of individuals living parallel lives of isolation but who collectively impose tastes and opinions more effectively than the greatest despots ever hoped to do. Thus individualism as Tocqueville understands it is fully compatible with a submissive conformity of the mind to the majority, a conformity that is the antithesis of genuine independence of mind. Such conformity is harmful to democracy and democrat, both as a citizen as a human being.

Precisely in its transcendent aspect, religion helps to lift the gaze above the immediate and ephemeral. It produces a habit of mind that, by considering daily a greater and higher whole, supports civic-mindedness. Even where there is no express link, there is a psychological link between religious duty and civic duty, both of which pull in the opposite direction of democratic individualism. One looks upward and outward, not only horizontally and inward. There is a related link between transcendent religion and the capacity to resist the tyranny of the majority. True independence of mind, and thus human greatness, are fostered by looking above what is merely human. They are fostered by a decidedly hierarchical outlook. This is a hard lesson for democrats who retain a deep admiration or longing for human greatness. Tocqueville, a friend of democracy, agrees with Nietzsche, an enemy of democracy, that democracy is inherently leveling and poor soil for greatness. It is aristocracy with its hierarchical outlook, with its contempt for equality and hence of mass opinion and the merely practical, with its capacity to desire and work toward great long-term ends, that better provides the necessary spiritual equipment for human greatness.

Individualism is a grave danger and a powerful inherent tendency in democratic society, but not an inevitability. Americans, Tocqueville says, "have combated the individualism to which equality gives birth with freedom, and they have defeated it" (486). By "freedom" Tocqueville in this context means political freedom, especially local self-government: "Local freedoms, which make many citizens put a value on the affection of their neighbors and those close to them, therefore constantly bring men closer to one another, despite the instincts that separate them, and force them to aid one another" (487). Americans combat individualism though associations as well. They join together constantly in associations of every sort, large and small, and for purposes broad and narrow, serious and trivial.

Americans also combat individualism through what he calls "the doctrine of interest well understood" (*la doctrine de l'intérêt bien entendu*), and what he describes reminds us of Locke's shift in moral doctrine discussed in the previous chapter. Americans are not moved by virtue or drawn to splendid sacrificial acts, as aristocratic human beings are inclined to be. Instead, democratic human beings make many small sacrifices, which they interpret as not sacrificial at all but instead as the best means of serving their own interest. Morality thus understood is less beautiful, but more accessible to all. It is also more suitable to democratic times, as minds become more exclusively occupied with calculations of self-interest: "No power on earth can prevent the growing equality of conditions from bringing the human spirit toward searching for the useful and from disposing each citizen to shrink within himself. One must therefore expect that individual interest will become more than ever the principal if not the unique motive of men's actions; but it will remain to know how each man will understand his individual interest" (503). Tocqueville thus suggests that individualism *in some form* is indeed inevitable in democratic society, but its worst manifestations can be combated.

But the doctrine of interest well understood is inadequate by itself, as becomes plain in the following chapter, entitled "How the Americans Apply the Doctrine of Self-Interest Well Understood in the Matter of Religion." The bulk of the chapter again is not apparently on the subject announced in its title, but rather on the vital importance of religion if the doctrine of self-interest well understood is to combat individualism effectively.

If the doctrine of self-interest well understood had only this world in view, it would be far from sufficient; for there are a great number of sacrifices that can find their recompense only in the other world; and whatever effort of mind that one makes to prove the utility of virtue, it will always be hard to make a man who does not wish to die live well. It is therefore necessary to know if the doctrine of self-interest well understood can be easily reconciled with religious beliefs. (504)

Tocqueville says that it can be so reconciled, despite the risk of turning religion into a calculation for eternal profit and thereby degrading it. For, even though genuinely religious human beings are not motivated by self-interest alone, nevertheless "interest is the principal means religions themselves make use of to guide men, and I do not doubt that it is only from this side that they take hold of the crowd and become popular" (505).

But in the American case, is that interest located in this world, as religion supports mores for the sake of commerce, or the next, as would be required to supplement the doctrine of interest well understood? Once again, Tocqueville emphasizes the worldliness of American religion: "Not only do Americans follow their religion out of interest, but they often place in this world the interest that one can have in following it." Moreover, whereas he had said that Catholic priests in America try to make use of their parishioners' worldly interests in order to direct them "constantly" to their eternal interests, it is not clear that the same can be said of the clergy of the Protestant majority.

American preachers constantly come back to earth and only with great trouble can they take their eyes off it. To touch their listeners better, they make them see daily how religious beliefs favor freedom and public order, and it is often difficult to know when listening to them if the principal object of religion is to procure eternal felicity in the other world or well-being in this one. (505–06)

Tocqueville never does affirm that American religion fills the gap left by self-interest well understood oriented toward earthly goods. It remains a grave question for him whether American religion on the whole, being predominantly this-worldly in orientation, is capable of doing so.[4]

The next chapter turns immediately to the power that overwhelms American religion's otherworldliness, and once again we return to "the taste for material well-being in America," which forms the general topic of the next few chapters. In these chapters, Tocqueville tells us that among democratic peoples, "the love of [material] well-being shows itself to be a tenacious, exclusive, universal, but contained passion" (508). It is contained because its "objects are small," and yet "the soul clings to them: it considers them every day and from up close; in the end they hide the rest of the world from it, and they sometimes come to place themselves between it and God" (509). This taste, as we have already learned, "is not the enemy of regular mores; for good mores are useful to public tranquility and favor industry." Tocqueville then *almost* repeats what he has said about the connection between religion and mores: "Often, indeed, it comes to be combined with *a sort of religious morality*; one wishes to be the best possible in this world without renouncing one's chances in the other" (emphasis added).

The next chapter is one of the most important in the book for Tocqueville's treatment of religion in America: "Why Certain Americans Display

---

[4] Cf. Manent 1996, 91: "For religion to have proper force, it is necessary for men to be devoted to it for itself and not for its social utility or by love of the political institutions to which it is fused."

Such an Exalted Spiritualism." Here, in the context of an extended discussion of the taste for material well-being, which itself is in the context of the predominant worldliness of American religion, Tocqueville reports:

One finds here and there in the heart of American society souls altogether filled with an exalted and almost fierce spiritualism that one scarcely encounters in Europe. From time to time bizarre sects arise that strive to open extraordinary roads to eternal happiness. Religious follies are very common there. (510)

"This," Tocqueville says, "should not surprise us." It should not surprise us in light of the following two considerations, which Tocqueville had indeed already made sufficiently plain.

The first of these considerations reiterates what he had said in volume 1 regarding the "real power of religion":

Man did not give himself the taste for the infinite and the love of what is immortal. These sublime instincts are not born of a caprice of his will: they have their immovable foundation in his nature; they exist despite his efforts. He can hinder and deform them, but not destroy them. The soul has needs that must be satisfied; and whatever care one takes to distract it from itself, it soon becomes bored, restive, and agitated amid enjoyment of the senses. (510)

The way of life inherent to democracy and pursued in America with only those restraints necessary to facilitate it is not finally a humanly satisfying life. The body has needs, to be sure, and its delights are real delights. But a life devoted exclusively to the needs and delights of the body is not a fully human life. The democratic soul, too, has a deeper need, unalterably rooted in human nature and evident even when considered "from a purely human point of view" (284). That need is somehow for "the infinite," tied to "a love of what is immortal" (510), and rooted, it seems, in the finitude of human life (283–84).[5]

Now, in volume 1, his observation about the natural human longing for the eternal was made with a view to the suggestion, or at least the implication, that this longing was *more powerful* in Americans generally owing to the separation of religion from politics. Here, his observation on the growth of the religious instinct is limited to a few individuals and leads to a very different view of American religiosity more broadly, directing us to the second consideration: "One should therefore not be astonished if, *in the heart of a society that thought only of the earth*, one

---

[5] Cf. Plato's *Symposium*, 204e1–205a8, 206a3–13. Cf. also Hobbes's *Leviathan* XI.1: "The object of man's desire is not to enjoy only once, and for one instant of time, but to assure forever the way of his future desire."

encountered a few individuals who wished to regard only heaven" (510–11, emphasis added). Despite the prevalence of religion (or at least "a sort of religious morality") in America, American society, which is to say the vast majority of the American people, is "uniquely preoccupied" with material goods. Tocqueville thus indicates that American religion in its predominant form – in its profoundly democratized form – fails to speak adequately to the natural human need for the eternal. There exists such a stifling imbalance in favor of material goods, one that American religion does not adequately correct, that from time to time the profound spiritual needs erupt in "a few individuals" in novel and bizarre forms of otherworldly religion. Tocqueville's implicit commentary on the dominant mode of American religion can be seen in his conclusion to the chapter:

If the social state, circumstances, and laws did not restrain the American spirit so closely in the search for well-being, one might believe that when it came to be occupied with immaterial things, it would show more reserve and more experience and would moderate itself without trouble. But it feels itself imprisoned within limits from which it is seemingly not allowed to leave. As soon as it passes these limits, it does not know where to settle, and it often runs without stopping beyond the bounds of common sense. (511)

Tocqueville here goes as far as he ever does in *Democracy in America* in indicating the extent of the concessions religion in America has made to democratic instincts.

One lesson of this chapter is that, contrary to what he had asserted in volume 1, the profound human desire for immortality is not enough to maintain, let alone strengthen, religion in its essentially transcendent orientation. The picture that emerges in volume 2 is more complicated and puzzling. We are faced in particular with a puzzle regarding the effect of the natural human desire for immortality on the majority, in whom it does not erupt in strange and radically otherworldly religions. Few Americans are overtaken by the spiritual need that Tocqueville says they, as human beings, naturally possess. If Tocqueville is correct about this need, how can he explain the life of the majority? Hobbes and Locke might plausibly say that the goods Tocqueville sees pursued by "the freest and most enlightened men placed in the happiest condition that exists in the world" (511) would have a claim to being the true natural goods; the "needs" they forget are evidently false; and the bizarre religious follies are precisely that, and not evidence of a supposedly suppressed human nature. Where does Tocqueville find evidence of this allegedly natural need among that large number who busy themselves so single-mindedly, as he himself observes, with material concerns? How is the natural need of the soul manifest in the *democratic* soul?

With these questions in mind, we turn to the next chapter, where the evidence in question is to be found precisely in the restlessness, the "feverish ardor" (511), with which Americans pursue material goods. Americans have produced the material conditions for happiness, and yet they are not happy. Indeed they are spurred to generate the material abundance that they do precisely because they sense, even if they are not quite aware, that material abundance does not make them happy. But they attribute their lack of satisfaction to having not acquired enough, or not having acquired it as quickly as possible. For Tocqueville, the spiritual poverty of the democratic way of life can be seen in its relation to death, concern for which is the natural root of religion. Americans tend to be oblivious of death, and yet are still somehow spurred constantly by their mortality:

The inhabitant of the United States attaches himself to the goods of this world as if he were assured of not dying, and he rushes so precipitately to grasp those that pass within his reach that one would say he fears at each instant he will cease to live before he has enjoyed them... He who has confined his heart solely to the search for the goods of the world is always in a hurry, for he has only a limited time to find them, take hold of them, and enjoy them. His remembrance of the brevity of life constantly spurs him. In addition to the goods he possesses, at each instant he imagines a thousand others that death will prevent him from enjoying if he does not hasten. This thought fills him with troubles, fears, and regrets, and keeps his soul in a sort of unceasing trepidation that brings him to change his designs and his place at every moment. (512)

Americans, as Tocqueville describes them, are generally unmindful of the prospect of a life after death, yet the agitation surrounding death despite or because of the attempt to turn away from or quiet that agitation through material acquisition suggests that they are not at bottom indifferent to death and thus to the prospect of an afterlife. To repeat from earlier: "The soul has needs that must be satisfied; and whatever care one takes to distract it from itself, it soon becomes bored, restive, and agitated amid enjoyment of the senses" (510). The Tocquevillian seed of religion cannot be completely hidden. Yet the capacity to recognize the root of the agitation, and thus the capacity for self-knowledge, is not something democracy is well suited to cultivate. Tocqueville soon renews his call to preserve religion in democratic times, and it is clearer than it had been before that what is called for is an *act of preservation*: "When any religion whatsoever has cast deep roots within a democracy, guard against shaking it; but rather carefully as the most precious inheritance from aristocratic centuries; do not seek to tear men from their old religious opinions to substitute new ones, for fear that, in the passage from one faith to another, the soul finding itself for a moment empty of belief, the love of material enjoyments will come to spread through it and fill it entirely" (519).

Let us summarize what we have seen so far. Tocqueville argues that religion is vital for any political society, but particularly for democratic society. For democratic society tends to foster certain instincts that become dangerous as they become increasingly exclusive and that religion is uniquely capable of combating. In particular, democracy tends to produce human beings whose concerns center narrowly on themselves, particularly on their own material interests and enjoyments. This is dangerous for society as people lose sight of their dependence on and responsibilities to the greater political and social whole of which they are a part. They may then become willing to abandon those responsibilities along with their freedom to a despotic state, which does not ask, and even prefers, that they contain their concerns to individual material pleasures. Democratic society also produces dangerous instincts with respect to the prospects for human greatness, as tastes, ambitions, and moral sensibilities are coarsened and lowered. Religion functions to combat these tendencies by fostering mores, especially in the form of moral restraints placed on the desire for material well-being. Religion also is capable of refocusing the soul on objects that transcend material well-being, thus serving to elevate and ennoble the soul. These benefits are plain even from a strictly human point of view: almost any religion, even a false one, is preferable to no religion.

Religion plays a prominent role in American life, giving American democracy a tremendous asset that in European democracy is not only weakening, but at risk of disappearing owing in part to an accidental and misguided animosity to religion on the part of its principal advocates, but owing also to the inherent tendencies of democracy itself. So America is blessed to have religion firmly planted in its history and mores, but it is not clear to what extent American religion fulfills the functions that Tocqueville hopes it can fulfill in a healthy democratic society. There is a strong public opinion in favor of religion in America, rooted in the correct opinion that religion is vital for maintaining mores, which are vital for maintaining a free society. But whereas Tocqueville wishes to see religion awaken tastes and passions apart from and above those of commercial society, Americans prize the utility of religion precisely for the sake of its usefulness in commercial society. Moreover, religion's capacity to elevate cannot be separated from its ultimate orientation to what transcends our mundane material lives – in a word, heaven. It is particularly in this function that American religion appears weak. The problem, for the majority at least, does not appear to lie in unbelief in the otherworldly or transcendent so much as in a pervasive distraction borne in the almost exclusive preoccupation in their daily lives with material well-being, which crowds out what remains of religion's most basic transcendent element. Even when turning from commerce to religion on Sunday, the message and content of religion have themselves been deeply affected by democratic society, such that even the clergy are more inclined to speak of the worldly benefits of belief than anything beyond this world. So while American religion appears strong from the outside, owing to the universal support of public opinion, it is far from clear how spiritually vital it truly remains in the American soul.

In Tocqueville's journal entries and letters from his time in the United States, we can see these questions emerge vividly as they first confronted him. Less than a week after his arrival, he made the following entry in his journal:

> By and large they seem to be a religious people. It is clear that no one thinks of ridiculing religious practices, and that the goodness and even the truth of religion is universally admitted in theory. How far is their life regulated by their doctrine? What is the real power of religious principle over their souls? How can the variety of sects not breed indifference, if not externally, then at least within? That is what remains to be known. (May 15, 1831; Pierson 1996, 67)

Tocqueville's answers to these questions a short while later are remarkable. His most sustained reflections on religion in America during his visit appear in a letter of June 19, 1831, to Louis Kergorlay. There Tocqueville goes further than he would again in writing in questioning what lay behind the external religiosity of Americans. He admits that "the state of religion among this people is the most curious thing to examine here" (Boesche 1985, 48). Americans appear externally an extremely religious people. He observes the "practical exactitude" that accompanies religious practice, commanded "imperiously" by law, "and opinion, much stronger than the law, compels everyone to appear at church and to abstain from all amusements." He observes that Protestant ministers (in good Lockean fashion) "occupy themselves only with treating the platitudes of morality"; "you hear them speak of morality; of dogma not a word, nothing that would shock a neighbor, nothing that could reveal a hint of dissidence" (48–49). Americans are supremely tolerant, and "it is an incredible thing to see the infinite subdivisions into which the sects have divided themselves in America." But "this so-called tolerance ... in my opinion, is nothing but a huge indifference," and "it is evident that here, generally speaking, religion does not move people deeply." Their strict external practice of religion Tocqueville attributes to the following attitude: "If it does not do any good, people seem to say, at least it can do no harm, and besides, it is proper to conform to the general rule." Going still further: "Either I am badly mistaken or there is a great store of doubt and indifference hidden underneath these external forms." And perhaps most remarkable to a reader of *Democracy in America*: "Political passion is not mixed, as it is in our country, with irreligion, but even so religion does not have any more power." Tocqueville speculates that American Protestant sects, "the core of the population," are caught on an unstable middle ground between Catholicism and deism and that thinking Protestants will gravitate toward one or the other (49–51).

Did Tocqueville radically change his view of American religion between the time of his visit and the writing of *Democracy in America* over the next few years? Does he not point to this same American religion as evidence that democratic freedom and enlightenment need *not* lead to a weakening of religion? The ambiguities of the passage in question, however, are now more readily apparent: "The philosophers of the eighteenth century explained the gradual weakening of religion in an altogether simple way. Religious zeal, they said will be extinguished as freedom and enlightenment increase." The weakening of belief as Tocqueville describes it cannot be characterized as altogether simple. And how precisely do Americans refute this altogether simple account? "In America one sees one of the freest and most enlightened peoples of the world eagerly fulfill *all the external duties of religion*" – just as he describes them doing to Kergorlay. If his view of religion did in fact moderate by the time of his writing *Democracy in America*, it did not evidently change radically.

If, then, his view did not change radically, as we have seen evidence in our earlier interpretation that it did not, why, when writing for a general audience, would he have had it appear that American religion was stronger than he in fact believed it to be? As we have distinguished the theoretical view of religion in Hobbes and Locke from their practical policies regarding religion (as "political philosophy" can imply both a philosophic view of politics as well as philosophy that is politically engaged or attuned), so too we must distinguish between Tocqueville's political science as analysis and as a practical application based on that analysis. The ambiguities surrounding Tocqueville's view of American religion concern his analysis of the facts. His practical recommendation of the utility of religion for democratic society is relatively unambiguous. The application of his political science, which required supporting religion, is in some tension with a frank depiction of the facts as he describes them privately to Kergorlay, which may have led Tocqueville not to penetrate the external appearance of American religion as directly in the book.[6]

Be that as it may, Tocqueville does write of a more substantial religious strain in America in a letter, again to Kergorlay, from 1847. His view that religion has been enormously weakened in America, both politically and "in the depth of souls," remains: "The march of time, the developments of well-being, . . . have, in America, taken away from the religious element three-quarters of its original power" (1985, 193). And yet on the basis, apparently, of recent reports from Kergorlay, Tocqueville says that "all that remains of it is greatly agitated." This agitation is caused by "the habits of political liberty and the movement that it has given to all things." These circumstances do not, however, indicate a tidal shift. For we must not forget that the desire for material well-being is the "mother passion" in America, stronger than the political and religious passions. And Tocqueville tells Kergorlay that once political liberty "is well

---

[6] Cf. J. S. Mill, "Utility of Religion," in *Three Essays on Religion*, 1885, 69–70: "It has sometimes been remarked how much has been written, both by friends and enemies, concerning the truth of religion, and how little, at least in the discussion of the controversy, concerning its usefulness. This, however, might have been expected; for the truth, in matters which so deeply affect us, is our first concernment. If religion, or any particular form of it, is true, its usefulness follows without further proof. If to know authentically in what order of things, under what government of the universe it is our destiny to live, were not useful, it is difficult to imagine what could be considered so. Whether a person is in a pleasant or unpleasant place, a palace or a prison, it cannot be otherwise than useful to him to know where he is. So long, therefore, as men accepted the teachings of their religion as positive facts, no more a matter of doubt than their own existence or the existence of objects around them, to ask the use of believing it could not possibly occur to them. The utility of religion did not need to be asserted until the arguments for its truth had in a measure ceased to convince. People must either have ceased to believe, or have ceased to rely on the belief of others, before they could take that inferior ground of defence without a consciousness of lowering what they were endeavouring to raise. An argument for the utility of religion is an appeal to unbelievers, to induce them to practise a well meant hypocrisy, or to semi-believers to make them avert their eyes from what might possibly shake their unstable belief, or finally to persons generally to abstain from expressing any doubts they may feel, since a fabric of immense importance to mankind is so insecure at its foundations, that men must hold their breath in its neighborhood for fear of blowing it down."

established, and exercised in a peaceable milieu, it impels men to the practice and the taste of well-being, to the care and passion for making fortunes; and as a repercussion, its tastes, its needs, its cares extinguish religious passions." But "these are distant and secondary results of political liberty," and there is no absolute truth regarding the effect of political liberty on religion. One must ever consider particular circumstances, and the circumstances in America are unusual.

Tocqueville's comments to Kergorlay about the effect of the peaceful pursuit of material well-being (the social state sought by Hobbes and Locke) on religion serve to return our attention to the dangers he fears could await. For "the practice and taste of well being scarcely harm political passions less than religious passions" (1985, 193). This is because there is a kinship between political and religious passions:

On both sides general goods, immaterial to certain degree, are in sight; on both sides an ideal of society is pursued, a certain perfecting of the human species, the picture of which raises souls above contemplation of private interests and carries them away. For my part, I more easily understand a man animated at the same time both by religious passion and political passion than by political passion and the taste for well-being. The first two can hold together and be embraced in the same soul, but not the second two. (192)

Democracy fosters a taste for political liberty. That is, what political passions remain incline strongly in the direction of political liberty, as Tocqueville found that they still strongly did in the United States. But democracy also threatens to extinguish political passions, leaving only small and limited private passions.

Returning to *Democracy in America*, this potential shrinking and leveling of the democratic soul raise in Tocqueville's mind the specter of a "kind of oppression with which democratic peoples are threatened" which "will resemble nothing that has preceded it in the world" (2000, 662). This would be the despotism of the schoolmaster, not the tyrant. Individuals may gladly come to pass on more and more matters beyond their immediate private concern to a gentle central power, whose management of affairs that once attracted their now emaciated political passions is made more attractive by being applied more equally than if more local decision makers had applied their judgment and will independently. If one is unashamed to make one's own material well-being one's overriding goal, why trouble oneself over distant affairs that can be uniformly managed, provided the managers are sufficiently competent? In one of the darkest passages in *Democracy in America*, Tocqueville writes: "In vain will you charge these same citizens, whom you have rendered so dependent on the central power, with choosing the representatives of this power from time to time; that use of their free will, so important but so brief and so rare, will not prevent them from losing little by little the faculty of thinking, feeling, and acting by themselves, and thus from gradually falling below the level of humanity" (665).

These perpetual children, reminiscent of Nietzsche's last men, would certainly be content with the rule of a benign leviathan. Tocqueville's equanimity and practical moderation in comparison to Nietzsche result from both his appreciation of the genuine goods he found in democracy – its fairness, a relative naturalness of manners and family life, industry and ingenuity – as well as his greater respect for the elevated and elevating character of Christianity, and indeed of almost any religion. The most important difference between them, however, is Tocqueville's assurance that man's nature is not radically malleable by society or history, and that his "taste for the infinite and love of what is immortal … have their immoveable foundation in his nature" (510).

We thus return to the importance of protecting and fostering religion in democracy to the degree and in the manner possible. The religion that is possible may not be the religion that focuses on the deepest needs of democratic human beings, but it remains bound to a religion that is thus spiritually elevated and intellectually passionate. That connection to the truly elevated has not been severed as would be the case with pantheism or metaphysical materialism. Tocqueville's political science requires identification of the defects and dangers inherent in democracy with a view to, if not avoidance of the harm, at least mitigation of it. The goods democracy tends to produce need no encouragement; it is democracy's weaknesses that need attention.

Tocqueville would have us protect religion as our invaluable inheritance. The goods of religion are evident "even if one wants to pay attention only to the interests of this world" (417). Rare indeed are those individuals in whom the loss of religious faith does not enervate the soul, when the soul "despairs of being able to resolve by [itself] the greatest problems that human destiny presents" and is "reduced, like a coward, to not thinking about them at all." Such a loss of faith "slackens the will and prepares citizens for servitude."

Accordingly, Tocqueville concludes, "if [man] has no faith he must serve, and if his is free he must believe" (418–19).[7]

And so we return again to Tocqueville's genuine admiration for American religion. Tocqueville has the remarkable capacity to do justice to the good and the bad in things democratic, as in things aristocratic. It is true that he admits being tempted to regret the loss of aristocratic society and the greatness and beauty one is more likely to find there. But he also confesses that in the presence of such greatness and beauty he is likely to ignore the far greater quantities of poverty and ignorance that one finds in aristocratic society. This extreme inequality seen clearly and altogether is not only ugly but unjust, insofar as it is not natural but the product of a particular sort of society, one built upon myriad artifices. Democracy is in this way more just, "and its justice makes for its greatness and its beauty" (675). Thus Tocqueville strives to see it, to see the whole as God sees the whole. Because democratic society places such powerful obstacles in the way of such striving, what is most precious in American religion is that it retains pointers to what is above us and immaterial, thus carrying a reminder of our deepest need as human beings and serving as a beacon to our innermost natures.

---

[7] In the course of discussing freedom of the press, Tocqueville says: "A great man [Pascal] has said that *ignorance is at both ends of science*. Perhaps it would have been truer to say that profound convictions are found only at both ends and that in the middle is doubt...One can reckon that the majority of men will always stop in one of these two states: they will believe without knowing why, or not know precisely what one must believe. As for the other species of conviction, reflective and master of itself, which is born of science and raised in the very midst of agitation of doubt, it will ever be given only to the efforts of very few men to attain it" (179).

Conclusion

Despite important political disagreements between Jefferson, Hobbes, and Locke, we have seen a common strand in the transformation of religion that each sought. They sought a religion disdainful of the doctrinal disagreements that had profoundly divided believers, a religion that pushes aside those divisive questions as unanswerable. Consequently, we see a religion with minimal theology; a religion with minimal requirements for salvation, which is loosely defined or undefined, and is in any case a personal or private matter, if it retains any place at all. We see, in fact, a religion that is focused less on salvation than on basic morals; not a high-minded virtue, but more broadly attainable and socially useful morals. We see a religion disinclined to quarrel over doctrine and eagerly supportive of temporal goods, particularly civil peace and order; a religion seemingly tailor-made for toleration (in Locke's doctrine) or complaisance (in Hobbes's; *Leviathan* 15.17). We see a religion with little inclination to proselytize, let alone persecute. We see a reorientation to worldly goods that would later become associated with secularization, but still within the frame of and supported by religion.

What Tocqueville observed in American religion resembles what we have just described to a remarkable degree. The character of American religion owes a great deal to the distinctive character of Puritanism; yet what Tocqueville observes is not Puritanism, but a religion transformed. Tocqueville attributes that transformation to the influence of democratic society, not to Enlightenment philosophy (although he is not unaware of Enlightenment influence in America [696]). But whereas Hobbes, Locke, and Jefferson see religion chiefly as a political problem requiring management, and hence transformation in the direction described, Tocqueville sees it as a positive and indeed vital political benefit, particularly in democratic times. It is, indeed, precisely traits that Hobbes, Locke, and Jefferson promote that most concern Tocqueville in America's democratized religion: the materialism and worldliness, the obscuring of a transcendent or otherworldly orientation, the slide into indifference.

And yet Tocqueville does not reject democratized religion. On the contrary, he recognizes that if religion is to remain a real force in democratic times, it must democratize. The risk of democratization is an excessive weakening or hollowing. Leaving people with no spiritual anchor amid the continual flux inherent to democratic life risks opening the door to despotism. An excessively weak or hollow religion also leads, according to Tocqueville, to "bizarre ... religious follies" characterized by "an almost fierce spiritualism" (510). Would he, then, have been surprised by the appeal of a reactionary religious despotism where democratic religion had grown too thin? However that may be, he is concerned with maintaining spiritual depth with a view to strengthening and supporting democracy. American Catholicism appears to be a model for Tocqueville of a religion that had adapted to democratic times while retaining its spiritual essence and clear pointers to an end that transcends the ephemeral worldly goods on offer almost everywhere else.

Tocqueville's disagreement with our representatives of Enlightenment thought over our religious lives is connected to their disagreement over our political lives. For Tocqueville, political society ought not to be about simply promoting or protecting private life, let alone private acquisition. Tocqueville presents us with a much stronger notion of citizenship than do the social contract theorists Hobbes or Locke, according to whom human beings by nature are not political animals, but instead free and independent individuals. According to the social contract doctrine, our natures do not incline us toward membership in political society. By nature we are not, nor do we long to be, parts of a whole greater than our individual selves. The only reason for entering political society is for the protection of one's own private welfare. Political society is an unwelcome necessity in the face of a naturally dreadful human condition. This helps us see how Hobbes could have found such extreme deference to sovereign authority a plausible political program. Locke crucially amends Hobbes's doctrine by adding a very un-Hobbesian right of revolution, an appeal to liberty, and by placing the people in supreme authority over the government; and yet no substantial political duties follow from this amendment. Participation in political life (which in any substantial way falls to representatives)[1] serves to keep government focused on the job given it by the individuals that created it. A government doing its job will allow its citizenry to return to the private – the natural arena of their concerns. Accordingly, just as we are naturally indifferent to the heavens above, so too are we naturally indifferent to the political world above.

Tocqueville is not a social contract theorist. He does not begin from individuals in "nature," somehow complete prior to the influence of a particular political society. Although he, too, is interested in human nature, that nature must be approached by way of observing human beings as products of some sort of distinctive social condition – either democratic or aristocratic. Man in the state of nature is replaced in Tocqueville's political science by the contrast between democratic man and aristocratic man.[2] Individualism, the detachment from society, thus appears as simultaneously a peculiar product of democratic society and an aberration, rather than, as for Hobbes and Locke, the best feasible approximation of our naturally self-interested liberty.

But this is not to say that human beings for Tocqueville are simply social or determined by social influences. Tocqueville's liberalism has at its core an independence of mind that requires a transcendence of social influence, preparation for which is not among democracy's strengths. Tocquevillian political science serves to improve democracy, but it is ultimately neither democratic nor aristocratic and would seek to protect aristocratic society from its excesses just as it seeks to protect democratic society. Central to Tocqueville's concern for religion is the role it plays in fostering individual human greatness, which entails the capacity to look up beyond public opinion. Independence of mind is in the first place for the sake of the individual himself; but it is also vital for that critical distance from democracy (and aristocracy) required by Tocquevillian political science. Tocqueville admits that he often addresses "severe words to ... democratic societies" (400). But the best and most honest guide stands at a remove: "Men do not receive the truth from their enemies, and their friends scarcely

---

[1] Note that for Hobbes the sovereign is not a ruler, but a representative of the collective private interests of the subjects (*Leviathan* 16).

[2] Cf. Mansfield and Winthrop 2000, xxvi–ii.

offer it to them; that is why I have spoken it." We could say that the best democratic citizens are not those whose minds are wholly given over to democracy. By drawing attention to that need of the soul that democracy tends to truncate or stifle, Tocqueville seeks to preserve and strengthen democracy and to ennoble the lives of democrats as human beings.

Bibliography

Adams, Arlin M., and Charles J. Emmerich. 1990. *A Nation Dedicated to Religious Liberty: The Constitutional Heritage of the Religion Clauses*. Philadelphia: University of Pennsylvania Press.

Ahrensdorf, Peter J. 2000. "The Fear of Death and the Longing for Immortality: Hobbes and Thucydides on Human Nature and the Problem of Anarchy." *American Political Science Review*. 94(3): 579–93.

Aronson, Jason. 1959. "Critical Note: Shaftesbury on Locke." *American Political Science Review*. 53(4): 1101–04.

Ashcraft, Richard. 1969. "Faith and Knowledge in Locke's Philosophy." In *John Locke: Problems and Perspectives*, ed. John Yolton. Cambridge: Cambridge University Press.

Ayers, Michael. 1991. *Locke*. London: Routledge.

Backus, Isaac. 1871. *A History of New England with Particular Reference to the Denomination of Christians Called Baptists*. Two Volumes. Newton, Mass.: Backus Historical Society.

––––––. 1968. *Isaac Backus on Church, State, and Calvinism: Pamphlets, 1754–1789*. Edited by William G. McLoughlin. Cambridge, Mass.: Harvard University Press.

Bacon, Francis. 1915. *The Advancement of Learning*. London: J. M. Dent and Sons.

Baldwin, Alice. 1928. *The New England Clergy and the American Revolution*. Durham, N.C.: Duke University Press.

Bartlett, Robert C. 2001. "On the Politics of Faith and Reason: The Enlightenment Project in Pierre Bayle and Montesquieu." *Journal of Politics*.

Bayle, Pierre. [1697] 1969. *Dictionnaire Historique et Critique*. 16 volumes. Geneva: Slatkine Reprints.

––––––. 2000. *Political Writings*. New York: Cambridge University Press.

Berger, Peter. 1999. *The Desecularization of the World: Resurgent Religion and World Politics*. Grand Rapids, Mich.: Eerdmans.

Biddle, John C. 1977. "John Locke's Essay on Infallibility: Introduction, Text and Translation." *Journal of Church and State.* (19): 301–27.

Boesche, Roger. 1987. *The Strange Liberalism of Alexis de Tocqueville.* Ithaca, N.Y.: Cornell University Press.

Brown, Stuart. 1996. "Locke as Secret 'Spinozist': The Perspective of William Carroll." In *Disguised and Overt Spinozism around 1700*, ed. Wiep Van Bunge and Wim Klever, 213–34. Leiden, The Netherlands: E. J. Brill.

Casanova, Jose. 1994. *Public Religions in the Modern World.* Chicago: University of Chicago Press.

Coleman, John. 1983. *John Locke's Moral Philosophy.* Edinburgh: Edinburgh University Press.

Craiutu, Aurelian. 2005. "Tocqueville's Paradoxical Moderation." *Review of Politics.* 67(4): 599–629.

Cranston, Maurice. 1957. *John Locke: A Biography.* London: Longmans.

Creppell, Ingrid. 1996. "Locke on Toleration: The Transformation of Constraint." *Political Theory.* 24(2): 200–40.

Cooke, J. W. 1973. "Jefferson on Liberty." *Journal of the History of Ideas.* 34(4): 563–76.

Dewey, John. 1974. "The Motivations of Hobbes's Political Philosophy." In *Thomas Hobbes in His Time.* Minneapolis: University of Minnesota Press.

Dunn, John. 1969. *The Political Thought of John Locke.* Cambridge: Cambridge University Press.

Dworetz, Steven. 1990. *The Unvarnished Doctrine: Locke, Liberalism, and the American Revolution.* Durham, N.C.: Duke University Press.

Edwards, Jonathan. 1959. *A Treatise Concerning Religious Affections.* New Haven, Conn.: Yale University Press.

Engeman, Thomas S. and Michael P. Zuckert, editors. 2004. *Protestantism and the American Founding.* Notre Dame, Ind.: University of Notre Dame Press.

Forde, Steven. 2001. "Natural Law, Theology, and Morality in Locke." *American Journal of Political Science.* 45(2): 396–409.

———. 2004. "John Locke's Natural Religion." Presented at the Annual Meeting of the American Political Science Association, Chicago.

Forster, Greg. 2005. *John Locke's Politics of Moral Consensus.* New York: Cambridge University Press.

Galston, William A. 1987. "Tocqueville on Liberalism and Religion." *Social Research.* 54: 500–18.

Gauthier, David P. 1969. *The Logic of Leviathan.* Oxford: Clarendon Press.

Geraint, Parry. 1978. *John Locke.* London: George Allen and Unwin.

Grant, Ruth. 1987. *John Locke's Liberalism.* Chicago: University of Chicago Press.

Habermas, Jurgen. 2010. *An Awareness of What Is Missing: Faith and Reason in a Post-secular Age.* Translated by Ciaran Cronin. Malden, Mass.: Polity Press.

Hancock, Ralph C. 1991. "The Uses and Hazards of Christianity in Tocqueville's Attempt to Save Democratic Souls." In *Interpreting Tocqueville's Democracy in America*, ed. Ken Masugi, 348–93. Lanham, Md.: Rowman & Littlefield.

Hatch, Nathan O. 1989. *The Democratization of American Christianity*. New Haven, Conn.: Yale University Press.

Helm, Paul. 1973. "Locke on Faith and Knowledge." *Philosophical Quarterly*. 23: 52–66.

Hobbes, Thomas. 1839. *Opera Philosophica quae Latine Scripsit*. Edited by William Molesworth. 5 volumes. London: John Bohn.

———. 1840. *The English Works*. Edited by William Molesworth, 11 volumes. London: John Bohn.

———. 1994. *Leviathan, with Selected Variants from the Latin Edition of 1688*. Edited by Edwin Curley, Indianapolis: Hackett.

———. 1999. *The Elements of Law Natural and Politic*. Edited by J. C. A. Gaskin. Oxford: Oxford University Press.

Hoekstra, Kinch. 1997. "Hobbes and the Foole." *Political Theory*. 25(5): 620–54.

Holifield, E. Brooks. 2005. *Theology in America: Christian Thought from the Age of the Puritans to the Civil War*. New Haven, Conn.: Yale University Press.

Hood, F. C. 1964. *The Divine Politics of Thomas Hobbes: An Interpretation of Leviathan*. Oxford: Clarendon Press.

Hopkins, Samuel. 1810. *The Life and Character of the Late Mr. Jonathan Edwards*. Portland, Maine: Lyman.

Hume, David. 1949. *An Inquiry Concerning Human Understanding*. Chicago: Regnery.

Israel, Jonathan. 2001. *Radical Enlightenment: Philosophy and the Making of Modernity, 1650–1750*. New York: Oxford University Press.

———. 2006. *Enlightenment Contested: Philosophy, Modernity, and the Emancipation of Man, 1670–1752*. New York: Oxford University Press.

Jefferson, Thomas. 1904. *The Writings of Thomas Jefferson*. 20 volumes. Edited by Albert Ellery Bergh and Andrew A. Lipscomb. Washington, D.C.: Thomas Jefferson Memorial Association.

———. 1943. *The Complete Thomas Jefferson*. Edited by Saul K. Padover. New York: Tudor.

———. [1787] 1954. *Notes on the State of Virginia*. Edited by William Peden. Chapel Hill: University of North Carolina Press.

Johnston, David. 1986. *The Rhetoric of Leviathan: Thomas Hobbes and the Politics of Cultural Transformation*. Princeton, N.J.: Princeton University Press.

Jolley, Nicholas. 1999. *Locke: His Philosophical Thought*. Oxford: Oxford University Press.

———. 2007. "Locke on Faith and Reason." In *The Cambridge Companion to Locke's Essay Concerning Human Understanding*, 436–55. Cambridge: Cambridge University Press.

Josephson, Peter. 2002. *The Great Art of Government: Locke's Use of Consent*. Lawrence: University Press of Kansas.

Kant, Immanuel. 1970. *Political Writings*. Cambridge: Cambridge University Press.

Kateb, George. 2009. "Locke and the Political Origins of Secularism." *Social Research*. 76(4):1001–34.

Kepel, Gilles. 1994. *The Revenge of God: The Resurgence of Islam, Christianity, and Judaism in the Modern World*. University Park: Pennsylvania State University.

Kessler, Sanford. 1983. "Locke's Influence on Jefferson's 'Bill for Establishing Religious Freedom.'" *Journal of Church and State*. 25(2): 231–52.

———. 1994. *Tocqueville's Civil Religion*. Albany, N.Y.: SUNY Press.

Koch, Adrienne. 1943. *The Philosophy of Thomas Jefferson*. New York: Columbia University Press.

Koritansky, John C. 1986. *Alexis de Tocqueville and the New Science of Politics*. Durham, N.C.: Carolina Academic Press.

Kraynak, Robert. 1980. "John Locke: From Absolutism to Toleration." *American Political Science Review*. 74(1): 53–69.

———. 2001. *Christian Faith and Modern Democracy*. Notre Dame, Ind.: University of Notre Dame Press.

Laslett, Peter. 1960. "Introduction." *Two Treatises of Government*. Edited by Peter Laslett. Cambridge: Cambridge University Press.

Lawler, Peter Augustine. 1993. *The Restless Mind: Alexis de Tocqueville on the Origin and Perpetuation of Human Liberty*. Lanham, Md.: Rowman & Littlefield.

Leckey, W. E. H. 1866. *History of the Rise and Influence of the Spirit of Rationalism in Europe*. Two Volumes. New York: Appleton.

Lively, Jack. 1962. *The Social and Political Thought of Alexis de Tocqueville*. Oxford: Clarendon Press.

Lloyd, S. A. 1992. *Ideas as Interests in Hobbes's* Leviathan. Cambridge: Cambridge University Press.

Locke, John. 1954. *Essays on the Law of Nature*. Ed. Wolfgang von Leydon. Oxford: Clarendon Press.

———. 1958. "A Discourse of Miracles." In *The Reasonableness of Christianity, with A Discourse of Miracles and Part of A Third Letter Concerning Toleration*, ed. I. T. Ramsey, 78–87. Stanford, Calif.: Stanford University Press.

———. 1960. *Two Treatises of Government*. Edited by Peter Laslett. Cambridge: Cambridge University Press.

———. 1968. *The Educational Writings of John Locke*. Edited by James L. Axtell. Cambridge: Cambridge University Press.

———. [1690] 1975. *An Essay Concerning Human Understanding*. Edited by Peter H. Nidditch. Oxford: Clarendon Press.

———. 1983. *A Letter Concerning Toleration*. Indianapolis: Hackett.

———. [1707] 1987. *A Paraphrase and Notes on the Epistles of St. Paul to the Galatians, 1 and 2 Corinthians, Romans, Ephesians*. Edited by Arthur W. Wainwright. 2 Volumes. Oxford: Clarendon Press.

———. 1990. *Questions Concerning the Law of Nature*. Translated by Robert Horwitz, Jenny Strauss Clay, and Diskin Clay. Ithaca, N.Y.: Cornell University Press.

———. 1999. *The Reasonableness of Christianity: As Delivered in the Scriptures*. Edited by John C. Higgins-Biddle. Oxford: Clarendon Press.

Luebke, Fred C. 1943. "The Origins of Thomas Jefferson's Anti-Clericalism." *Church History*. 32(3): 344–56.

Macauley, Thomas Babbington. N.d. *The History of England from the Accession of James II*, vol. 1. New York: Harper and Brothers.

Manent, Pierre. 1996. *Tocqueville and the Nature of Democracy*. Translated by John Waggoner. Lanham, Md.: Rowman & Littlefield.

Mansfield, Harvey C. 1971. "Hobbes and the Science of Indirect Government." *American Political Science Review*. 65(1): 97–110.

———. 1979. "On the Political Character of Property in Locke." In *Powers, Possessions, and Freedom: Essays in Honour of C. B. Macpherson*, ed. Alkis Kontos, 23–38. Toronto: University of Toronto Press.

Mansfield, Harvey C. and Delba Winthrop. 2000. "Editors' Introduction." *Democracy in America*. Translated by Mansfield and Winthrop. Chicago: University of Chicago Press.

Marsden, George. 1990. *Religion and American Culture*. San Diego: Harcourt Brace.

———. 1994. *The Soul of the American University*. New York: Oxford University Press.

Marshall, John. 1994. *John Locke: Resistance, Religion, and Responsibility*. Cambridge: Cambridge University Press.

Martinich, A. P. 1992. *The Two Gods of Leviathan: Thomas Hobbes on Religion and Politics*. Cambridge: Cambridge University Press.

———. 1997. *Thomas Hobbes*. New York: St. Martin's Press.

McClure, Kirstie. 1996. *Judging Rights: Lockean Politics and the Limits of Consent*. Ithaca, N.Y.: Cornell University Press.

McConnell, Michael. 1990. "The Origins and Historical Understanding of Free Exercise of Religion." *Harvard Law Review*. 103(May): 1409–1517.

McKenna, Antony. 2003. "Clandestine Literature." *Encyclopedia of the Enlightenment*, ed. Alan Charles Kors, vol. 1. New York: Oxford University Press.

McLoughlin, William G. 1967. *Isaac Backus and the American Pietistic Tradition*. Boston: Little, Brown.

———. 1968. "Isaac Backus and the Separation of Church and State in America." *American Historical Review*. 73(5): 1392–1413.

Mill, John Stuart. 1885. *Three Essays on Religion*. London: Longmans, Green, and Co.

Miller, William Lee. 2003. *The First Liberty: America's Foundation in Religious Freedom*. Washington, D.C.: Georgetown University Press.

Mitchell, Joshua. 1990. "John Locke and the Theological Foundation of Liberal Toleration: A Christian Dialectic of History." *Review of Politics*. 52(1): 64–83.

———. 1999. *The Fragility of Freedom*. Chicago: University of Chicago Press.

Moore, J. T. 1978. "Locke on Assent and Toleration." *Journal of Religion*. 58(1): 30–36.

Myers, Peter C. 1998. *Our Only Star and Compass: Locke and the Struggle for Political Rationality*. Lanham, Md.: Rowman & Littlefield.

Nadon, Christopher. 2006. "Absolutism and the Separation of Church and State in Locke's *Letter Concerning Toleration*." *Perspectives on Political Science*. March: 94–102.

Newlin, Claude. 1962. *Philosophy and Religion in Colonial America*. New York: Greenwood Press.

Nuovo, Victor. 2003. "Locke's Christology as a Key to Understanding His Philosophy." In *The Philosophy of John Locke: New Perspectives*, ed. Peter R. Anstey, 129–53. London: Routledge.

Owen, J. Judd. 1999. "Church and State in Stanley Fish's Antiliberalism." *American Political Science Review*. 93(4): 911–24.

———. 2001. *Religion and the Demise of Liberal Rationalism: The Foundational Crisis of the Separation of Church and State*. Chicago: University of Chicago Press.

———. 2004. "The Task of Liberal Theory after September 11." *Perspectives on Politics*. Vol. 2(June): 325–30.

———. 2005. "The Tolerant Leviathan: Hobbes and the Paradox of Liberalism." *Polity*. 37(1): 130–48.

———. 2007. "Locke's Case for Religious Toleration: Its Neglected Foundation in the *Essay Concerning Human Understanding*." *Journal of Politics*. 69(1): 156–68.

———. 2007. "The Struggle between 'Religion and Nonreligion': Jefferson, Backus, and the Dissonance of America's Founding Principles." *American Political Science Review*. 101(3): 493–503

———. 2010. "John Toland and Leo Strauss on Esoteric Writing." In *Recovering Reason: Essays in Honor of Thomas L. Pangle*, ed. Timothy Burns, pp. 209–21. Lanham, Md.: Lexington Books.

Pangle, Thomas L. 1988. *The Spirit of Modern Republicanism: The Moral Vision of the American Founders and the Philosophy of Locke*. Chicago: University of Chicago Press.

———. 1992. "A Critique of Hobbes's Critique of Biblical and Natural Religion in *Leviathan*." *Jewish Political Studies Review*. 4(2): 25–57.

———. 2010. "Why Has the West Lost Confidence in Its Foundational Principles?" In *Religion, the Enlightenment, and the New Global Order*, ed. John M. Owen and J. Judd Owen, pp. 74–106. New York: Columbia University Press.

———. 2010. *The Theological Basis of Liberal Modernity in Montesquieu's* Spirit of the Laws. Chicago: University of Chicago Press.

Parker, Kim Ian. 2004. *The Biblical Politics of John Locke*. Waterloo, Canada: Wilfred Laurier University Press.

Powell, H. Jefferson. 1993. *The Moral Tradition of American Constitutionalism: A Theological Interpretation*. Durham, N.C.: Duke University Press.

Powell, Milton, editor. 1967. *The Voluntary Church: American Religious Life (1740–1865) Seen through the Eyes of European Visitors*. New York: Macmillan.

Rabieh, Michael S. 1991. "The Reasonableness of Locke, or the Questionableness of Christianity." *Journal of Politics*. 53(4): 933–57.

Rawls, John. 1996. *Political Liberalism*. New York: Columbia University Press.

Richards, Peter Judson. 2001. "'A Clear and Steady Channel': Isaac Backus and the Limits of Liberty." *Journal of Church and State*. 43(3): 447–82.

Rivers, Isabel. 2000. *Reason, Grace, and Sentiment: A Study of the Language of Religion and Ethics in England 1660–1780*. New York: Cambridge University Press.

Russell, Paul. 1993. "Epigram, Pantheists, and Freethought in Hume's Treatise: A Study in Esoteric Communication." *Journal of the History of Ideas.* 54(4): 659–73.

Sandler, Gerald. 1960. "Lockean Ideas in Thomas Jefferson's Bill for Establishing Religious Freedom." *Journal of the History of Ideas.* 21(1960):110–16.

Shaftesbury, The Third Earl, Anthony Ashley Cooper. 1746. *Letters of the Earl of Shaftesbury, Author of the Characteristicks.* Glasgow: R. Foulis.

Sheldon, Garrett Ward. 1991. *The Political Philosophy of Thomas Jefferson.* Baltimore: John Hopkins University Press.

Sigmund, Paul. E. 2005. "Jeremy Waldron and the Religious Turn in Locke Scholarship." *Review of Politics.* 67(3): 407–18.

Smith, Christian. 2003. *Soul Searching: The Religious and Spiritual Lives of American Teenagers.* New York: Oxford University Press.

Smith, Steven B. 1997. *Spinoza, Liberalism, and the Question of Jewish Identity.* New Haven, Conn.: Yale University Press.

Snyder, David C. 1986. "Faith and Reason in Locke's Essay." *Journal of the History of Ideas.* 47: 197–213.

Spellman, W. M. 1997. *John Locke.* New York: St. Martin's Press.

———. 1988. *John Locke and the Problem of Depravity.* Oxford: Clarendon Press.

Strauss, Leo. 1953. *Natural Right and History.* Chicago: University of Chicago Press.

Tarcov, Nathan. 1981. "Locke's 'Second Treatise' and 'The Best Fence against Rebellion.'" *Review of Politics.* 43(2): 198–217.

———. 1984. *Locke's Education for Liberty.* Chicago: University of Chicago Press.

Tessitore, Aristide. 2002. "Alexis de Tocqueville on the Natural State of Religion in the Age of Democracy." *Journal of Politics.* 64(4): 1137–52.

Tocqueville, Alexis de. 1955. *The Old Regime and the French Revolution.* Translated by Stuart Gilbert. New York: Random House.

———. 1981. *De la Démocratie en Amérique.* 2 volumes. Paris: Garnier-Flammarion.

———. 1985. *Selected Letters on Politics and Society.* Edited by Roger Boesche. Translated by James Toupin and Roger Boesche. Berkeley: University of California Press.

———. 2000. *Democracy in America.* Translated by Harvey C. Mansfield and Delba Winthrop. Chicago: University of Chicago Press.

Thomas, Keith. 1971. *Religion and the Decline of Magic: Studies in Popular Belief in Sixteenth and Seventeenth Century England.* New York: Oxford University Press.

Toland, John. 1720. "Clidophorus, or Of the Exoteric and Esoteric Philosophy." In *Tetradymus,* 63–100. London: Brotherton, et al.

Waldron, Jeremy. 1988. "Locke: Toleration and the Rationality of Persecution." In *Justifying Toleration,* ed. Susan Mendus, 61–86. New York: Cambridge University Press.

———. 2002. *God, Locke, and Equality: Christian Foundations of John Locke's Political Thought.* Cambridge: Cambridge University Press.

Walker, D. P. 1964. *The Decline of Hell*. Chicago: University of Chicago Press.

Warrender, Howard. 1957. *The Political Philosophy of Hobbes: His Theory of Obligation*. Oxford: Clarendon Press.

Witte, John. 2010. "The Enlightened City on a Hill: Puritan Sources of Enlightenment Doctrines of Law, Liberty, and Constitutionalism." In *Religion, the Enlightenment and the New Global Order*, ed. John M. Owen and J. Judd Owen. New York: Columbia University Press.

Wolfe, Alan. 2003. *The Transformation of American Religion: How We Actually Live Our Faith*. New York: Free Press.

Wolin, Sheldon. 2001. *Tocqueville between Two Worlds*. Princeton, N.J.: Princeton University Press.

Wolterstorff, Nicholas. 1996. *John Locke and the Ethics of Belief*. Cambridge: Cambridge University Press.

Wood, Neal. 1983. *The Politics of Locke's Philosophy: A Social Study of "An Essay Concerning Human Understanding."* Berkeley: University of California Press.

Woolhouse, Roger. 2007. *Locke: A Biography*. Cambridge: Cambridge University Press.

Wuthnow, Robert. 1998. *After Heaven: Spirituality in America since the 1950s*. Berkeley: University of California Press.

———. 2006. *American Mythos*. Princeton, N.J.: Princeton University Press.

Yarbrough, Jean. 1998. *American Virtues: Thomas Jefferson on the Character of a Free People*. Lawrence: University Press of Kansas.

Yolton, John. 2004. *The Two Intellectual Worlds of John Locke*. Ithaca, N.Y.: Cornell University Press.

Zetterbaum, Marvin. 1967. *Tocqueville and the Problem of Democracy*. Stanford, Calif.: Stanford University Press.

Zuckert, Catherine H. 1981. "Not by Preaching: Tocqueville on the Role of Religion in American Democracy." *Review of Politics*. 42(April): 259–80.

———. 1992. "The Role of Religion in Preserving American Liberty: Tocqueville's Analysis 150 Years Later." In *Liberty, Equality, and Democracy*, ed. Eduardo Nolla, 21–36. New York: New York University Press.

Zuckert, Michael P. 1994. *Natural Rights and the New Republicanism*. Princeton, N.J.: Princeton University Press.

———. 1996. *The Natural Rights Republic: Studies in the Foundation of the American Political Tradition*. Notre Dame, Ind.: University of Notre Dame Press.

———. 2002. *Launching Liberalism: On Lockean Political Philosophy*. Lawrence: University Press of Kansas.

———. 2004. "Natural Rights and Protestant Politics." In *Protestantism and the American Founding*, ed. Thomas S. Engeman and Michael P. Zuckert. Notre Dame, Ind.: University of Notre Dame Press.

Index

162 *Index*

Locke, John (cont.)
on prophecy, 105–106
Puritan Christianity influenced by, 6
Reasonableness of Christianity, 84–91
religiosity of, 60–62
on religious disputes, 67, 110–111
on religious doubt, 103–112
on religious indifference, 111
religious tolerance for, 62
on salvation, 63, 65, 67
on Scripture, 79–84
Second Treatise of Government, 100
Spinoza as influence on, 61
*Thoughts Concerning
Education*, 96
on traditional revelation, 79
Two Treatises of Government, 68–70
on virtue, 96
on zealotry, 66

Madison, James, 1
Manent, Pierre, 126
Martinich, A. P., 26
materialism
as Christian doctrine, 15
Jefferson and, 14–15
Tocqueville on, 139, 144
in U.S., 139
McKenna, Antony, 104
McLoughlin, William, 3, 6–7
metaphysical liberalism, x,
Miller, William Lee, 1–2
miracles
Hobbes on, 41
for Hume, 104–105
in *Inquiry Concerning Human
Understanding*, 104
knowability of, 82
proof of, 104
as supernatural events, 81–82
Mitchell, Joshua, 62
moral law, 89
for Locke, 93
moral science, 91–92
civil law and, 95
divine law and, 94–95
moral virtue, 54
morality
in *Essay Concerning Human
Understanding*, 91–102
evil and, 91, 93
foundations of, 90
good and, 91, 93
for Locke, 88
providence and, 102
More, Thomas, 39
Morton, Nathaniel, 118

Mosaic Law, 47
covenant theology influenced by, 5
Murat, Achille, 126

natural laws, 31, 93
as doctrine, 68–69
in *Essay Concerning Human
Understanding*, 69
natural liberty, 5–6
natural religion, 31–37, 53
natural revelation, 72–73
natural theology, 70–71
nature
invention of commonwealth and, 38
in *Leviathan*, 37–40
religion and, 37–40, 123–127
state of nature as fictional, 38–39
Notes on the State of Virginia (Jefferson),
10–11, 19–20

original revelation, 79

paganism, 54
*Paraphrase and Notes on the Epistles of
St. Paul* (Locke), 80–81
pluralism. *See* reasonable pluralism;
religious pluralism
political liberalism, ix
Backus and, xv
Enlightenment liberalism compared to, x
Jefferson and, xv
liberal democracy and, x
metaphysical liberalism compared
to, x,
religion in, x
transformative agenda of, xiv
The Politics of Locke's Philosophy
(Wood), 69
practical atheism, 56
Presbyterian Calvinism, 12
primitive Christianity, 12–13
rejection of Trinitarianism and, 18
prophecy, 46–47, 105–106
Protestants, in U.S., 128
Puritan Christianity, 5–6
in *Democracy in America*,
117–120
Locke as influence on, 6
as religious doctrine, 118–119
in U.S., 119–120
Puritans, 118
laws under, 119

rational Christianity, 14–15
Rawls, John, 3
political liberalism and, ix
on reasonable pluralism, xi

reason
  faith as contraindication to, 75, 77
  revelation and, 43–44, 78
reasonable pluralism, xi
Reasonableness of Christianity (Locke), xi,
    84–91
  doctrine of Christian salvation in, 84–85
  doctrine of hell in, 91
  Jefferson influenced by, 85
  righteousness in, 94
reflection, knowledge and, 73
religion. *See also* supernatural religion
  democracy and, in U.S., xv, 116, 120–133
  democratization of, 148
  direct action of, 127–129
  disputes over, 67, 110–111
  faith and, 42–43
  under First Amendment, 3–4
  for Hobbes, 22, 25–27
  indirect action of, 129
  as inheritance of aristocratic age, 145–146
  liberal theory and, xi
  natural, 31–37, 53
  natural state of, 37–40, 123–127
  perpetual fear and, 33–34
  philosophic method for, 115, 121–122
  in political liberalism, x
  political necessity of, 7–8
  political theory and, 25–26
  revelation in, 41–42
  separation from politics, 124
  sovereign establishment of, 22, 41, 47
  state of nature and, 37–40
  as threat to sovereign power, 35
  in U.S., 17–20, 108–109, 120–121,
    127–133, 140–144, 146
  utility of, 143
religiosity
  of Locke, 60
  in United States, xiii, 141–142
religious doubt, 103–112
religious freedom
  for Backus, 3–4, 9
  Calvinism from, 14
  for Jefferson, 4, 10–11
  in separation of church and state, 1
  third way of, 2
  in U.S., 3, 17–19
religious indifference, 54–56
religious pluralism
  Hobbesian Christianity and, 50
  for Jefferson, 20
revelation, religious
  in *Essay Concerning Human
    Understanding*, 72–73
  evidence of, 84
  for Hobbes, 41–42, 44–45

human role in, 77–78
  knowledge of God through, 73–79
  limitations of, 83–84
  original, 79
  reason and, 43–44, 78
  through Scripture, 79–84
  as sensitive knowledge, 73
  traditional, 79
righteousness, 94
Rogers, G. A. J., 63
Rome, religious tolerance in, 52–53
Rush, Benjamin, 13

salvation, religious, 63, 65
  doctrine for, 67, 84–85
  in *Reasonableness of Christianity*, 84–85
  requirements of, 84–85
Scripture
  anti-Scripturalism, 40
  in *Essay Concerning Human
    Understanding*, 79–84
  Hobbes treatment of, 44–46
  in *Leviathan*, 46
  religious revelation through, 79–84
Second Treatise of Government
    (Locke), 100
secularization theory, ix
  founding of sociology and, ix
  for Tocqueville, xiii
self-determination, liberty and, 9
self-interest, 24–25
  as doctrine, 135–136
  in Locke's moral science, 91–93
sensitive knowledge, 73
separation of church and state
  for Backus, 2–4
  for Jefferson, 2–4
  religious freedom and, 1
Short, William, 12, 14, 16
Sigmund, Paul, 61
Smith, James, 13–14
sociology, secularization theory and, ix
sovereignty
  establishment of Christian
    commonwealth, 50
  religion established by, 22, 41, 47
Spinoza, Baruch, xi, 61
Story, Isaac, 18
Strauss, Leo, 61
supernatural religion
  for Hobbes, 24–31
  for Hume, 108
  self-interest and, 24–25

Taylor, A. E., 26
temporal authority, 6
Theologico-political Treatise (Spinoza), xi

Lightning Source UK Ltd.
Milton Keynes UK
UKOW07n1825301214

243806UK00004B/38/P